Talk for Writing across the Curriculum

Talk for Writing across the Curriculum

How to teach non-fiction writing to 5–12 year-olds

2nd edition

Pie Corbett and Julia Strong

Open University Press

Open University Press
McGraw-Hill Education
8th Floor
338 Euston Road
London
NW1 3BH

email: enquiries@openup.co.uk
world wide web: www.openup.co.uk

and Two Penn Plaza, New York, NY 10121-2289, USA

First published 2011
First published in this second edition 2017

A catalogue record of this book is available from the British
Library

ISBN-13: 978-0-33-522688-7
ISBN-10: 0-335-22688-4
eISBN: 978-0-33-522689-4

Library of Congress Cataloging-in-Publication Data
CIP data applied for

Typeset by Transforma Pvt. Ltd., Chennai, India

Printed and bound in Great Britain by Bell and Bain Ltd, Glasgow

Dedication

This book is dedicated to all the teachers and local authority consultants whose enthusiasm and hard work in trialling the approach made the development of Talk for Writing possible. In particular, our thanks go to Pam Fell from Sheffield, Sue Bence and Sue Ross in Southampton, and Sheila Hentall and Val Cork from Lewisham, without whose help we would not have been able to develop Talk for Writing across the curriculum. We would also like to thank all the Talk for Writing Training Schools that have contributed to the development of Talk for Writing in recent years, without whose help this book could not have been updated. These schools can all be visited to see Talk for Writing in action. Visit www.talk4writing. com/training

Pie Corbett and Julia Strong

Praise page

"This latest update of Pie and Julia's best-selling book reflects changes in the curriculum, strengthening the *Talk for Writing* approach, using cold and hot tasks, showing new worked examples of how to apply *Talk for Writing* to each non-fiction type and placing formative assessment at the heart of the process. It is exciting to see how all the best ideas and findings in education are converging, evidenced in this latest 'up-to-the-minute' excellent publication."

Shirley Clarke, Formative Assessment Expert, UK

"The teaching of reading has always taken priority in policy and practice in literacy. Pie Corbett and Julia Strong have produced a very welcome counterweight to that dominance in their *Talk for Writing Across the Curriculum*. It is so refreshing to see suggestions for teaching to bring elements of language together, especially when done in such an entertaining and engaging way as this. This new edition makes a 'classic' even better."

David Wray, Emeritus Professor,
University of Warwick, UK

"This book celebrates the importance of talk in becoming and growing as a writer: talk to share ideas; talk to analyse text; talk to co-construct writing; and talk to evaluate writing. Throughout the book constantly underlines the importance of talk for learning and the many creative and rich ways talk can be used to help young writers internalise the rhythms and patterns of text. Full of practical ideas and activities, the teaching combines being creative and being critical in a wholly integrated way. An invaluable resource for primary school teachers!"

Debra Myhill, Professor of Education at the
University of Exeter, UK

Five of the many 5-star reviews from Amazon:

- **Awesome resource:** This book has totally changed the way I teach writing, fiction as well as non-fiction. It is incredibly inspiring and the methods recommended in it really engage and inspire the children. The DVD is great to watch too, very motivating. Can't recommend highly enough. Mrs F Richards, 2012.

- **A brilliant resource:** I never normally write reviews but this book is invaluable for teachers. Having less confidence in non-fiction writing, this book gives fun and innovative ways to teach it. The children are really engaged and look forward to each lesson. Also, the DVD helps in understanding some of the techniques described. Buy it! APY, 2012.

- **The greatest value ...** A must for any teacher and those with a passion for teaching writing. It qualifies the importance of talk to help children learn to write. The greatest value of this book is that it shows you how to stage the lead up to writing. Excellent resource. Teenabeena, 2014.

- **The best and most useful teaching book:** A lifeline, couldn't get through planning literacy units without it. So many good ideas. The best and most useful teaching book I have ever bought. Miss C Campbell, 2015.

- **Recommended for teachers:** The content of this book is exceptional and is ideal for schools developing oracy in their curriculum. The DVD complements the book. Lianne Blackburn, 2013.

Contents

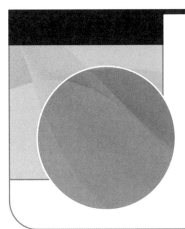

Video index related to chapters

Chapter 1: The impact of Talk for Writing and its origins

1. Maurice Leahy explains the difference the Talk for Writing approach has made to Carlton Hill Primary School, Brighton

Chapter 2: The Talk for Writing process

2. Assessment: bookending units with cold to hot tasks
3. The creative hook
4. Warming up the tune of the text

Chapter 4: Recount

5. Imitation: how to help young children internalise a simple recount text
6. Boxing up: the bridge from imitation to innovation
7. Shared writing showing how to innovate on the model
8. Imitation: how to help young children internalise a news recount
9. Boxing up the text
10. Co-constructing a recount toolkit
11. Year 2 teacher Jonny Gee embedding recount skills in history at Adswood Primary, Stockport
12. Using text mapping and actions to help Year 5 children recall historical information, Penn Wood School, Slough
13. Year 1 children imitating a science recount text about how plants grow, Penn Wood School, Slough
14. Louise St John using the Talk for Writing process to teach French at Victoria Road Primary, Plymouth

Chapter 5: Instructions

15. Warming-up-the-text games (for instruction text)
16. Illustrating how a unit builds from imitation to innovation to independent application (instruction text)
17. Oral rehearsal of instructions to help children recall maths processes and understand vocabulary

Chapter 6: Information

18. Reading as a reader: using drama and other activities to help children comprehend text
19. Brainstorming ideas to support innovation
20. Using boxing up to plan an innovation based on the model
21. The art of shared writing
22. Applying skills learnt through work on fictional information to real information
23. How older pupils can map a text and use the map to talk the gist of a text
24. Innovation: clumping and adding in extra information
25. The steps needed to reach independent application
26. The innovation stage: more advanced shared writing
27. A reception child from Selby Community Primary is helped by his mother to 'read' his text map about the Solar System
28. Pie demonstrating with a class how to use boxing up in history to plan information text about Queen Victoria
29. Pie demonstrating the shared writing that followed the planning

Chapter 7: Explanation

30. How the Talk for Writing approach suits all subjects
31. How living sentences can help children remember what has been explained in science
32. Year 1 children from Yew Tree Community School, Birmingham, using actions to recall technical vocabulary in science
33. A Year 1 child at Yew Tree Community Primary, Birmingham, explains what he has discovered about invertebrates
34. A Year 6 pupil from Yew Tree Community Primary School demonstrating how imitation is helping her understand the language of maths

Chapter 8: Persuasion

35. Imitation: internalising a persuasive text
36. Boxing up the text to understand structure and beginning to create a toolkit for persuasive writing
37. Children from Year 6 at Carlton Hill Primary School, Brighton, internalising the language of persuasion so that they can script a film promoting Arundel Castle
38. The children's final promotional film

Chapter 9: Discussion

39. Pie explains the potential of discussion text
40. A Year 6 pupil from Knowle Park demonstrates how talking the text gives her the language of discussion
41. The power of discussion text is illustrated by a Year 5 teacher and two pupils from Pegasus Primary School, Oxford

Guided tour

This book has been structured to help you understand the Talk for Writing process step by step in relation to each of the six key non-fiction text types so that you can adapt it to meet the varying needs of the subjects and the pupils that you teach.

The DVDs that accompany the book are a useful addition for anyone reading the book as well as for anyone who wants to provide staff training on the Talk for Writing approach. Please be aware that you can use this material to support training in your school but it cannot be used for commercial gain. The DVDs include video footage from two Pie Corbett conferences as well as showing Talk for Writing in action in a range of schools. They also include the teaching notes and handouts.

Making learning visual is key to the Talk for Writing approach. Chapters 2 and 4 to 9 are all structured around this image of the three stages of the Talk for Writing process, bookended by assessment. The different sections of this poster are then used as signposts to guide the reader through the structure of the approach.

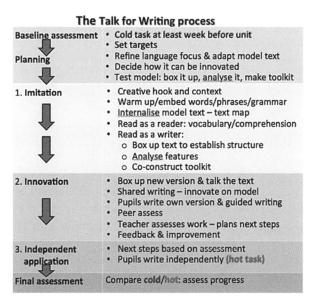

Figure P1   The Talk for Writing process

The following icons also help to guide the reader through some key regularly recurring features of the Talk for Writing process

	Warming up the tune of the text icon Throughout the Talk for Writing process, teachers are encouraged to devise activities that will first warm up and then consolidate the words, phrases and grammar that are key to the text being focused on, alongside warming up the content of the unit.
	The magpie icon Throughout the process, children are encouraged to store useful words and phrases as they arise through the activities, for future use just as a magpie hoards shiny objects.
	The links icon Linking sentences (and the parts of sentences) together with sentence signposts is the key to writing coherent text. The book is full of activities, flagged up by this links icon, to help the children internalise how to use linking techniques.
	Model text icon Without a model text, the children will not know what sort of writing they are trying to achieve.
	Talking the text icon Oral imitation of model text is essential if children are to internalise the language patterns that they will need to write.
	Boxing up icon Boxing up text is a simple device for analysing the structure of any text and then planning a new version.
	The toolkit icon Throughout each unit, the children are engaged in co-constructing a toolkit of the key language features of each text type.
	The **DVD icon** indicates where the DVD is particularly relevant.
	The **handout icon** indicates where it is useful to refer to a handout.
	The **stick figure icon** indicates where a child has commented on the approach.
	The **smiling face icon** indicates free-writing opportunities for children to choose what they write about and how they write it.

The impact of Talk for Writing and its origins

Why this book has been updated

Figure 1.1   Reception class at St George's, Battersea

In the five years since *Talk for Writing Across the Curriculum* was first published in 2011, there have been significant changes to the education landscape in England. In those five years, this book sold 42,000 copies: that's a lot of copies for a book about how to improve teaching, and says one very important thing about the teaching profession in the UK – teachers care greatly about the quality of the teaching and learning that they provide.

In those five years in England, a new curriculum has been published – significantly altering the focus for English teaching – phonics, spelling and grammar tests have been introduced, and the method for measuring attainment has been altered.

This book has been updated so that it relates to all of these changes, the key features of which are explained in Chapter 3, pages 59–67.

Another reason for the update is that, in those five years, the Talk for Writing approach has grown greatly in depth, breadth and understanding. More and more schools are applying the approach systematically and finding that not only is the children's attainment in English greatly increasing, but attainment is increasing right across the curriculum; an approach that started out as a way of internalising story pattern has turned out to have an underpinning process that can support learning for all ages in all subjects. Moreover, and importantly in these test-obsessed days, the children are enjoying their learning and becoming confident in their ability to learn, and the teachers are enjoying their teaching.

Curriculum and assessment requirements will come and go, but quality teaching and learning will always shine through.

The impact of Talk for Writing

See video clip 1.

'Irrespective of whether your school is outstanding or making the exciting journey from special measures, Talk for Writing is a whole-school philosophy to teaching and learning that will catalyse improvement and raise aspirations across the school. Its impact is felt in every area of the school, from the humdrum of the school's data to the vibrancy of the learning environments, excitement in the classroom atmosphere, the tangible buzz in the staffroom, and renewed enthusiasm for a profession and moral purpose we all believe in passionately.

It is not an intervention; it is a philosophy: a philosophy that impacts so much more than just the quality of children's reading and writing – although this it also does in bounds. Staff morale, a collaborative ethos, greater understanding of how children learn, and an environment where rapid success is seized on and celebrated are all fundamental by-products of the Talk for Writing approach.

Excellent teachers relish the inspiration it provides to be creative and develop a genuine depth to learning that is often talked about, but seldom realised. Teachers who are working on developing their pedagogy and skills benefit from the proven methods and strategies that Talk for Writing presents – enabling our teachers to teach and our children to learn.

Most importantly, it works. It just works. If Talk for Writing is led well with passion, dedication and a deep understanding of what exceptional learning looks like, it works. Attainment will rise, achievement will increase, teachers will feel proud of the success they have orchestrated and, most importantly, children will realised the potential we all know they have.'

James Munt, Executive Headteacher, Front Lawn Academy, Havant

'**St Matthew's C of E Primary School** in Nechells, Birmingham, is less than a mile from the city centre, in an area classified as high deprivation. The school population reflects the wider multicultural community, with 90% of children coming from minority ethnic groups and over 60% with English as an additional language. The very low attainment on entry presents a challenge for the delivery of literacy, but our children thrive in an environment where our values underpin their growth and development: Courage – Attainment – Pride. Talk for Writing has provided an excellent vehicle for facilitating the high expectations for our children to not only read and write well, but also develop their creativity and independence. In 2009, before the introduction of Talk for Writing, our SATS results were 34%, combined with English level 4+ 48% and maths level 4+ 52%. By 2013, outcomes at Key Stage 2 had soared – reading level 4+ 93%; writing level 4+ 97% and maths level 4+ 97%. St Matthew's achieved an Outstanding Ofsted grade in 2015: a testament that, for us, Talk for Writing is not just about writing or reading – it is about whole-school improvement.'

Paulette Osborne, MBE, Headteacher

'In 2008, before **Knowle Park Primary** became involved in the South 2gether Talk for Writing project, only around half of the children achieved level 4, the expected level in reading and writing at that time. The school is in an area of deprivation within a sprawling housing estate in Bristol; more than 50% of the children receive free school meals. The consistent Talk for Writing approach to the teaching of speaking, reading and writing has transformed the achievement of all our children. In the last three years (2013, 2014, 2015), we have achieved around 90% level 4+ for writing and reading and, in 2015, 42% achieved level 5 in writing and 45% in reading. Every child now leaves our school a confident speaker, reader and writer.

We have also started to see that the same principles can be applied to other areas of the curriculum. Teachers are now boxing up model text in geography, science and history as well as making toolkits for calculations in maths. It is common to see washing lines for many subjects, and the principles of modelling and sharing learning and collaboration are evident in all subjects.

One of the major impacts is the consistency of practice you see around the school. Each teacher, whether experienced or an NQT, has the plans, texts and resources from the previous year ready to pick up and run with. We try to keep the texts the same each year so that teams can make tweaks and improve them but not plan from scratch. The children benefit from this: as they transition from one year to the next, the agreed methods are there to be built on.'

James Walker, lead teacher for writing at Knowle Park Primary, Bristol and Talk for Writing trainer

'Talk for Writing has given **Harbour Centre** children access to the world of literary fact and fiction in a way that was not possible before. They have always loved stories but now they have the skills to author their own!'

Amy Peart, Headteacher, The Hythe Primary School, Surrey, linked to the SEND Harbour Centre

'We are able to make links across all aspects of the curriculum through Talk for Writing. Experiencing the text in a variety of ways really helps to embed it into the children's memories by making it memorable and relevant to them. It works so well for our pupils who all have significant learning and speech and language difficulties.'

Angela Humphreys (LAN Centre Manager) Harbour Centre, Surrey

At **Penn Wood Primary School**, in Slough, 87% of children have English as an additional language and, with its proximity to Heathrow, mobility is very high – for example, by the spring of 2016 mobility for Year 6 was 193%. The school has been on an improvement journey from 'Serious weaknesses' several years ago to achieving 'Good' with 'outstanding features' by 2014. Talk for Writing is a golden thread running through the inspection report and has been systematically applied across the school for several years to raise the children's language acquisition and subsequent attainment. In 2015, 95% of children attained Level 4+ at the end of Key Stage 2 and the school was in the top 10% of schools for Value Added in reading, writing and maths combined.

St George's Primary, Battersea, is on an estate within one of the most deprived areas in the country. Over 50% of the children have English as an additional language and over 60% are on free school meals. When Janet Hilary became head, the school was in special measures, results were dire and Ofsted described the Foundation Stage as 'utterly woeful'; a statement she could only agree with. The central focus of the school was to increase the language development of the children to provide them with a voice: Talk for Writing was one key to doing this. By September 2011, Ofsted graded the school as outstanding and in 2013 the school achieved 100% level 4 in all the tested areas with over 50% of children scoring level 5 in English.

The beginnings of 'talking the text'

It is impossible to write any text without being familiar with the language rhythms and patterns that it involves. Indeed, it is impossible to write a sentence pattern without being able to say it – and you cannot say it, if you haven't heard it. The language required for success at any writing task must become part of the children's linguistic repertoire. To achieve this, we have to structure units of work to provide the appropriate language patterns enabling the children to hear them and say them, read them and explore them so they really know the patterns well. It's like teaching a new language. Language is primarily learned through interactive 'hearing' and 'saying' and the richer and more varied the language patterns, the better the writing will be. This is particularly important if children do not come from linguistically rich homes and they are not read to. It's all about building up a bank of text types in their head so that the language patterns are familiar to them and become part of their linguistic competency. **This awareness of the need to provide, through imitation, a language template on which the child can build an independent voice lies at the heart of the Talk for Writing approach.**

Why reading matters

Unsurprisingly, the best writers in any class are always readers. Reading influences writing – indeed, the richness, depth and breadth of reading determines the writer that we become. If a child's reading is meagre, then their writing will inevitably be thin. Most teachers would be able to take a pile of children's books and rapidly work out which children read and which do not – for their writing will be an echo of their reading. In fact, it is even possible to work out their favourite author or type of writing, as their composition may well be a sub-version of Jacqueline Wilson, Anthony Horowitz or the non-fiction of Terry Deary.

Figure 1.2   A boy engaged in reading at Burnley Brow Primary School

- Children who are read to regularly before coming to school are the most likely to have success.

- Children who read for pleasure are also most likely to succeed – in literacy, but also across the curriculum because of the way in which reading develops the ability to think in the abstract.

A rich reading experience of stories, poems and non-fiction helps children to internalise a living library of non-fiction, poems and stories, like templates that can be used for their imagination. Avid readers acquire a store of patterns, rather like building blocks that can be used to compose. For instance, even the earliest stories of young children who have been read to involve them in drawing upon their reading as well as their immediate lives. Here is Poppy who is just three:

Well, Pops was going to collect some berries and some conkers and she was going to collect some fir cones then she met a monkey and then she met a tiger. Then she met her grandma. Then she met the elephant. Then she met the lion. Then she met her father and then she met her mummy. Then she went to Flopsy Mopsy. Then Flopsy Mopsy and Peter Rabbit went outside to collect some berries, fire cones and conkers and while they were walking they saw some coconuts falling to the ground and they collected some and then they went home. Then they played. When it was night the little girl went bed. It was morning time in the early evening so they went to playgroup.

Already her stories are full of everyday events such as picking berries in the autumn and the impending visit of her gran, mingled with the current favourite story of Peter Rabbit. Children cannot create out of nothing. There needs to be both rich experience, and a language bank inside the mind to draw upon.

Teachers may be tempted into thinking that children are unimaginative. The issue is usually not a lack of imagination: too often it is a lack of the building blocks of writing – with stories this would be characters, settings and possibilities. Imagination concerns manipulating what you know to create something new. However, it is not uncommon to find children arriving in school with a meagre diet of stories and rhymes, let alone non-fiction. Indeed, many professionals who work with young children believe that language deprivation is increasing. It is this concern about helping provide children with the language-rich environment that will enable them to thrive as writers and learners that led to the development of Talk for Writing.

The oral approach described in this book is based on how children learn language – through the **imitation**, **innovation** and **invention** of language. Constant experience of texts, both orally and in written form, helps children **internalise language patterns**:

- The text as an experience of memorable, meaningful images and ideas.
- The underlying template – the text or plot pattern.
- The rhythmic flow of the sentences – syntax.
- Phrasing and words.

The oral aspect of Talk for Writing was initially developed in 2003 through a 'Storymaking' project carried out at the International Learning and Research Centre, funded by the then DfES through the Innovations Unit, as well as being supported by the CfBT. It was co-led by Mary Rose and myself, Pie Corbett. This was an attempt to explore a systematic, cumulative and dynamic approach to language acquisition. Initially, narrative was used as a strategy for learning another language. The idea was simple – children orally learned a story in their home language before learning the same story in a second language. This was based on work carried out at the University of Rome by Professor Taeschner. Teacher research then focused on exploring the links between storytelling and writing.

Since then, many schools have found that daily storytelling can have a dramatic influence on progress in composition. For instance, the initial teacher research focused on 4- and 5-year-olds in Reception classes. At the start of the year, only 2% of the sample was able to retell a whole story; by the end of the year, 76% retold a whole tale in fluent standard English.

In a study carried out in Lewisham (reported in 'Stories to tell, stories to write', available from Lewisham Professional Development Centre, Kilmorie Road, London SE23 2SP), 100% of the primary-age pupils tracked made average progress in writing and 80% made three or more sub-levels of progress in one year. This was particularly impressive because the children being tracked were selected because they had been making less than average progress. A second study in

Lewisham (2010) found that a similar cohort of children made, on average, two years progress in one year, this time focusing on the impact of Talk for Writing on non-fiction writing.

It is worth noting that the teachers involved in the first project had attended a one-day conference on Storymaking, followed by support from their literacy consultants, while those in the second study received two full-days' training several months apart, plus interim support meetings. Complex developments require time, attention and support. The published booklet 'Stories to tell, stories to write' provides useful case studies that illuminate the teachers' and children's journeys as storytellers and writers. It also highlights the value of storytelling for children who have English as a new language as well as those who struggle.

A more recent study in Salford by teachers at St Thomas of Canterbury Primary School showed that the approach works powerfully for children who have English as a new language – indeed, compared with a control group in similar schools, those pupils benefiting from the 'talk write' approach on average made outstanding progress.

From storytelling into 'talking the text'

> 'Having done a lot of oral storytelling with Key Stage 1 children, I was a little sceptical about getting Year 5 children to stand up and get really involved in expressive oral retelling. How wrong I was!'
>
> *Maria Wheeler, teacher on Lewisham Talk for Writing across the curriculum project*

The approach was then built upon by groups of teachers across the country, trialling ideas which were then shared and shaped at conferences run by Julia Strong for the National Literacy Trust from 2005 until 2012. The impact was such that the Primary National Strategy funded a pilot project in 2008 where we developed the approach for fiction writing. The resulting Talk for Writing materials were then circulated to schools by the Strategy.

The breakthrough into applying the theory to non-fiction came from one teacher in Southampton who began to teach her class non-fiction texts orally before using shared writing to craft a new version with outstanding results, as can be seen below. This was then researched by a small team of teachers led by the local literacy consultants.

The initial sample below was written by a high-attaining Year 1 girl writing about 'bats':

Bats Han up side down.

Bats like new homes.

Bats like to eat inses.

Three weeks later, following the Talk for Writing process, the same girl wrote the following about hedgehogs:

> Hedgehog Facs.
>
> Hedgehogs are not pets.
>
> What are they like. They have sharp spins on ther bakes but undernif they are soft.
>
> What do they eat? They eat slipuriy slugs crushey bittls tickley spids and juciy catppl. They like frat too. They gring wort. Badgers are the alle anmls that eat hedgehogs.
>
> Did you now. Hedgehogs are nkctnl that mens they come out at nit. Hedgehogs hibnat that mens they sleep in the winter. Their nest is called a hibnacl. Ther babys are coled hogllos.
>
> And they can sime!

Similarly, a low attaining Year 3 boy initially wrote the following about hamsters:

> Hasds are riley sofd.
>
> Thay slep in the day.
>
> They hav shap tef.
>
> They sutums clum up and down.
>
> They eaten nus and druy bnuns.

Three weeks later, following the process, the same boy wrote:

> A lion is a type of cat with a lonig taol.
>
> They all look the same. They have a bodey of a cat and long her. Most lions are yellow.
>
> Lions usually live in loing grass in hot cutres like Africa and Asia.
>
> They eat all sizes of animals and sometimes kill cubs.
>
> If you want to see a lion you could sday buy loing grass where there are lions foot pris.
>
> When lions walk their heels don't touch the ground. They can run at speed of 30 miles an hour. The males roar and can be heard over five miles away. Males eat first.
>
> The most amazing thing a bault lion is that they are Excellent swimmers.

Importantly, both children had also gained confidence through the process, most notably the boy who moved from disliking writing, scoring his enjoyment of writing as 1/10 and seeing himself as a poor writer, to awarding it 10/10 and declaring himself a good writer.

Following the success of Talk for Writing with fiction, we managed to secure the interest of a number of authorities in piloting Talk for Writing across the curriculum. A small, but significant, handful of teachers on the Isle of Wight, in Bradford, Sheffield, Lewisham and Southampton experimented and fed back their experience of 'talking the text' with non-fiction. The idea of learning texts orally so that they act like a template for writing has now been developed considerably. Teachers draw on the importance of 'reading as a writer', using activities to warm up the tune of the texts being focused on, as well as using shared and guided writing to craft language. Of course, none of this works without finding the right subjects to write about, for we write best about what we know and what matters.

By 2012, we had sufficient confidence in the importance of the Talk for Writing process as the key to improving pupil attainment across the curriculum to set up Talk for Writing as an educational consultancy. This has enabled us to focus on developing and spreading the approach alongside building a network of Talk for Writing Training Schools while maintaining our key values and aims.

The centrality of non-fiction

Many teachers of literacy make great claims for the importance of narrative in helping children understand themselves and their world. Of course, non-fiction plays a similar and powerful role in children's development. The world of non-fiction allows us to talk about things that have happened to us, to explain how things work, to instruct others, to persuade and discuss as well as passing on information. It is a template to put upon our lives so that we can give order and reason to living.

While stories may be good for the human spirit and nourishing our soul, it is non-fiction that gets the job done! Without non-fiction talking, reading and writing, our complex world could not function. It helps us to live and work confidently, giving us control over what happens. Non-fiction is vital to the existence and development of society, not only because it helps us function but also because it reflects different key modes of thought. While children should be able to develop the ability to persuade, it is also important that they should be able to think about other people's viewpoints and make decisions based on evidence and reasoned argument.

Separate text types?

It is worth adding that many teachers like to teach non-fiction texts in their 'pure' forms. Of course, in the real world this rarely happens. A recount about a trip to the zoo might well also include descriptions of animals, information about the animals, and even a section where the writer begins to discuss whether or not zoos are a good idea. It is this richness of detail and information that allows the writer to engage the reader.

It is interesting to note that there are many similarities between the different types of non-fiction writing. Temporal sentence signposts will be found in almost any type of writing and are very common. Indeed, in many ways, constant reading of non-fiction and 'talking the text' over the seven years of primary education should allow nearly all children to be able to shift register, deploying the appropriate style they need in relation to audience and purpose. This is what skilled adult writers manage through familiarity with the appropriate voice they need for different situations. So, to improve the writing, many children need to read more widely, deeply and attentively. The richness of the reading shapes the writer we become. The grid on the following page brings out what the six non-fiction text types have in common rather than focusing on what separates them.

The next chapter takes you through how the Talk for Writing process can help children internalise the underpinning patterns of all the different non-fiction types of writing so that they can confidently turn their hand to any writing task, mixing and matching the features as required by the audience and purpose of the text they are writing.

Typical features the six non-fiction text types have in common

	Instruction	Recount	Explanation	Information	Persuasion	Discussion
Structure	• Beginning, middle, end • Chronological	• Beginning, middle, end • Chronological	• Beginning, middle, end • Chronological or logical • Headings	• Beginning, middle, end • Logical • Headings	• Beginning, middle, end • Logical	• Beginning, middle, end • Logical
Language features: Cohesion	• Time links	• Topic sentences • Time links	• Topic sentences • Causal links	• Topic sentences • Time and causal links	• Topic sentences • Emotive links	• Topic sentences • Causal and comparative links
Expression	• Impersonal • Technical language	• Impersonal/personal • Description	• Impersonal • Generalisers • Description to illustrate • Technical language	• Impersonal • Generalisers • Description to illustrate • Technical language	• Personal • Description to persuade	• Impersonal • Generalisers • Description to illustrate • Technical language

2

The Talk for Writing process

Talk for Writing is based on how children learn and places the learner, through formative assessment, at the heart of the planning, teaching and learning process. The term Talk for Writing not only describes all the talk that surrounds the teaching of writing but also the wider learning within a unit. It helps the children become better speakers, listeners, readers, writers and thinkers. It includes the way in which an effective teacher thinks aloud, articulating thought processes as well as demonstrating readerly and writerly

Figure 2.1   Imitating the text at Front Lawn Primary, Havant

processes. The children are engaged in talking through ideas and refining their spoken and written expression; by involving them in explaining to others, it enables the children to develop their understanding of whatever is being studied. And, of course, in the process it improves the children's reading: the more familiar you become with the tune of a text, the easier it is to read that sort of text because the language patterns are familiar to you.

Teaching non-fiction writing in Talk for Writing style is very similar to the teaching of narrative since it follows the same three key stages from **imitation** through **innovation** into **independent application**. In the same way that learning a story orally helps a child internalise a narrative pattern so that it is added to their linguistic repertoire, non-fiction texts can also be learned orally. The teacher creates a memorable, meaningful version of the text type being taught (at a level just above where the children are), building in the structure and age-appropriate language features.

The children are then taken on a journey from imitation to innovation to independent application for each of the key non-fiction text types. For an overview of the typical features of all the key non-fiction text types – see **Handout 2**, Appendix 2 on **DVD 2**.

We have found that children often come to understand the patterns of non-fiction text better if their initial experience is with fictional non-fiction – for example, beginning to understand the patterns of explanation text through a model focusing on why dragons died out before moving on to factual information about why the dinosaurs died out. In this way, the pattern of the language can be focused on without having to worry about the accuracy of the facts. This approach is illustrated in the non-fiction worked examples in this book. In addition, each teacher needs to pass the baton on to the next teacher so that when the children move up a year they are building on the non-fiction skills that they already have.

The theoretical essence is simple but the practice is always more complex. The art of effective teaching is being able to identify where the children are on their learning journey and providing the right skills for them to add to their repertoire through imitation and innovation so they can apply and develop them independently across the curriculum. In such a way, the children will achieve breadth and depth and will have mastered flexible writing skills that can be adapted to suit the needs of any writing task in any subject. Moreover, the approach can be adapted to suit the needs of all children of all ages:

> *It's really good for the children in our class who can't hear very well or talk very well because of all the actions and sign language we use. We can all join in. It gives me lots of ideas about my writing because it's sometimes hard to think by myself and it doesn't make sense. I like it best when we do quizzes about our text.*

Kai from the SEND Harbour Centre, Staines

> *Now my writing is high standard because I can organise properly and it doesn't jump around. I remember the class one and that helps to sort it in my head.*

Linda, pupil from Lewisham Talk for Writing across the curriculum project

> *Story maps help me with my writing because I always have a bank of words to use.*

Yusra, 8, St George's Primary School, Battersea, London

'I also find it helpful actually saying the words so I know what kind of words I can use for my own writing. It's amazing how much I've improved my writing, though I can't spell every word.'

Pupil from Sheffield Talk for Writing across the curriculum project

'When Pie Corbett invented story maps, it helped me with my writing because when I write in my book, I always know what to write.'

Jaime, aged 9, St George's School, Battersea, London

'Talk for Writing has helped me to sort out my thinking. I know how to write well now.'

Year 4 pupil, Burnley Brow

An overview of the Talk for Writing process

The Talk for Writing process is summed up by the image below:

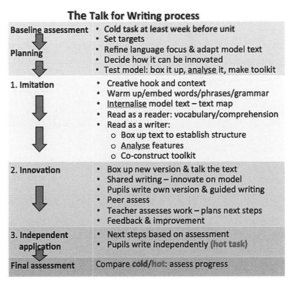

Figure 2.2

Each non-fiction chapter illustrates this process in practice so you can see how to adapt it to the type of text you want the pupils to be able to read, write and speak in. Appendix 1 (DVD 2) explains how the video clips support teacher training in the process.

Decide on the purpose of each unit

This is key to the child making progress. If we are not careful, we get sidelined by the allure of an interesting topic, for example pirates, and forget that the purpose of the unit is not to teach the children about pirates but to use it as a vehicle to teach essential transferable skills. So, the wise teacher will think through the points below:

- The **objective** of the unit (e.g. to develop recount writing skills). If the class has already been taught this type of writing in Talk for Writing style, the toolkit that was co-constructed with the class for this type of text will need to be located so that the unit builds on previous learning.

- An interesting **topic** that will deliver the objective.

- The **hook** that will engage the class with the topic.

- A **model text** that will provide the linguistic patterns that the class will be shown how to reproduce. This model will need to be located or written and will usually need to be adapted to suit the needs of the class.

Baseline assessment and planning: adjusting the language focus and the model text

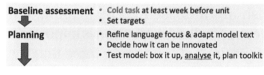

Figure 2.3

At least a week before beginning a unit it's a good idea to set an activity to establish what **baseline skills** pupils already have in relation to the objective of the unit. For younger pupils, you might want to call this *Have a go!* – the children's words could be recorded if they haven't started writing yet. For older pupils, we use Roz Wilson's term *cold task*. The pupils will need a familiar context (for instance, for explanation, if the area has been flooded recently, you could ask the children to explain what had caused the flooding) so that they have something to write about that they know about and that interests them. Warm up the topic with a brief discussion, but do not provide any teaching in how to write about this subject. This will help you pinpoint what specific skills to focus on in the unit to help the children progress.

If this writing were typical of the writing that resulted from this cold task,

Nearly everyone's house near me flooded in Janary, it was terrible. The river just rose and rose and kept on rising so anyway we tried to put sandbags in frunt of our door to stop the water getting in but it came up thrugh the toilet!!!! Everything downstairs was rouined, the carpits just had to be thrown away but I rescued our cat.

You would then know that your unit had to focus on:

Explanation features:

- The structure and focus of explanation text rather than falling back on recount writing in 'explain what happened' mode.

- The phrasing of explanation text especially causal language.

- The construction of complex sentences to explain things.

General language features:

- Writing in sentences and knowing where the sentences end.

- Linking sentences effectively.

- Including a variety of sentence structures.

- Appropriate punctuation avoiding comma splices.

- Modelling the type of vocabulary needed and how to spell it.

At the end of the unit, the children would be asked to do a similar piece of explanation writing, which is known as the **hot task** or *Show what you now know*. By comparing the cold and hot tasks, you can assess the progress made.

A note on cold tasks across the curriculum

The learning focus for units of work in English are all based on expression, not content. For units of work in other subjects, content as well as expression is important. Logically, you cannot set a sensible cold task for a unit of work on a topic that the children do not yet know anything about, as they would have nothing to write, so cold tasks across the curriculum may have to be based on the last piece of written work the children did for this subject – see page 181 for an illustration of this.

Bookending units with a cold and hot task

The idea is to bookend units of work with a cold and hot task so that the teacher, the child, the parents and anyone visiting the class can easily see the progress made within the unit – see Clip 2 on **DVD 1**. It is, therefore, useful to make it visually obvious where the opening cold task baseline is and where the hot task is at the end of the unit. You might want to get the children to write on appropriately coloured paper – e.g. pale blue for cold and pale orange for hot, and then stick the work in the books. An easier method, favoured by those who value their weekends, is to use coloured tabs or stamps – blue for the cold text, red for the hot – so anyone looking at the book can easily

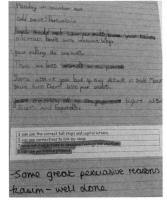

Figure 2.4   Kasim's cold task

locate the start and end of each unit and identify the progress made.

From the example of a cold task (see Figure 2.4), the teacher from Montgomery Primary School, Birmingham, could assess what persuasive writing skills this child already had and ensure that the planned unit would help the child make progress.

The highlighted targets below the cold task, help both teacher and child know what needs to be focused on. If you look at Figure 2.5 here, that the same child wrote at the end of the unit on persuasive writing, you can see that he has made considerable progress. The blank target grid is there to help the child reflect on his learning in relation to his targets.

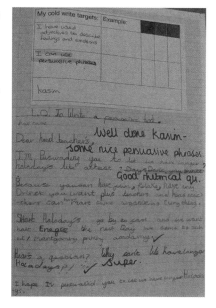

Figure 2.5   Kasim's hot task

Adapting your planning in the light of the cold task assessment

The cold task enables the teacher to assess the work of the whole class and identify the key skills that the class already has and how these could be developed within the unit, as well as any new skills to be introduced. These then form the targets throughout the unit. It might help to think of these targets as Rome and ensure that *all roads lead to Rome*. Also, note down specific skills that low attainers will need more help with and opportunities where the skills of higher attainers could be extended.

Then write or adapt the model text, as necessary, to illustrate the key features identified. Check that your model:

- **has all the language features you want to introduce** at the right level. If your class have been taught in Talk for Writing style before, decide how you will work with the class to add any new features to their already **co-constructed toolkit** for this text type. If this is their first time of using the approach, then plan how you are going to co-construct your toolkit of features with the class progressively throughout the unit (see pages 27–30);

- **has the language features you want to embed** at the right level to help the children work towards mastery;

- **is not too long** (maximum 400 words).

Stage 1: The imitation stage

1. Imitation

- Creative hook and context
- Warm up/embed words/phrases/grammar
- Internalise model text – text map
- Read as a reader: vocabulary/comprehension
- Read as a writer:
  - o Box up text to establish structure
  - o Analyse features
  - o Co-construct toolkit

Figure 2.6

This first stage is the most important stage as this lays the pattern of language in the children's heads. If this stage is rushed, the children will not have internalised the patterns sufficiently to be able to innovate and then use them independently.

The creative hook

Figure 2.7   Scrooge's counting house

Begin the unit with a hook to motivate the children – see Clip 3 on **DVD 1**. Amazing sets relating to the topic can be constructed. More simply, this could be a filmed message from someone marooned on an island asking for instructions on how to build something, or from the teaching assistant who has been captured by a giant asking the children to write a letter to persuade the giant to let her go. One Christmas, St Vincent de Paul School in Liverpool hired an actor to sack the headteacher and cancel Christmas. This was the hook for a wide range of non-fiction writing across the school, including persuading Scrooge to reinstate Christmas. Interestingly, the children were far more concerned about the loss of their headteacher than they were about Christmas. The head had to be reinstated by lunchtime as the reception children were so upset!

Warming up the words, phrases, sentence patterns and grammar

It is vital that the children understand what the words mean, otherwise this could just become an exercise in rote learning and hollow chanting. The teacher has to think about how to make sure that the children understand what they are saying.

This is crucial because generative grammar cannot work without understanding. Generative grammar is the underlying principle that underpins 'talking the text'. It is the brain's extraordinary ability to internalise the underlying patterns of language through the constant experience of hearing sentences and then using those patterns to create new utterances. A child who hears and begins to join in with and say a sentence such as, 'We are discussing whether or not football should be played in the playground' may ultimately internalise the pattern as part of their language store, recycling the underlying pattern to create a new statement such as, 'We are discussing whether or not we should have a school uniform.'

Look at your model text and decide which words, phrases and grammar will need warming up so that when the children hear the words they will know what they mean – see Clip 4 on **DVD 1**. And, of course, how are you going to help them spell these words? Think about the key phrasing that underpins this sort of text. The sentence signposts that link the text together, as illustrated here,

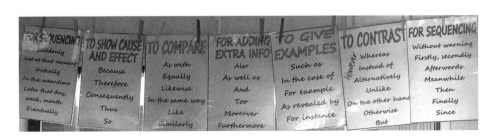

Figure 2.8   Using a washing line to display key sentence signposts

courtesy of Front Lawn Primary, Havant, will be crucial – see Appendix 3 on **DVD 2** for an explanation of the different sorts of connecting phrases. If the children are still not secure in constructing compound or complex sentences, or introducing sentences in a variety of ways, what activities will help them learn how to do this and punctuate their sentences correctly? What grammatical terms do you need to introduce to help them talk about their learning and apply their understanding in their writing? Chapters 4 to 9 have many examples of these sorts of activities. The more these activities are oral and engaging, the more chance there is of the children internalising the language that they need for success within the unit. *Jumpstart! Grammar* is full of entertaining grammar activities that could easily be adapted to fit the focus of any unit. As you introduce or reinforce a feature, help the children remember it by adding it to the toolkit along with examples (see the section on toolkits on pages 27–30).

Time has to be spent loitering with the text at this early stage. If the teacher dashes on, then the children's writing may well disappoint. Apart from learning the text orally, as explained below, the children need to play around every day with the information and language patterns, interacting and imitating as much as possible. The more the text is processed in different ways, the more likely it is that the children will learn the information but also internalise the language.

To interact with the text there are, therefore, two strands that need attention:

- mingling with the information.

- interacting with the language patterns.

To this end, we have devised a number of games and activities that can be played on a daily basis as 'starters' to warm up and then help embed the tune of the text. It is worth the teacher thinking about what the children might find difficult to learn and where there might be challenges in the writing. This should focus attention on what needs to be addressed through the games and activities. This shifts the teaching from becoming a range of entertaining games to focusing upon what needs to be learned in order to help children make progress. It is the assessment influencing the teaching that sharpens and clarifies the learning experience. And, of course, many of these activities will lead to short-burst writing activities, thus ensuring creative writing is done every day even when the focus is on internalising text orally.

> *When Pie Corbett came to teach us, I didn't think that it would help by just throwing in random ideas. However, as he went along, I realised it allowed us to become more creative. This has helped my writing because I now think about every word I use and the effect it would have on the reader.*
>
> Dujour, aged 9, St George's Primary,
> Battersea, London

To help children internalise language patterns you might:

- Rehearse specific spelling patterns that will be needed for this writing.

- Put key sentence signposts (words and phrases that help link text and tell the reader the direction in which the text is heading) and other language features onto cards and rehearse them. When playing the drama games suggested below, make sure that children use the 'non-fiction' language. You could even give a simple score for the correct use of different features.

- Play 'linking phrase of the day' where you all have to try and slip the sentence signpost into classroom conversation and activity (*because, this leads to, therefore, on the other hand, moreover* etc.).

- Take a pattern such as an adverb starter (*amazingly, usefully, incredibly, weirdly, helpfully*) and challenge the children to see who can 'use' that construction during the day.

- Try sentence games where you change bland language, extend sentences, alter sentence openings, drop in or add on information, trim back wordy sentences as well as 'sentence doctor' errors.

- Play rapid sentence games where you write up a key pattern and then children have to invent sentences using the same pattern. Imitate sentences orally first and then in writing (using mini-whiteboards), e.g.

  - *The apple falls because of gravity.*

  - *The dragon sneezes because of the dust.*

  - *The hippo floats because of its water wings.*

- Practise short-burst writing using images related to the topic to build up focused descriptive writing skills as well as a greater understanding of the context of the unit.

To help children understand the information, among other things, you might:

- Interview a child in role as 'Professor Know-it-all' – the world expert.

- Have a panel of experts on the topic.

- Carry out a mock TV interview about the topic.

- Hold 'back-to-back' mobile phone conversations about the topic.

- Hot seat experts.

- Make a list of 'amazing facts'.

- Box up 'Did you know?' facts (Did you know that the Romans ate dormice?).

- Create a display of 'False or True?' (False or True – the Romans ate Rats . . . False – they ate dormice, stuffed!).

- Present information as a news broadcast.

- Play 'spot the true fact' where the teacher gives false facts with one truthful nugget and the children have to decide which is true.

- Turn information into an illustration or diagram.

- Transform information into bullet points.

- Create a 'fact file' using small cards that each have a 'blistering fact'.

Internalising the model text

> *Dear Pie Corbett, I am writing to you because I think your ideas about how to get children to stand up and say stories is brilliant. I used to hate writing. It was boring listening to the teacher groan on and on because I would just sit there and do nothing. Also then it was hard. Now I love it because it is so much more easy and I produce more work. I think it's got easier because our teacher teaches us all the things and then we learn stories that include all the things. I also feel more confident . . .*

Pupil's letter presented as evidence of impact by teacher on the Sheffield Talk for Writing across the curriculum project

The children internalise the pattern of language of the model text by learning it orally. The teacher speaks the text in a lively manner and the children join in with both the speaking of the language and the actions that make it memorable. The children do not see the text at this stage, but there is a text map to act as a reminder plus actions to reinforce specific language patterns as well as the meaning.

The class works on internalising the text over a number of days until it begins to become second nature, with the teacher increasingly handing over to the class – see Clip 6 on **DVD1**. It is crucial for the patterns to be 'over-learned' if they are to actually become part of the child's linguistic repertoire. As the text becomes embedded in the children's long-term working memory, the teacher moves from whole-class imitation to group performances down to trios and pairs. Pairs sit facing each other with the text maps or mini washing lines between them – saying the text at the same time like a mirror, using actions. There are many ways to vary the learning of a text, e.g.

- Say it in pairs like a mirror.

- Pass it round the circle.

- Perform it like a tennis match – word for word, chunk for chunk, or sentence by sentence, back and forth.

- Mime it.

- Say it as fast as possible – babble gabble – racing to see who can get to the end first.

- Pass it up and down a line.

- Present the text as a group, using PowerPoint or other forms of illustration.

Many schools build in regular opportunities for children to talk their text, presenting the information to other classes and even performing in assembly. The provision of audience and purpose is always a spur to learning, refining and honing the use of language.

The initial stage of 'talking the text' mirrors the stage where children learn to retell a known tale. Where children are unfamiliar with a text type or struggle with literacy, it is worth spending time helping the children internalise the basic patterns of the text – in the long run, this pays off because you will see the patterns reappearing in their own writing. This is rather like putting a writing frame into the children's minds in a memorable, meaningful manner.

This is key to the success of the whole process. Time spent on ensuring the children have internalised the pattern of the text they will write will pay dividends. You may find the following useful in helping you to do this as well as looking at video clips 5 and 8 to see how Pie does this.

A note on drawing text maps

Figure 2.9   An example of a simple text map

Draw a text map that sums up the overall flow of the text. It's important to keep the map and the drawings simple, as fussy over-detailed maps with an image for every word are much harder to 'read'. Soon the children will be drawing their own version: the more daunting your map is, the less they will feel capable of drawing their own. (The instruction text map to the left, from Warren Farm Academy in Birmingham, is ideal. The simple pictures mean that you can immediately start to 'read' it.)

It's important to think about the needs of your class and draw the text map that will best help them. Some schools choose to box up each sentence with a clear full stop at the end. If many children in the class are new to the English language, this increased level of scaffolding supports the children in understanding how to structure and punctuate their sentences.

Top tips for imitating the text

- Make certain you and your teaching assistant have learned the model text very well so that you can lead the storytelling with gusto.

- Draw a simple text map; do not have an icon for every word.

- Devise a few actions that will help everyone remember the key language patterns and content. The children will enjoy joining in with this and suggesting better actions. Avoid too many actions.

- Once the preparations are in place, immerse the children thoroughly in the model text. Remember, you are the model so say the words clearly, with expression, and make the movements with energy so everyone can enjoy joining in. Keep looking at the text map to support you and the class: this is not a memory test.

- Get the children to sketch their own text map as this will help imprint the text in their heads. Outlaw clip art – not only does this waste hours of time but it also breaks the connection between hand and brain.

- Finally, remember to focus on getting the children to intonate the text properly; and remember, if they sound dull, that's because you sounded dull. Increasingly, hand over to the children so they can talk the text independently with enthusiasm.

Figure 2.10   In conclusion

A note on key actions

It is useful to have set actions across the school for the key sentence signposts like *first*, *after that*, and *finally*, and display them both to support the children in using them and to remind the teacher to model their use and extend the range (see **Handout 7** in appendix 3, **DVD 2** for suggested gestures to illustrate these linking words. Substitute pictures of children for the pictures of Pie, like the example to the right from Selby Primary School, North Yorkshire, that forms part of a set of key language for science investigations – see **Handout 8** in appendix 3, **DVD 2**. Each year, the range of linking phrases should be extended; the visual resource could accompany the class to be built on each subsequent year.

A note on punctuation

Some teachers like to get the children to voice the punctuation of the text so the children may say something like this: *Are you ever bored at the weekend, question mark.* Inserting words to vocalise all the punctuation removes the meaning from the text and makes it sound very strange. The whole point is to embed the pattern of language and so they need to hear the pattern of the language in a meaningful way. Expression helps children 'hear' the punctuation. To help children remember the punctuation, it is probably better to use actions, like punching the air for full stops, or stamping out the stop. Hand movements to indicate commas, for example, for dropped in information, are particularly useful.

Once the children have internalised the text, there are two key steps that help bridge the move from imitation to innovation: reading as a reader and reading as a writer, which includes co-constructing the toolkit for the type of text focused on.

1a) Reading as a reader

Of course, after a while, the children will need to see what the text looks like when it is written down. The longer this moment can be delayed, the more likely the children are to have internalised the patterns. If the children know the text intimately, then it will mean that even those who struggle with reading have access to the written version, as they already know what it is going to say. This removes the barrier that reading problems can produce when studying a text and helps the child become a reader since prior knowledge is key to deciphering text meaningfully. 'Reading as a reader' aids comprehension – see Clip 18 on **DVD 1**.

Below is a simple model text for introducing how to teach instructions. To aid understanding not only would all the relevant props be available – for instance, a puppet theatre, puppets, all the items named in the ingredients – but, more importantly, the children would have been involved in making puppets so the instructions have real meaning.

> **How to make a puppet**
>
> Have you ever wanted to entertain your friends? If so, read these instructions and soon you will be able to put on a puppet show for them.
>
> **You will need:** a piece of felt, pins, marker pens, large needles, coloured thread, ribbons, buttons, wool and a pair of scissors.
>
> **What to do:**
>
> 1. Fold the felt in half.
> 2. Draw the shape of your puppet on the felt.
> 3. Cut it out carefully.
> 4. Put in some pins to stop it moving.
> 5. Sew round the edges but leave the bottom open for your hand.
> 6. Draw on a face.

7. Decorate the body.

Now you are ready to perform for your friends. Why not make a cast of characters and write a play? Have fun!

A key aspect during this initial stage is to ensure children understand the vocabulary plus the specific teaching of comprehension. This might involve oral comprehension through discussion or more formal setting of questions. Read the text carefully line by line, exploring vocabulary and deepening understanding through questioning and discussion. There are many other ways to help children deepen their understanding of texts. Typically, they would involve:

- Talking about the text (oral comprehension). An excellent book explaining how to open up discussion on text so that the children co-construct understanding rather than trying to work out the answer they think you want to hear, is Aidan Chambers' *Tell me*, published by Thimble Press, which explains the underpinning techniques of what is sometimes referred to as book talk.

- Discussing the audience and purpose.

- Analysing who wrote the text, what did they need to know to do this – and why did they write it.

- Filling gaps – cloze procedure – taking out key language features such as linking words or phrases.

- Comparing sentences or paragraphs and discussing which is most effective and why.

- Sequencing – splitting up sentences, paragraphs or even whole texts for children to reassemble – this helps confirm the organisation of language.

- Improving – provide weak sentences or paragraphs and the children have to 'improve' them.

- Annotating – reading paragraphs carefully and annotating them, searching for different features or commenting on impact.

- Focused vocabulary work relating to the passage.

1b) Reading as a writer

To lead into the next phase of **innovation**, the children must first be involved in analysing the text that they have internalised. There are two key aspects that the teacher has to ensure happen:

- understanding the underlying structure of the text through the very simple device of boxing up;

- recognising and understanding the ingredients that helped to make the writing effective and collecting these in a toolkit of ingredients.

Boxing up text to understand structure

Boxing-up text
(e.g. information text about an animal)

Heading for each section	Key points
Introduction State what type of animal	• lion • type of cat
Appearance (what it looks like)	• ... • ...
Habitat (where it is found)	• ... • ...
Diet (what it eats)	• ... • ...
Habits (what it does)	• ... • ...
Conclusion (Round off text, e.g. with an amazing fact)	• ...

Figure 2.11   Boxing up text

First show the children how to box up the text. This involves the children in using a problem-solving approach to see if they can identify how the text is organised and box it up into a grid accordingly – see Clips 6 and 9 on **DVD 1**.

Boxing up has proved to be an invaluable, simple way of helping pupils first understand the structure of a text and then use a similar structure to plan their own text. Create a two-column grid with as many rows as there are paragraphs or sections in the text. Then involve the class in identifying what the heading would be for each.

Where there are paragraph headings, this might be relatively simple. Often, there are obvious topic sentences that clearly indicate the subject matter found in each section. Carry out the boxing up with the children so that they problem solve the text and co-construct the pattern.

What is a topic sentence?

Usually, the topic sentence is the first sentence in a paragraph. The sentence tells the reader what the topic of the paragraph will be about. All the other sentences develop the topic mentioned. For instance, if a paragraph starts with, 'Lions have a limited diet', then the rest of the paragraph will be about the diet of lions. A topic sentence is like the subheading to a paragraph that has been turned into a sentence. Therefore, with small children, start with a subheading and show them how to turn it into a topic sentence.

The children work in pairs to identify the structure of the text. Then a boxed-up grid may be drawn (see below) that will act as a planner. The one below indicates how all text has a beginning, middle and end. The second column is initially blank, ready for new information to be added or notes to sum up the key points of the model text.

An example of how to box up

Below is a boxed-up version of 'How to make a puppet'

Heading for each section	Key points
Beginning Introduce what is going to be made with a hook	• entertain friends • follow these instructions • put on puppet show

Middle	
A. What to do	• list of materials
B. What to do	• list all stages in order
End	
Round off	• ready to perform

Where children are working on a text type for the first time, working out the basic underlying pattern is very handy as it leads the children into writing something similar with a predetermined structure.

However, the danger of this approach is that the children may become over-reliant on the model – even to the extent that they cannot write without first filleting a text. For this reason, it is important to lead the children into a stage where they also begin to think for themselves about their audience and the purpose, constructing their own boxing-up grids – what 'clumps' of information do we need and in what order should they come?

It is worth considering that all non-fiction actually shares the same overall structure. All non-fiction text should begin with an **opening** to introduce the subject matter in an engaging way to hook the reader's attention. This is then followed by the **middle** or main body of the text. This is generally organised into clumps so that the information or ideas are clustered sensibly (logically or chronologically) into specific sections – usually presented as paragraphs. Finally, there is always some form of **ending** in which the writer might summarise, make a concluding point, remind the reader of the relevance of the information to their own lives or perhaps leave the reader gasping at a final killer fact!

You can adapt the boxing-up approach to support understanding of any text. A good paragraph of non-fiction text should have a beginning, a middle and an end, just like a longer text has; equally, the structure of a long text can be boxed up via sections rather than paragraphs. Once children have understood this process, you can use it to box up the class novel so that the children can see the underlying structure.

Co-constructing the toolkit

Once the children have understood how the text is structured, the children will benefit from using a problem-solving approach to identifying key language features that might be useful for 'when we write our one'. This is rather like 'raiding the reading' or magpieing – stealing good ideas. Use a range of methods to help them analyse all the ingredients that contribute to making the text effective. Underlining and highlighting are useful techniques as children search for the basic ingredients of the text type such as linking phrases or powerful descriptive phrases. This becomes easier if they look at how several writers have tackled a type of writing, for they can generalise the sorts of patterns that typically appear.

Once a new feature has been identified, get the children to explain what they have just learned and add the feature to your **toolkit of ingredients** for this particular type of text; examples can be displayed on the washing line to support understanding. In this manner, a toolkit for each text type can be co-constructed with the children listing the ingredients to choose from to make this sort of writing effective – see Clip 10 on **DVD 1**.

It may also help if children are introduced to the fact that there are basically four things that you have to do to try to ensure that any piece of writing works.

Ingredients for success for any writing

Plan it	• Remember audience and purpose – you have to engage and interest your reader. • Box up your ideas, including a beginning with a hook, a middle and an end.
Link it	• Introduce your ideas with topic sentences. • Link your ideas, with good sentence signposts. • Read it aloud to check that it flows.
Express it	• Use a range of sentence types and structures. • Select just the right words to say what you want to say.
Check it	• Read it aloud and see if it sounds good – does it hold your interest? – does it say what you wanted it to say effectively? • Check your spelling and punctuation is correct.

These generic ingredients could then become part of the children's inner toolkit around which they can build the specific features relating to the type of writing focused on.

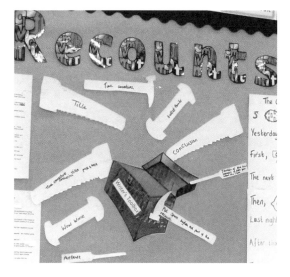

Figure 2.12   Toolkit display for recount text

Beware of disembodied tick lists of features

Co-constructing toolkits is much more effective than listing a series of success criteria and sticking them in the children's books. These lists are often meaningless to the children because they have not understood what the features mean. If they are involved in co-constructing the lists, and if the toolkits include examples of what the features mean, then they will support the children's learning. If you were asked to write some interesting information about an animal and were given the following success criteria to include:

- fronted adverbials;

- the subjunctive mood;

- semicolons;

- the past progressive;

you would not find the list helpful; neither do the children. If the list had been co-constructed with meaningful features for this type of text supported by useful examples, then it could help.

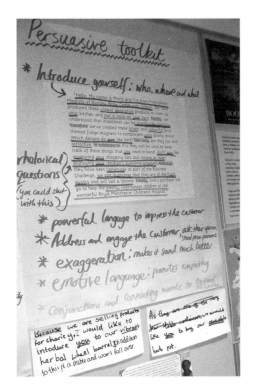

Figure 2.13   Persuasive toolkit

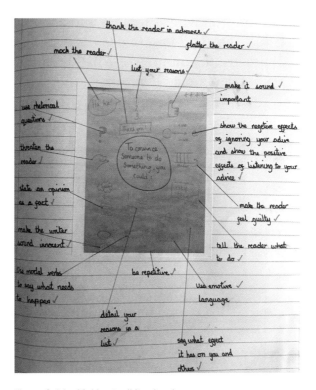

Figure 2.14   Making toolkits visual

Toolkits in reception and Year 1 are often called *Writing Secrets* and are very visual. As the children grow older, these toolkits are further developed so that the features are added to year on year. In this book, we have illustrated toolkits split into four key ingredients, *Plan it*; *Link it*; *Express it*; *Check it*, as this simple list helps children remember the key ingredients of all effective writing. Different teachers have chosen different visual ways of developing this idea to suit the needs of their classes. At St Joseph's in Derby, they have laminated tools that allow teachers to change the toolkits depending on the focus of the writing

(Figure 2.12). At Burnley Brow, Lancashire, the Year 6 teacher made the key features very visible by analysing the model text with the class and colour-coding the features (Figure 2.13). At Penn Wood, all the toolkits are highly visual and are displayed on washing lines in icon form. The visual toolkits are also stuck in the children's books and they have to annotate them to show they understand what they mean, as illustrated by Figure 2.14 from a Year 6 unit on persuasion.

The basic toolkits for each type of non-fiction text are easier than those for key story types like suspense because the underpinning structure and features tend to be more consistent and it is easier for the children to grasp the pattern. More confident writers should also look at other examples to broaden their frame of reference.

Everyday toolkits

Many schools have also developed what might be called *Everyday*, *Always* or *All the time toolkits*. These are features like writing in sentences that begin with a capital letter and end with a full stop. Such features always apply whatever text is being focused on. The ones pictured below are from Maidwell Primary in Northampton where Years 1 and 2 are taught together. The picture enables us to see how these *All the time toolkits* can be built on year by year to ensure progress is planned into units of work. In this way, the children are aware of the underpinning features that must always be present in their writing and that they must check for carefully when reading their writing through.

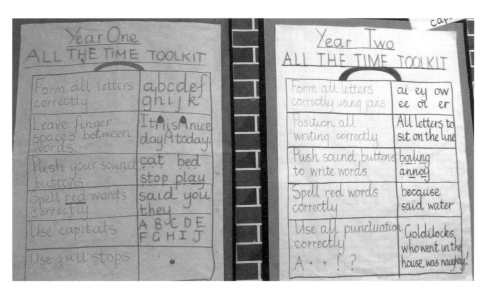

Figure 2.15   Everyday toolkits displayed for Years 1 and 2

Display the toolkits on the washing line or working wall so they support the children when they start to write and encourage them to jot down key features and favourite words in their writing journals.

What is a writing journal?

These act as a 'writing thesaurus'. Each type of writing will need a section. Into this the children stick the basic model, boxed up to show the organisation, the writing toolkit of ingredients plus useful banks of words, sentence patterns, tips, hints and reminders. The benefit of the journal is that it acts as a reminder or reference point when children are writing across the curriculum and it is personal, as illustrated in Figure 2.16 by this page from a child's writing journal from East Hunsbury School in Northampton. Below that is the reversible toolkit journal used at Maidwell, a small rural primary in Northamptonshire: one way round is for English; turn the book over for maths.

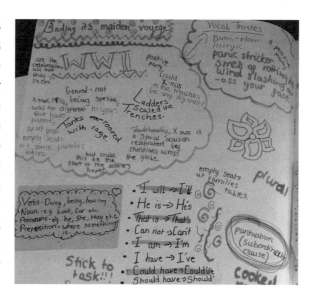

Figure 2.16   Page from a child's writing journal

Typically, children will be noticing the use of such features as:

- topic sentences and headings that help to show the reader how the text is organised, e.g. *appearance, diet, habitat*;

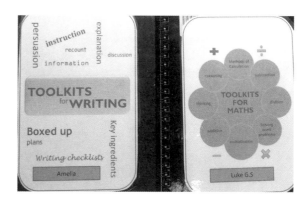

Figure 2.17   Reversible toolkits for English and maths

- sentence signposts that help to steer the reader through the text, e.g. *however, on the other hand, This leads to . . .*;

- generalisers that help the writer to sum up facts in general terms, e.g. *most, typically, the majority of*;

- persuasive devices such as 'boastful adjectives', e.g. *magnificent, marvellous*;

- 'bossy' verbs (imperatives) that allow a writer to push the reader to a viewpoint or instruct the reader: *Remember . . . Do . . . Avoid . . . Ensure . . . .*

Making the learning visible

By the end of the imitation stage, all of the learning that the children have experienced so far should be visible on the learning wall or washing line. The children should be able to see the model text, the boxed-up plan, the co-constructed toolkit and any word or phrase banks that have been created to help them with their learning. It also, of course, helps the teacher and the teaching assistant to remain focused on the key learning targets.

The persuasion washing line (Figure 2.18) from Front Lawn Primary in Havant shows a boxed-up text map, the model text (with capital letters in red to draw the children's attention to them) and a toolkit of the key persuasion features the unit has covered so far. In Maidswell, Years 5 and 6 share the same classroom. Their

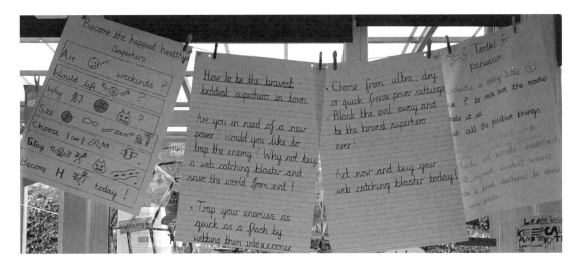

Figure 2.18   Using a washing line to make learning visible

working wall (see Figure 2.19) displays the boxed-up planning, the model information text, and examples of the language of comparison, a feature that the unit was focusing on.

Figure 2.19   Using a working wall to make learning visible

Working in partnership with your teaching assistant (TA)

The approach works best when the teacher and the TA work in partnership actively supporting the children's learning. While one is teaching, the other can be visually drawing out the key learning points for the children by, for example:

- magpieing useful words and phrases onto flip charts;
- drawing text maps in response to the pupils' ideas;
- listing the key ingredients for success as they arise out of discussion with pupils;

- boxing up the text in response to pupil input;

- adding ideas to flip charts.

All of these resources can then be used as posters on the writing wall or washing line supporting the children's writing. If the resources are created in front of the children and are co-constructed out of their discussions, they will be meaningful.

Figure 2.20   The dual approach

The picture to the right from Yew Tree Community School, Birmingham, shows the dual approach in action. The teacher is scribing up the shared writing while the TA is putting useful words on the whiteboard. See Clip 42 on **DVD 2** of Claire Jepson, a teaching assistant explaining how useful it has been to be a part of the school's Talk for Writing development team.

By this point, the children should be very familiar with the overall pattern of the model they have internalised and its various language features – they will have heard, spoken, read, discussed and played with the sentence types till they have begun to become part of their linguistic repertoire. It would be ideal to end this stage with some sort of enthusiastic performance to other classes or, with younger classes, invite the parents in at the end of the day and get them to join in. The language patterns can then be further embedded at home and all the family can have fun – see Chapter 11 on involving the family.

Stage 2: The innovation stage

2. Innovation

- Box up new version & talk the text
- Shared writing – innovate on model
- Pupils write own version & guided writing
- Peer assess
- Teacher assesses work – plans next steps
- Feedback & improvement

Figure 2.21

Once the children have become familiar with the original text they are ready to move into the second phase, which involves using the original as a basis for creating something new – so that they can write their own version. Do not move on to innovation till the original model is deeply embedded as you cannot innovate on something that is only vaguely known.

The idea is that the children draw upon the underlying structure and language features of the original model to enable them to create their own version about a different topic. To put it simply, the children might have already spent a week learning all about foxes, including learning orally a basic text. This is then used as a basis for writing a new text about badgers.

By this point the original model will be displayed, with the text boxed up and annotated – accompanied by lists of the key ingredients as well as writing reminders, techniques and tricks which have all been drawn out of discussions with the children. These should be on the washing line or working wall so that the teacher can refer to them, as well as being inside the children's writing journals for their own personal reference.

The teacher will need to plan a new starting point, avenue for investigation or experience to act as a basis for the children's writing. All of us write best about what we know about – and what matters to us. This is especially true of non-fiction. Children can only write powerfully when they really have deep understanding and something to say – if their knowledge is thin, then the writing can only be flimsy. This is why 'topic work' often helps to improve non-fiction writing because the children's immersion in a topic helps to build up their knowledge, understanding and views in a way that makes them 'experts' on the topic. It also often means that children come to their writing with the enthusiasm of the expert and so they are more likely to be committed to trying hard.

Shared planning: boxing up the plan for the innovation

The boxed-up grid from the original model can be used as a basic planner. See Clip 20 on **DVD 1**. New information needs to be gathered and organised onto the planning grid. Different approaches to gathering information will have to be modelled and practised, e.g.

- Note-taking.

- Listing questions before finding answers.

- Interviewing visitors and experts.

- Writing or emailing for information.

- Skimming and scanning information books and texts.

- Watching TV/film and taking notes.

- Using the internet.

- Using trips and outings to gather information.

- Using the school grounds, locality and community to discover information, views and ideas . . .

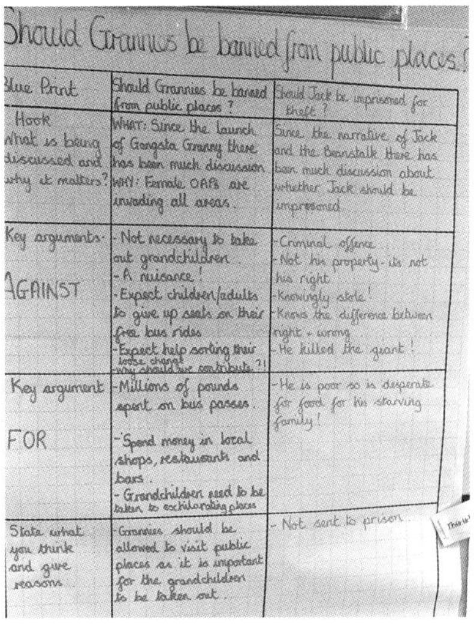

All of this has to be underpinned by learning how to judge whether a source is reliable as well as double-checking with other sources.

The great thing about boxing up is that it not only allows you to analyse the model text but you can then add in additional columns and use the same structure to plan your innovation on the model. The children can then add another column and plan their innovation. The boxed-up discussion displayed in Front Lawn Primary in Havant clearly shows the underpinning structure of discussion in the left-hand column of the grid. The next column shows

Figure 2.22   Using boxing up to plan innovation

how this can be applied to the discussion topic about grannies. The final column shows how the same underpinning structure can be used for a different discussion topic (Should Jack be imprisoned for theft?)

> ❝Boxing up works across all text types and genres. Making this a key component for all text analysis and planning for writing helped children feel in control of learning as each text type could be dealt with in the same way.❞
>
> *Teacher from Lewisham Talk for Writing non-fiction project*

Depending on the children's needs, it can be useful to draw a new text map and to 'talk the new text' in pairs, refining ideas and trying out different ways of expressing ideas, views and information. Reference should be made back to the original to check for useful language features that might be recycled. Pairs can come to the front and present their text orally, receiving feed back from the teacher and class. This acts as a model so that pairs feed back to other pairs, working as response partners, identifying where an oral text works effectively as well as making suggestions for improvement.

During innovation, it is important to keep playing spelling and sentence games so that the children have plenty of oral and written practice in the language features that they will need when they come to write. It can also be handy to play drama games to develop a text further with fun activities such as interviewing experts or role-playing TV programmes, which tune the children into the language they will need to use. One simple game is to work in pairs and use the phrase, 'tell me more about', which encourages the children to develop and extend ideas prior to writing.

Shared writing

The teacher may then use the planning grid to move from an oral version into writing. During shared writing with the class, the text will be further refined, often referring back to the original model or models. It is important for the teacher to involve the children in the composition, taking suggestions and pushing the children to refine their ideas so that they are fluent, coherent and effective. At all times, the teacher needs to bear in mind the level that the text should be written at – which should be above the standard of the children. To put it simply, if the children are writing at what teachers in England understand as level 2, then the class composition must be at level 3.

Of course, life is never this simple, and there are no classes where children are all writing at the same level. This is why teachers use guided writing to group children according to their need and to teach them at their level. Many teachers find it useful to develop a text over several days, focusing on different aspects. Key points need to be referred to and included so that the shared writing is an opportunity to teach progress. During shared writing, the teacher or the children may explain why one idea is more effective than another. The teacher pushes the children to generate possibilities and to judge what would work best. Everyone should be drawing on the original model, as well as the list of ingredients, whilst being driven by using their writing techniques to make the composition powerful. See Clips 7, 21, 26 and 29 on **DVD 1** as examples of this. **Handout 4** (see **DVD 2**, Appendix 2) may also be useful here as it lists the sort of phrases you use to involve the children in shared writing. One very useful tip when composing is to model for the children how to use a dotted line under any words that they may find hard. This has two important effects:

- First, it illustrates that when composing it is not a good idea to break your flow and start looking words up in a dictionary; keep writing and check the spelling later.

- Second, it shows that they must never 'dodge' a good word they wish to use because they can't spell it. This is also very useful for the teacher and the TA when children suggest words that they may have difficulty in spelling.

The quality of the shared writing will determine the progress the children make. Shared writing must be interactive – if it is not, it rivals watching paint dry. One useful approach is to provide the children with whiteboards on which they are regularly required to jot down ideas following short opportunities to share ideas with a partner in order to provide thinking time. Shared writing is absolutely key to the process. Without it, writing is not being taught. The children have to experience the thoughts that go through a writer's head as they try to select just the right word or phrase to express exactly what they are trying to say. This helps the children generate a range of language choices. What changes would make it more effective? The most important thing is to constantly model for the children the importance of reading their work aloud to check first that it flows, and secondly that it sounds right. This helps the children move from generating to judging. It is worth remembering that there is no such thing as a 'wow word'. The power of a word or a sentence depends on the context it is in. Bill Bryson's book *A Walk in the Woods* ends with the sentence *And so we did*. In context, it is the perfect ending. Equally, there never was such thing as a level 5 connective; but there very much is an effective linking phrase used appropriately in context that can help bring writing to a higher level.

Constant rereading helps to ensure that the writing flows coherently as well as being a chance to spot mistakes or clumsy writing that jars on the ear. Part of the success of writing is the ability to capture the 'tune' of the text type so that the sentences flow rhythmically in the right register. Pausing to reread helps children 'hear' where editing is needed.

As we have noted, boxing up is a useful strategy because it encourages children to write in paragraphs. The language ingredients will help to link ideas and the sentences to be written in an appropriate style. However, all of this has to become servant to the overall purpose of the writing, bearing in mind the intended 'reader'. We use our writing style to create an effect.

Occasionally, the teacher will wish to 'demonstrate' during the composition. By this, I mean that the teacher explains aloud some new or difficult feature that has been introduced to the children. Often aspects of progress are introduced in this way so that the teacher shows children how to do something, before having a go together until ultimately children attempt something similar themselves.

The final text is read through and edited. It helps to make the odd mistake or build in a typical weakness so that a discussion may be opened up that relates to something that the children then look for in their own writing. It is worth bearing in mind that shared and guided writing are teaching episodes, so they need to be well planned. It is useful to write out your own version, ensuring that it is pitched at the right level, including the features that you wish to draw to the children's attention. Of course, the children will generate different ideas, but the pre-written text gives the teacher both confidence and a useful reminder to focus on any specific teaching points.

Shared writing is not a question of quickly just doing the introduction. The teacher has to show, through involving the class in the process, how to write the whole text. **Handout 3** in Appendix 2 on **DVD 2** focuses on the art of shared writing. It lists all the ingredients that contribute to successful shared writing. It may be useful to look at this list and reflect on which aspects you think you do well and which ones may need sharpening up. Ideally, be brave enough to have yourself filmed while shared writing and reflect on what aspects have worked really well and what aspects might need improving.

> ❝The most important elements of the process, however, were the shared writing and communal retelling of our shared text.❞
>
> *Maria Wheeler, class teacher from a Talk for Writing project*

The shared writing from Maidwell Primary School, Northampton, for the joint Year 5 and 6 class, illustrates the power of using a different colour to edit text in order to illustrate how you alter text to achieve just the effect that you want.

Moving away from the model – the road to becoming an independent writer

Shared writing should be developed progressively to illustrate to children how to move away from the model. The more confident writers in Years 5 and 6 will be innovating in such a way that they are only using the underlying structure (e.g. how to box up persuasion) and using the related writing toolkit

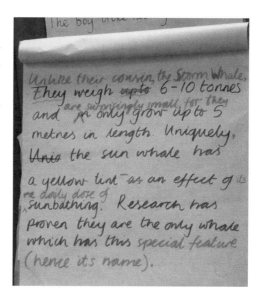

Figure 2.23   Editing shared writing in a different colour

(e.g. persuasion) to create the effect that they want. Indeed, whilst their writing is arising from direct teaching through the shared writing, it is in many ways moving towards invention. Very confident writers might launch straight into their writing and be brought onto the carpet for a review on the second or third day. In this way, the teacher may gradually adapt the pattern of teaching to challenge and support different children. Having said that, where standards are modest, the children will need to hug closer to the model for longer.

There are many different ways to innovate on a text. It is worth considering which form of innovation is appropriate for the class and children that you teach. At first, most teachers cling too tightly to the model and over-control children's writing. Whilst this may happen with the first couple of innovations when a teacher first uses Talk for Writing, it is important to become more adventurous, otherwise the teaching will hold back the writing.

To put it simply, in upper Key Stage 2, children should **not** be using simple substitution or hugging closely to a model unless they are new to the country or have very particular needs. They should be using the underlying text structure and related toolkit and becoming increasingly creative with their compositions, drawing on their wider reading, ideas and imagination. By the same token, more confident children at Key Stage 1 will be writing text based on the original but increasingly adding and altering so that they have drawn upon the full range of their reading and imagination.

Levels of innovation

Young children can have great fun retelling a text and making it their own by choosing simple substitutions. This could involve changing names, places, objects or creatures. By the same token, older children who struggle may benefit from a special form of substitution that is known as 'hugging closely'. At this stage, the child sticks very closely to the sentence structure of the original. This should be modelled sentence by sentence so that the children are writing on mini-whiteboards as the teacher writes and no one is moving on until sentences are completed and punctuation sorted. For example:

Model text	Shared writing – hugging closely	Child's version
Last week, we all went to the Country Museum. First, we looked at the tractors. They had enormous wheels.	Yesterday, we all went to the Toy Museum. First, we looked at the dolls. They had shiny faces.	Last Friday, our class went to the Toy Museum. First, we looked at the teddy bears. They had very big heads.

'Hugging closely' gives confidence, but for more confident writers it would be boring and become a trap that limits writing. Once children have grasped simple substitution, they can be shown how to embellish by adding additional detail:

> Last week, as part of our class project, we all went to Warwick Doll Museum.

> For me, the most interesting section was on teddy bears because they had changed so little over the years.

As a result, the writer would still hug closely, but begin to embellish.

Last Friday, to help us with our project on the history of toys, our class visited the Warwick Doll Museum.

The section I liked best was on automatons because it was great to see them in action.

Over time, the children will have been shown how to add in and on to text to achieve different effects, as well as how to change viewpoint, tense and text type. The aim is to achieve confident writers who can spin their text in whatever direction the audience and purpose requires.

In the following example, the basic idea still lurks under the writing, but this confident writer is now embellishing and experimenting by building description and adding personal responses.

If you are doing a project on the history of toys, you may want to visit Warwick Doll Museum. It's more interesting than the name might suggest. Not only is it full of fascinating exhibits with much loved and often somewhat-dishevelled toys staring at you from all corners but it includes whole rooms of automatons.

As you may have guessed, the section that made the biggest impression on me was . . .

The temptation for the teacher and the child is to stay with substitution and 'hugging closely' because this gives the illusion of success, but true independence and development in writing will not occur unless children move on to adding and altering, drawing on their full range of reading and working at their imaginative fingertips. At Watermoor Primary, they call this 'shaking hands'. In other words, the children decide which parts of a text they should 'hug closely' and where can they 'shake hands' with the text, which means moving away and making it more their own. At Duston Primary in Northampton, they have created an invention indicator that has been adapted below. The children have to identify where they think they are on the indicator with the aim of reaching independent invention.

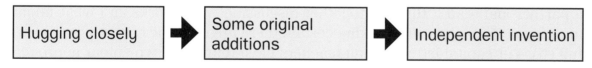

Hugging closely ➡ Some original additions ➡ Independent invention

It is important to move children through different forms of innovation so that they are increasingly challenged, but also gain confidence in manipulating what they know in order to create something new. Innovation is about practising transferable language patterns that, in the end, children will be able to draw upon in order to create. Make sure that you make the following patterns explicit:

a. **Big text patterns** – *e.g. explanation writing/discussion writing.*

b. **Toolkits** – *e.g. how to explain clearly how to make information interesting, etc.*

c. **Basic written style** – *e.g. word choice, sentence variation, etc.*

By Year 6 they should have mastered the various ingredients of the different text types so that they would be able to transfer text that has been presented, say in information style, and convert it into news recount. Over time, they should be able to write much more sophisticated text and mix and match text features as appropriate because, in real life, most non-fiction text is an amalgam of at least two of the non-fiction text types.

Children plan and write their own version

Shared writing is then followed immediately by the children attempting their own composition – perhaps working on the writing over several days, section by section. Ultimately, the final copy may be put into a booklet, onto the school's website, displayed, or turned into some form of presentation. This encourages attention to detail and focuses the mind on the need to present writing as accurately and powerfully as possible, taking good account of the need to inform, persuade, explain or instruct an audience.

If you are share writing a five-section piece of text, it is often most effective to share write it one section at a time over five days so that the children quickly have the opportunity to plan, text map, talk through and write their own paragraphs using the washing line, the model text and the shared writing to support them.

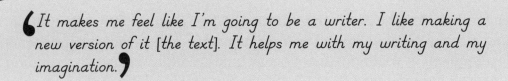

It makes me feel like I'm going to be a writer. I like making a new version of it [the text]. It helps me with my writing and my imagination.

Sarrinah, Harbour Centre, Staines

Peer assessment

Once they have completed a paragraph, ask the children to share their work with a partner and read it through together discussing what works and what might need improving, alongside making certain there are no basic errors like missing full stops or capital letters. Many teachers have found the two-colour approach useful here – say pink for perfect and green for growth. The colours chosen don't matter as long as there is consistency across the school.

The teacher can then assess the work and adapt the following day's shared writing in the light of what the children need. Once the sections have been completed, you might want to ask the children to read their work through, checking it carefully, and write their own comment about how well they think they have completed the task. This is a good way of ensuring the children become increasingly responsible for the quality of their own work and correcting their own errors, and it also gets the dialogue going about what needs to be done to improve their work.

Using assessment to guide your planning

At this stage the teacher will be taking home 30 pieces of writing all on the same topic (such as foxes), using the same information. Obviously, there will be a variety of sophistication in the way that the children have tackled the composition, but in essence everyone will have written something fairly similar. The teacher is now in the position of being able to consider two key aspects:

- How well did the children tackle the writing as writers?

- How effective was the writing?

The answers to these questions will inform the next piece of teaching which should be focused on what the children need in order to improve. Do they need to work on the actual business of being a writer – gathering and sorting ideas, concentrating whilst writing, referring to the plan as well as their journals, or editing? Additionally, what is there in the actual writing that has worked well, and what needs to be attended to next, in order to improve?

The 'marking'/'assessment for learning' should clearly let the child know what has worked well, but also point them towards what needs to be done next. This allows the teacher to increasingly draw the children into working together to develop their repertoire as a writer. The assessment also helps to focus the teacher on what needs to be emphasised in the next stage of 'independent application'.

The teacher can then decide which features to revisit and strengthen later, and which feature will be focused on immediately the work is handed back to the children. If this feature has been identified, say by a simple green line down the relevant section in the margin, then the teacher can begin the lesson with an activity related to this feature. When the books are given back, the children can immediately improve this feature of their work. If work that has been marked is handed back and the children aren't immediately required to improve it, then all the time spent marking has been wasted.

To provide feedback, 'visualisers', iPads, or any other electronic method of getting the children's work on screen, are very powerful. This means that the teacher and the children can use the children's writing to consider what has worked well, and to discuss what needs to be improved. **Handout 5** on **DVD 2**, is full of phrases supporting self-assessment and may be useful here. The teacher models the language to help the children reflect on what works and what needs to be improved so that the children learn to use the same

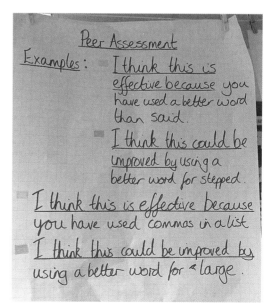

Figure 2.24   Model sentence starters to support peer assessment

phrases and reflect on their work. After such support, a pupil's work could be projected on screen and the author explain the choices that they have made, followed by the class being involved in suggesting possible improvements. The more practice the children get at reflecting on the quality of work and how to improve it, the more they will develop their own editing skills.

The teacher can model how to be a successful 'response partner' with the whole class. The picture above from Front Lawn Primary (see Figure 2.24) provides pupils with the sort of sentence patterns they will need when commenting on each other's work. The basic routine for being a response partner is as follows:

- The author reads their work to their partner, perhaps explaining what they were trying to do.

- The partner discusses with the author what 'works well'.

- One or two places might be identified where improvements could be made.

- Final decisions are always left to the author.

- Time is then provided to allow the author to make the changes they have selected.

If the children's work lacks coherent links, the best activity to support their development with this key feature is sentence combination. This involves providing the children with a series of simple sentences in logical but unconnected order about whatever topic is being focused. The task is to combine them into coherent well-linked sentences – see pages 177–178 for an example of this. The Bill and Betty tactic is another good idea to use at this point. At break time, the teacher in role as Bill or Betty puts work up on the flip chart that mirrors the errors typically made by the children. The children's job, once break is over, is to suggest how the work can be improved. One teacher famously reported hearing one boy saying in all seriousness to another child that Bill's writing seemed to be improving.

One of the contributions that the Transforming Writing project (see pages 72–73) made to the development of Talk for Writing was mini-lessons. Mini-lessons are just that! These work best when the teacher is marking the books and notices that there is some form of common inaccuracy, error, misconception or weakness. So, the next day/lesson, the teacher teaches directly to the common error and the children make relevant improvements. These are usually short-burst, very focused, and the children adapt their writing immediately. There are three possible formats:

a. *'I want these children to come to join me for a mini-lesson on . . .'*

b. *'This morning there will be three mini-lessons – but you can only come to one – choose the one that you feel you most need to attend.'*

c. *'Tomorrow we can have three mini-lessons – what do you want me to teach you?'*

Mini-lessons can be taught by the teacher, a teaching assistant, or by a confident writer working with several peers explaining an aspect of writing.

> ❝Yes I like writing more because I like the flow of writing. It feels good in a way. I'm concentrating and listening more and that has helped my writing.❞

Hope, pupil from Lewisham Talk for Writing across the curriculum project

Stage 3: The independent application stage

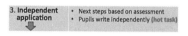

| 3. Independent application | • Next steps based on assessment |
| | • Pupils write independently (hot task) |

Figure 2.25

In this stage, the children move towards becoming more independent.

Let us imagine that the children have been working on a set of instructions.

Imitation – Initially, they learned orally and read a set of imaginative instructions titled 'How to trap a dragon'.

Innovation – They then used this as a basis for composing and writing a set of instructions titled 'How to trap an ogre'.

Independent application – Finally, the teacher allows the children to write their own set of instructions in which they have to 'trap' any mythical or fantastical creature.

This leads the children towards becoming increasingly independent until, in the end, everyone is writing the same text type but choosing topics that interest and intrigue them, or that they know about.

The teacher will still have to use shared writing to teach, but now has the advantage of having read the children's instructions at the 'innovation' stage and observed them in the course of writing. This means that the shared writing can now focus on aspects of the process that need reinforcing, as well as aspects of the actual writing that need revisiting and strengthening. The assessment drives the shared writing and allows the teacher to consider what groupings are needed for guided writing.

Another aspect of this stage that the teacher uses would be to throw into the melting pot several more models so that the children can consider how different writers tackle writing the text type. This might allow children to add more to the list of ingredients or techniques, thereby beginning to broaden their repertoire.

The children can then use their boxing-up skills to start planning their independent work around the same writing focus. They can use their text-mapping skills to people their boxed-up planning with ideas, and can then talk their text with their partner and adapt their ideas in the light of this, if they choose. Then, when they begin to write, they will know what they are trying to say and how they want to say it.

Once again, when they have finished their independent writing they could read it aloud and discuss it with a partner, improve it as they think best, give it a final check through and write a comment on how well they think they have written the piece.

The stage of 'independent application' might look somewhat different with different classes. Confident writers will need high-quality shared writing as a focus. This might be supported by reading as writers a variety of high-level texts which can then be drawn upon and imitated. Less confident classes may have to revisit the whole process of gathering their information, drawing and telling, before moving into boxing up and rehearsing ideas, followed by shared, guided and independent writing. Some children may be best advised to 'hug closely' to the original model. The amount of scaffolding required is in direct relation to what the children need in order to gain success. The important thing is to work towards weaning them off the scaffolding.

Have you tasted it?

Do you like cooking? You may well have had that experience of following a recipe to the letter but still finding the meal tasteless.

In many schools, teachers are (understandably) driven to teach whatever is the latest version of levels, rather than teaching writing. The language of the professional SATs or grammar test marker has crept into the classroom and, rather than children writing in order to communicate powerfully – to explain, inform or narrate – they write to achieve a level or proficiency in the use of the fronted adverbial. In these circumstances, teaching writing can be reduced to the level of a checklist of features that have to be included. And to follow the cooking metaphor further, you can use all the ingredients – but you can only tell if it has worked by eating the meal!

The creative generation of sentences in writing has to be balanced constantly by rereading to listen to whether it 'sounds right' – whether powerful communication is developing. Often, you can hear whether writing works just by reading it aloud. Sometimes it will be hard to explain why something works or does not – and you have to resort to saying, 'Well, it just doesn't sound quite right.' One boy referred to this as 'testing out our writing'. This means that an important aspect of the writing process will be reading writing aloud to a partner or in a circle. Usually teachers do this after the children have finished writing, but it can be very helpful during the writing – perhaps after each paragraph.

Certainly, we can look for a well-structured piece that includes the expected ingredients and even a few writing techniques . . . But in the end, the key question has to be – does the writing fulfil its brief at the level of composition and effect?

- Does it tell the reader what happened in an interesting, amusing and engaging way?

- Does it clearly instruct someone in how to do something successfully?

- Does it inform the reader about a topic in an engaging manner so that the reader wants to read on and find out more, and can use the information?

- Does it clearly explain how something works or why something happens?

- Does it persuade you to a viewpoint so that you are convinced?

- Does it provide a reasoned discussion that has helped the reader think about the subject?

Tick lists will only get you so far. In non-fiction, the writer has to consider how to express the subject matter in a way that will hook the reader's interest and hold them, handcuffed to the page, intrigued, amused . . . and totally engaged.

The end of unit assessment

Final assessment	Compare cold/hot: assess progress

Figure 2.26

This independent writing can act as the hot task – showing what they now know. Once it has been assessed by the teacher, the teacher can look back at each child's cold task to assess what progress has been made. The teacher can then decide what general language features will need to be particularly focused on in the next unit in English, as well as which features will need to be further developed across the curriculum so that the children have the opportunity to broaden and deepen the range of their writing. When the work is handed back, apart from focusing on whatever feature the teacher has selected for the children to improve, the children can then look at their cold task and at the hot task and reflect on the progress they have made.

A good way of testing if they really have internalised the process is to wait a month or so and set a similar task to see if they can do it independently.

Encouraging real independence, creativity and invention

If children are to become effective creative writers who enjoy writing, they will need the motivation that comes from being able to choose their own topic and writing about it as they choose. At the end of units, it is a good idea to plan in free writing opportunities when the children know in advance that they will have the freedom to write in the way they select about what interests them.

Applying the approach across the curriculum

Once the text type has been taught in the manner described, then the teacher begins to look for opportunities to revisit and apply what has been learned across the curriculum.

This is crucial because, if a text type is only taught once during a year, then it is unlikely that the children will truly have internalised the patterns of language and added them to their writing repertoire. The more that a text type is revisited, the more likely the children are to embed their learning so that the style of writing becomes internalised, broadened and developed. Chapters 4 to 9 end with a section on how to embed each text type across the curriculum – see clip 30, which introduces how the approach works across the curriculum. Clips 11–14, 17 and

27–34, 43 show children using the approach across the curriculum from reception to Year 6.

Writing journals are handy at this point as they should be organised so that they contain a section for each type of writing. In every section there should be at least one model, pitched at the right level, plus a reminder of the overall structure, the ingredients, as well as any writing techniques or tips. In this way, the journal becomes a writing thesaurus, which is referred to – ensuring the children's learning in literacy does not slip away through lack of use . . . 'use it or lose it'.

Box up Maths Steps to Success for Solving Problems	
Beginning – Plan it!	Read the question. Pick out the key information and what it is asking you do to.
	Decide what operation you will need to use. Is it a one, two or three step problem? At each step, do you need to add, subtract, multiply or divide? Do you need to use trial and error to work it out?
Middle – Work it out!	Go through the possible solutions. Remember to do this systematically or in steps. What strategies will you use at each step? Always include your jottings or working out.
End – Check it!	Check your working out You could use a calculator or the inverse operation.

Figure 2.27   Boxing up in maths

Again, the teacher should still use shared and guided writing, if aspects deserve revisiting, though the focus in the children's minds should be just as much taken up with the new subject matter as they are with revisiting and refining old techniques.

The key ingredients underpinning the Talk for Writing process are relevant to all subject areas, as outlined on pages 76–78. The picture here, from St Matthew's, Birmingham, shows how boxing up has been adapted to suit planning how to tackle maths problems. This approach was first developed by secondary maths teachers Zeb Friedman and Helen Hindle in a Talk for Writing project in Brighton and Hove, and is now used by many primary schools.

If the new subject matter requires recalling a lot of facts, it will be very useful to use the text-mapping approach to help the children recall all these facts. Teachers have found that if the children use text mapping as a form of note taking, it greatly strengthens their ability to remember key facts.

'Talk for Writing has ensured every child in my class can succeed. It is inclusive, fun and engaging. I love teaching Talk for Writing and the pupils enjoy the active lessons too. From a maths point of view, the pupils have been able to access more mathematical challenges that deepen their understanding though the use of text mapping and vocabulary sheets.'

Amy Rogers, Year 1 teacher and maths coordinator, Dashwood Academy, Banbury

How this approach can help secondary schools

Where the Talk for Writing approach has been applied systematically in secondary schools, it has proved very successful for all ages and all subjects. This underlines the importance of embedding and developing the approach across the curriculum in primary schools. The more pupils use the approach to underpin their expression across the curriculum, the greater the improvement in their communication skills will be, as well as their self-confidence and their ability to think and discuss any subject. In other words, it will help them achieve the breadth and depth that underpins mastery. These quotations from secondary schools underline the potential of the approach across the curriculum.

> *I have had a look through the evaluation sheets and, to be honest, they brought tears to my eyes.*
>
> Brighton secondary literacy consultant summing up feedback from a training day in which teachers across the curriculum showed how they were integrating the approach into their teaching

> *I talk to the pupils on a regular basis and ask them is the Talk for Writing approach useful? They tell me a resounding Yes. It is very useful. It helps them to learn and it's been an ideal vehicle for us.*
>
> Paul McAteer, Executive Headteacher, Slough and Eton C of E Business and Enterprise College

> *The students feel pride in their own improvement and success . . . It's slashed the time we have to spend on marking . . . There's a real sense of 'Let's see what we can do now' – and there's much more conversation about teaching and learning now.*
>
> Hiri Arunagiri, Head of Science, Slough and Eton

> *Making notes in a box on the five key ideas has totally changed the way we teach. It's revolutionised the way the students can answer the unit four questions . . . It's even transformed accountancy! . . . We feel like we are walking on water.*
>
> Head of Business Studies, Slough and Eton

> *At last a literary consultant who really understands the phrase 'across the curriculum' rather than trying to make us all English teachers.*
>
> Conference delegate

> 'It was a real pleasure participating in the project team session and the school is really excited that this is the key strategy for the development of our teaching and learning. We had some fantastic feedback from staff who did the training and it was great to be able to go straight into a whole staff session and express this . . . The English team thought their day was fantastic and already have lots of ideas!'
>
> *Vicki Shaw, Project team leader and Deputy Head at Rainham Girls School*

> 'Just thought I would offer a quick update. As planned, we are continuing to reinforce the strategies that you brought to us and ensuring that strategies are implemented across the school. During a recent LA review, the renewed and consistent focus on literacy was highlighted as much improved practice. Thanks again – you have left us with a strong legacy.'
>
> *Deputy Headteacher, Whitehaven*

For those interested in extending the approach across the primary curriculum in Years 5 and 6, or across the secondary curriculum, the book to get is *Talk for Writing Across the Secondary Curriculum*, by Julia Strong. However, this book (*Talk for Writing Across the Curriculum*) will be invaluable for English teachers in Key Stage 3 and literacy coordinators in secondary schools. By following its approaches to teaching non-fiction text, it will not only enable English departments to benefit from and build on best practice in primary schools, but will also provide the perfect way of helping children transfer their skills across the curriculum. To see a taster of how the Talk for Writing process can be adapted to suit the needs of all subjects and for students of all ages – see Clip 23 on **DVD 1**.

If you are interested in learning more about this, contact: julia.strong@ Talk4Writing.com

How this approach supports pupils whose mother tongue is not English

Schools with English as an additional language (EAL) pupils of all ages have found the Talk for Writing approach invaluable for supporting the language development of these pupils. This can best be expressed by the schools themselves:

> 'In the past few years, our EAL percentage changed from 0% to 50% in some cohorts. 2016 saw our first Talk for Writing cohort leave Year 2 having started their journey in reception. This cohort was 25% EAL and had little or no English when starting with us. By the end of Year 2, 90% had achieved a Level 2B+ in writing.

In 2015, we had a reception cohort of 50% EAL, again with little or no English for the vast majority. By the end of reception, 67% had achieved the writing Early Learning Goal and were at a Good Level of Development. The imitation and innovation processes immerse EAL pupils in a vocabulary-rich environment that scaffolds the English language through embedding and internalising language structures, resulting in a quick acquisition of skills and a confidence to write in English.'

Ian Clennan, Headteacher, Selby Community Primary School, North Yorkshire

'Burnley Brow Community School is a larger than average two-form-entry nursery and primary school in an inner urban area of Oldham that has significant pockets of social and economic need. At over 99% EAL, almost all our children are of Bangladeshi heritage; most enter the nursery with very little English. In 2011, we started using the Talk for Writing approach in English lessons across the school. In September 2014, we revamped our English curriculum, placing Talk for Writing at the forefront of our provision throughout school, incorporating high-quality formative assessment and 'mini-lessons' in order to provide fully-personalised learning for all our children. Using core story patterns and non-fiction texts from Year 1 to Year 6, we immerse our learners in the text in order to equip them with the tools and empower them with the creativity and confidence to become effective independent writers across the curriculum. We have seen a huge improvement in the children's confidence to speak and develop their story language. Only one month after revamping our provision, Ofsted commented that: 'pupils enjoy writing and the changes to the way in which pupils develop a piece of writing are having a positive effect on their standards, particularly at Key Stage 2'.'

Suzanne Wootton, English Subject Leader, Burnley Brow Community School

'Talk for Writing had been fully embedded across Brackenhill Primary School. It equips our children, the majority of whom are EAL, with a vocabulary and structure that supports their development and success in writing.

Talk for Writing has been enthusiastically embraced by staff (as it is such fun to teach in this way), embraced by children (as they can see their success) and embraced by parents who are delighted at the confidence their children show as they perform their oral stories.

As a school, we can see children's language and writing developing as a result of Talk for Writing and then we start to see this transferring into independent writing. The bottom line, though, is that in 2012 100% of pupils made two levels of progress and 60% of pupils made three levels of progress in writing by the end of Key Stage 2. Talk for Writing works; it is as simple as that.'

Helen Metcalf, Headteacher, Brackenhill Primary School, Bradford

This was written in 2013. The school has since gone from strength to strength: in 2012, 68% of children achieved level 4 or above in reading, writing and maths; by 2015 this had reached a very impressive 93% (17% above the local authority average and 13% above the national average).

In conclusion: the potential of the process

Because the Talk for Writing approach (moving from imitation to innovation to independent application) is based on how human beings learn, it can be adapted to support the learning needs of pupils and students of all ages within all subjects across the curriculum whether the focus is practical or theoretical.

This is illustrated here by an example showing how the approach can support the creative arts. St Matthew's C of E Primary, in Nechells, Birmingham, has a topic week every term where two subjects are focused on in depth and skills learned in English can be applied and strengthened across the curriculum. For example, Year 6 did a project week in spring 2016 shared between art and geography. The art topic focused on drawing and graffiti.

1. The skills focused on at the imitation stage are clear from this picture. 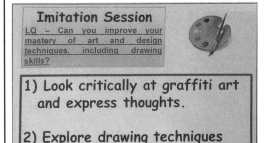 Figure 2.28 The imitation stage	2. Early on in the unit, the art vocabulary the children were to use was mind mapped and illustrated so the children understood the terminology. 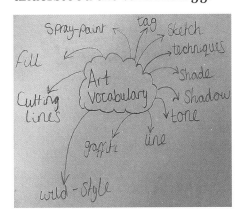 Figure 2.29 Art vocabulary
3. During the imitation stage, the children looked at examples of graffiti art and the teacher modelled for them her thoughts when responding critically to a piece of graffiti. In my-turn/ your-turn style, she then involved the children in expressing their own reactions. This enabled the children to annotate an image of graffiti art and express their reactions.	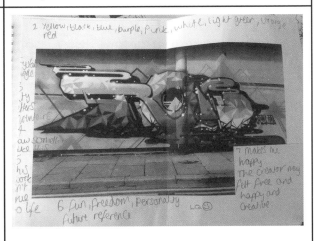 Figure 2.30 How to annotate an image

4. The children then worked on specific drawing skills alongside understanding the technical terms that describe them as illustrated here.	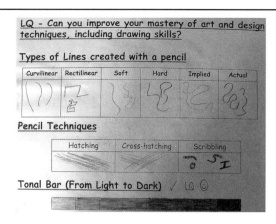

Figure 2.31   Practising drawing skills |
|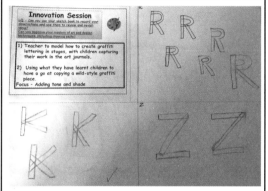

Figure 2.32   The innovation stage | 5. At the innovation stage, the teacher modelled the steps to go through to create graffiti lettering, with the children practising these skills in their art journals. |
| 6. The children then put their skills into practice by recreating a graffiti tag before commenting on how well they felt they had completed the task. |

Figure 2.33   Putting the skills into practice |
|

Figure 2.34   The independent application stage | 7. By the independent application stage, you can see that this child has been able not only to design his own graffiti tag but also to attempt the extension task by adding tone and shadow to his design. |

8. The independent application stage was strengthened by a visit from a professional artist who helped the children develop their graffiti skills. The children were involved in evaluating how this experience had helped them.

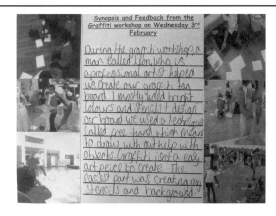

Figure 2.35   Evaluating the artist workshop

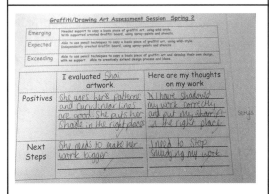

Figure 2.36   Assessment and next steps

9. At the end of the week, the children reflected on their learning by evaluating each other's work as well as their own.

A word about key resources

- The **interactive whiteboard** is handy, as model texts can be clearly displayed and annotated.

- **Flip charts** are essential for the shared and guided writing.

- The **writing wall** or **a washing line** should be used to display texts, word lists, sentence patterns and drafts.

- **Visualisers** (or web cams or iPads) are very handy for reviewing children's writing.

- **Mini-whiteboards** are essential for spelling and sentence games.

- A **digital camera** is handy for capturing trips, visits, visitors and making displays lively.

- **Voice recorders** are useful for interviews and developing ideas.

- **Handwriting books and lined flip-chart paper** provide excellent support for the teaching of handwriting.

- *Talk for Writing in the Early Years*, Pie Corbett and Julia Strong.

- *Talk for Writing in Secondary Schools*, Julia Strong.

- *Jumpstart! Literacy; Jumpstart! Grammar; Jumpstart! Poetry.*

The political context and research background for Talk for Writing

Anyone concerned with teaching in England in the past 60 years will have noticed that what goes around comes around, often repackaged as new. So any attempt at outlining the political context and research background for Talk for Writing is littered with elephant traps. Magpieing good ideas is at the heart of effective teaching and learning and each reader will have their own interpretation of the origin of ideas and the influence of political context. What follows is an attempt to summarise the research and policy context that influenced its initial and continuing development.

Interestingly, despite the wide range of approaches to teaching, standards of literacy in this country did not change significantly between the end of the war and the early 1990s after which they did begin to rise. The introduction of the national curriculum in 1989, with its focus on ten subjects, combined with the introduction of **national testing**, signalled a significant shift towards centralisation in education. National tests were introduced over a number of years (1991–98) for the purpose of testing children at the end of Key Stages 1–3 (when the children were aged 7, 11 and 14) on nationally regulated educational standards. In 1992, the introduction of league tables added a significant edge to the testing.

By 1996, concern over standards led the Conservative Government to set up the **National Literacy Project** to raise standards of literacy in primary schools by improving the quality of teaching through more focused literacy instruction and effective classroom management. Meanwhile, in May 1996, the Labour Party, in opposition but hoping to become the next government, set up a Task Force to develop a strategy for substantially raising standards of literacy in primary schools in England, called *The Reading Revolution*. Following Labour's election in May 1997, this transmogrified into the less romantic-sounding **National Literacy Strategy (NLS)**. A key element of the strategy was the expectation that from September 1998 all primary schools in England would teach a prescribed literacy hour. The leader of the Strategy, John Stannard, had led the National Literacy Project. Strangely, initially it only focused on reading and writing – it had very clear targets for developing these important skills, but no targets for speaking and listening – the very skills which are needed to underpin effective reading and writing.

National testing (SATs) was made even more onerous by the introduction of national targets linked to the league tables. The Strategy was an unprecedented intervention in classroom teaching methods – representing the first England-wide policy on teaching literacy and describing term by term how reading and writing should be taught. It particularly focused on phonics to help children learn to read and text type to scaffold children's ability to write appropriately for a range of audiences and purposes. Its emphasis on direct, interactive teaching with termly objectives and dedicated literacy time had substantial support from research into school management and school improvement.

The Framework required primary teachers to teach a daily English lesson, referred to as the Literacy Hour, in which pupils were taught for the first half of the lesson as a whole class, reading together, extending their vocabulary, looking at the phonetics of words, learning grammar, punctuation and spelling, and emphasising work at word, sentence and text level. Each lesson was to begin with clear objectives.

By 2002, evidence that the approach was too restrictive was mounting. Ofsted, the body inspecting schools, warned the Government of a 'serious narrowing of the primary curriculum' in most schools. Meanwhile, there was an ever-increasing cry from all sides of the profession to get rid of the league tables and the SATs. These fell on deaf ears in England, but in Wales the SATs system was gradually dismantled.

The ensuing years in England saw a number of tweaks to the system, including slight name changes to confuse the unwary. The year 2006 saw the publication of the **New Primary Framework**. This was generally welcomed as it was more flexible and helped teachers plan lessons and access resources more creatively and effectively. Structured teaching and learning in longer sequences and units of work strengthened the identified cycle of 'review-teach-practise-apply-review' and included guidance on developing spoken English. In 2009, before its election defeat, the Labour Government had announced that the **National Strategies** were to be discontinued from 2011.

Did standards improve?

National targets for state primary schools in England were a central feature of the strategy. The initial target was that by the year 2002, 80% of 11-year-olds would reach the expected standard for their age in English. In 1997, only 63% of 11-year-olds reached this standard. By 2005, it reached 79% and then began to plateau, finally reaching the 2002 target of 80% by 2007.

In 1999, Professor Roger Beard's review of research, and other related evidence about the efficacy of the strategy, confirmed the promise of the National Literacy Strategy to raise standards and improve the life chances of many children. However, he reported that evidence from school inspection indicated that several aspects of literacy teaching may need to be modified or strengthened in many schools in order to implement the Strategy, including an increase in direct teaching and in the time pupils spend on texts, greater use of balanced teaching approaches that also provide for extension, the use of systematic phonics, and more attention to the teaching of writing. He emphasised that teachers' subject knowledge may at times need strengthening in order to implement the NLS with understanding and insight.

Test results in the early years of the Strategy indicated that children were making more progress with reading than writing. And, worryingly, although the 2001 PISA (Progress in International Reading Literacy) survey of 10-year-olds found that English pupils were on average among the best readers internationally, they also had a poorer attitude to reading and read less often for fun than pupils in other countries. As a result, the National Strategy began to put more emphasis on reading for pleasure – an emphasis maintained by the 2006 revision of the primary curriculum. Such an emphasis is central to the Talk for Writing approach, as motivation is key to learning. Interestingly, teachers developing the Talk for Writing approach have commented how its emphasis on helping children come up with the best phrase has also motivated them to read: 'It's raised my children's enthusiasm for reading. They've become avid readers so they can find good phrases to use.'

What did the official evaluators of the Strategy conclude?

Researchers, led by Michael Fullan from the University of Toronto, were brought in by the then Department for Education and Skills to evaluate the literacy and numeracy strategies over three years. Their final report, *Watching and Learning 3*, published in 2003, concluded that the strategies had been generally well-implemented and well-supported by schools. Teaching had improved substantially since the strategies were introduced. Significantly, the report emphasised that unrealistic targets were lowering staff morale and concluded that high targets for 11-year-olds in maths and English were becoming counterproductive and narrowing the curriculum.

Research on non-fiction writing

There has been relatively little research focusing on non-fiction writing. However, in 1992, members of the Primary Language team at the University of Exeter School of Education began the *Exeter Extending Literacy Project*. Their objectives included concern that when reading and writing across the curriculum, children encounter and are expected to produce a wide range of written text types, but that this text range is hardly ever considered as an issue by teachers. Their practical findings about how to support the reading and writing of non-fiction were later written up by Wray and Lewis in *Extending Literacy*, a seminal text that helped underpin the Literacy Strategy. Their findings included writing frames to support coherence. Though very useful in scaffolding children's writing, teachers have increasingly felt that writing frames do not help pupils internalise the language patterns necessary to support their independent writing. Talk for

Writing has been developed precisely to help children internalise text-appropriate language patterns so that they can apply them independently in their formal speaking and writing.

Over ten years later, in 2006, the Evidence for Policy and Practice Information Centre, at the University of London, conducted a systematic review to answer the research question: 'What is the evidence for successful practice in teaching and learning with regard to non-fiction writing for 7–14 year olds?' Results showed that certain conditions are either assumed or have to be in place to create a climate for successful practice. These include a writing process model in which students are encouraged to plan, draft, edit and revise their writing and peer collaboration. These processes help to scaffold and model a dialogue that will become internal and constitute 'thought'.

Such an approach is key to Talk for Writing, which uses focused talk combined with shared planning and writing to help children internalise the formal specific language patterns that are needed to write the full range of non-fiction text effectively.

Why did writing progress lag behind?

The lack of progress in writing by 2000 led Ros Fisher, Maureen Lewis and Bernie Davis to conduct two studies on what was holding back progress. They established a link between children's performance, the way writing is assessed, and the methods teachers use to interpret the writing component of the NLS. In schools where reading scores were high, children who made less progress in writing may not have got the support they needed. They importantly concluded that, 'Where teachers made full use of shared and guided sessions to model and scaffold children's writing development, children's writing showed good progress.' Building teacher confidence in shared writing is key to Talk for Writing. Despite the Strategy's emphasis on this element for several years, many teachers comment on never having seen it well demonstrated and lack confidence in how to do it effectively. This feature is therefore included not only in Chapters 2 and 4 to 9, but is also demonstrated on the **DVD** (see clips 10, 20, 21 and 26).

Research on grammar teaching

The Literacy Hour played a leading role in reintroducing grammar teaching to schools, and the dissemination of quality resources like *Grammar for Writing* helped primary teachers understand grammar and how to teach it. However, the Qualifications and Curriculum Authority produced a fascinating overview, *The Grammar Papers*, stating that there is little research evidence to actually prove its efficacy. In 2004, the English Review Group of the EPPI-Centre looked into *The effect of grammar teaching (syntax) in English on 5 to 16 year olds' accuracy and quality in written composition*. Interestingly, it reported that there was no evidence to counter the prevailing belief that the teaching of the principles underlying and informing word order or syntax has virtually no influence on the writing quality or accuracy of 5- to 16-year-olds. However, in 2001, R. Hudson had also looked at the research evidence relating to grammar teaching and writing skills. This review found that a clear focus on subordinate and main clauses can support children in understanding punctuation. This characteristic may be significant, as it seems to be missing from the negative studies and is present in many, if not all, of the positive ones.

Talk for Writing does not focus on the minutiae of grammar but rather concentrates on modelling the pattern of language required for a range of writing tasks so that pupils internalise appropriate patterns of language, including how to subordinate clauses. It also provides an easy-to-follow approach to identifying the generic key features of non-fiction writing to help pupils transfer learning in literacy lessons across the curriculum. However, given the introduction of grammar tests in 2014 that, increasingly, are focusing on the naming of parts (see page 66), we would suggest that the technical names are introduced and used in line with the curriculum so that the children become accustomed to them, but these should not form the objectives for children when writing. For example, an objective might be *Make your writing engaging by varying the way sentences begin* rather than *Begin your sentences with fronted adverbials*. You would, of course, teach the children how to drop in information at the front of sentences and model how this is always marked off by a comma. Given the strange requirements of the test, you would also explain that this is known as a fronted adverbial, but the focus would remain on what makes the writing effective rather than on an obscure, recently coined grammatical term.

Interaction matters

A few years into the strategy, researchers were reflecting concern that the Strategy was too focused on reading and writing to the exclusion of speaking, listening and thinking. Research from the universities of Cambridge, Durham and Leicester showed that just 1 in 10 of the spoken contributions that children made during the national literacy hour was longer than three words – and only 5% were longer than five words.

A paper in the *Cambridge Journal of Education* reported that uninterrupted 'interactions' of more than 25 seconds between teachers and one child or small groups had declined dramatically since the introduction of the literacy hour. In 1996, these dialogues made up around a quarter of the communication between pupils and teachers during Key Stage 2 lessons. But during the early years of the literacy hour, this type of communication had dwindled to only 5% at Key Stage 2 and 2% at Key Stage 1.

The Strategy recognised these shortcomings, such that speaking and listening objectives were included in the redrafting of the strategy, and speaking and listening as well as thinking skills became a focus of Strategy training.

Pupil–teacher interaction is what matters

In late 2008, research findings were published by Professor John Hattie, from Auckland University, following 15 years of analysing education research.

His research is outstanding, not least because it is based on 80 million students from 50,000 studies. His findings are significant enough to enable him to state unequivocally that **raising the quality of pupil–teacher interaction is key to effective learning**. The top-rated approaches to achieving this are summarised as:

- Pupils assessing themselves by reaching a view on their levels of understanding.

- Setting work that is one step ahead of current level.

- Using formative assessment to decide next steps.

- Teacher clarity – being explicit about what to do.

- Reciprocal teaching – pupils take turns in teaching class.

- Teacher credibility.

Professor Hattie commented: 'A teacher's job is not to make work easy. It is to make it difficult. If you are not challenged, you do not make mistakes. If you do not make mistakes, feedback is useless.'

Effective pupil–teacher interaction, including formative assessment, lies at the heart of the Talk for Writing approach, with the teacher using assessment to guide the next piece of teaching so that the pupils move confidently and competently from imitation to innovation to independence. Moreover, raising pupil expectations of what they can achieve works hand in hand with raising pupil confidence. As one boy expressed it, 'Mr Corbett has makes me push, push, push until I find just the right word.'

Professor Hattie's conclusions echo the findings of another unequivocal body of educational research that is very relevant to writing, since it shows the centrality of formative assessment (sometimes known as assessment for learning) to pupil progress. *Inside the Black Box* by Paul Black and Dylan Wiliam, a magnificently written research summary, includes the following conclusion: 'Feedback to any pupil should be about the particular qualities of his or her work, with advice on what he or she can do to improve, and should avoid comparison with other pupils' – a timely reminder in these target-driven times not to confuse formative with summative assessment. Two very useful resources for teachers that build on these findings are *Active Learning Through Formative Assessment* and *Unlocking Formative Assessment*, both by Shirley Clarke. Many teachers have found these a real lifesaver as they so succinctly guide you into achieving a formative approach to providing constructive feedback on work and involving the children themselves in their own learning. Shirley Clarke advised on the Transforming Writing project (see page 72) that helped strengthen how formative assessment underpins the Talk for Writing process.

All the research into what works in education emphasises the centrality of interaction to learning – of enabling pupils to do it themselves – and of providing the oral-based support activities that give pupils the confidence to express themselves coherently right across the curriculum.

National changes to primary literacy in England since 2011

First and foremost phonics

Following the change of government in 2010, schools were advised by the Department for Education (DfE) to follow the 2000 curriculum until it was reviewed.

From 2012, two years before the arrival of the new curriculum, the DfE introduced the Phonics Screening Check for the end of Year 1. This was later extended to Year 2 for the pupils who had failed the first check. Three years later, in July 2015, the DfE published the final report from the National Foundation for Education Research three-year evaluation into whether it had had any impact on the standard of reading and writing. They found evidence that it had impacted on phonics teaching and classroom practice, including faster pace, more time devoted to the teaching of phonics, and drilling pupils in the kind of pseudo words used to test pupils' skills in decoding unfamiliar words. Interestingly, there is little evidence that schools are teaching systematic synthetic phonics to the exclusion of other reading strategies. Many schools still believe that a phonics approach to teaching reading should be used alongside other methods, a view that we would support. Phonics is necessary, but not sufficient.

When it came to the important question of whether it had actually had an impact on what matters, the standard of reading and writing, the answer would appear to be no. Phonics attainment, as measured by scores on the check, has improved: 74% of Year 1 pupils reached the expected standard of phonic decoding in 2014 compared with only 58% in 2012. However, when they looked at pupils' reading and writing scores over the same four years, there were no improvements in attainment or progress that could be clearly attributed to the introduction of the check. Despite millions being spent on materials and training, there has only been a tiny percentage improvement in reading at Key Stage 1.

How the new curriculum for English differs from its predecessor

In early 2013, a draft new national curriculum was issued with the final version appearing at the end of that year to be implemented from September 2014. There are many positive aspects to England's new curriculum for English, as outlined in the document entitled *English Programmes of Study: Key Stages 1 and 2*. One of the most welcome aspects is its emphasis on encouraging a love of reading. However, the most striking thing about it is the number of pages devoted to spelling and grammar, as opposed to everything else. You only have to glance at the index of this 88-page document to see something is amiss: 30 of those pages are devoted to a detailed listing of often somewhat obscure spellings, with a further 34 devoted to grammar, including a glossary of terms. This doesn't leave much room for everything else. And when you examine the details, you come across all sorts of strange anomalies, like the suggestion that bullet points are only introduced in Year 6 whereas, if you ask primary teachers, they'll often tell you they introduce them in Year 1, if not in reception. But then, of course, no primary teachers were involved in the working party that established the primary curriculum for English, so it's not surprising if quite a few things don't seem to fit.

It would, however, be hard to argue with the opening aims of the document, except perhaps that it makes no reference here, or anywhere else, to the fact that we are now communicating in a rapidly changing digital age:

> *The overarching aim for English in the national curriculum is to promote high standards of language and literacy by equipping pupils with a strong command of the spoken and written word, and to develop their love of literature through widespread reading for enjoyment. The national curriculum for English aims to ensure that all pupils:*
>
> * *read easily, fluently and with good understanding;*
>
> * *develop the habit of reading widely and often, for both pleasure and information;*
>
> * *acquire a wide vocabulary, an understanding of grammar and knowledge of linguistic conventions for reading, writing and spoken language;*
>
> * *appreciate our rich and varied literary heritage;*
>
> * *write clearly, accurately and coherently, adapting their language and style in and for a range of contexts, purposes and audiences;*
>
> * *use discussion in order to learn; they should be able to elaborate and explain clearly their understanding and ideas;*
>
> * *are competent in the arts of speaking and listening, making formal presentations, demonstrating to others and participating in debate.*

The underpinning idea is not to tell teachers 'how to teach', but to concentrate on 'the essential knowledge and skills every child should have' so that teachers 'have the freedom to shape the curriculum to their pupils' needs'. Again, there is nothing to argue with here as long as the skills teachers are asked to concentrate on are the right skills.

What the new curriculum says about non-fiction

Since this book focuses on non-fiction, let's look at the key changes for non-fiction in the new curriculum. The previous curriculum placed significant emphasis on helping children understand the underpinning ingredients of the six main non-fiction text types. The new curriculum takes a very different broad-brush approach to non-fiction. On page 29 of the document, which outlines the writing requirements for Years 3 and 4, in the notes and guidance (non-statutory) section, there is this paragraph summing up the approach:

> *Pupils should continue to have opportunities to write for a range of real purposes and audiences as part of their work across the curriculum. These purposes and audiences should underpin the decisions about the form the writing should take, such as a narrative, an explanation or a description.*

This statement begins well enough. Unfortunately, whoever wrote it did not understand that description is not a form of writing like narrative or explanation, but a feature that would be found in most forms of writing. The only text type that is very thin on description is instructions.

But, in practice, the curriculum relating to non-fiction is broad enough to allow schools to interpret this as they choose and to continue to focus on helping children understand the different non-fiction text types and to broaden and deepen these skills across the curriculum. However, we would perhaps take issue with the assumption behind the highlighted section of this extract:

> *By the end of Year 6, pupils' reading and writing should be sufficiently fluent and effortless for them to manage the general demands of the curriculum in Year 7, across all subjects and not just in English,* **but there will continue to be a need for pupils to learn subject-specific vocabulary***. They should be able to reflect their understanding of the audience for and purpose of their writing by selecting appropriate vocabulary and grammar.*

This would suggest that the language patterns of all the various subjects taught across the curriculum can be taught within the English curriculum and that it is only the technical vocabulary that needs attending to. We would argue that although the underpinning language patterns of the different text types in their pure and hybrid forms should be taught within English, there is far more to the tune (the frequently used language patterns) of many other subjects, for example science, maths and history, than just the specific vocabulary. To write about history you need to understand long- and short-term causes, and this is much better taught within the context of history than within the English curriculum where it would have to be crowbarred in. If the programme of study is right, then secondary teachers of every subject other than English only have to worry about the vocabulary of their subject and leave how to express it to the English department. If this erroneous perspective is followed to its logical conclusion, there is no hope for the concept of literacy across the curriculum. Why it is important for teachers to consider the tune of the subject they are teaching is illustrated in relation to experiments in science on pages 74–75.

The shifting sands of assessment

As any writer knows, to be able to write a summary effectively you have to fully understand the information that you are attempting to summarise. And, of course, it helps if what you are trying to sum up is clear and logical. The more I read the documents on changes in assessment facing teachers in England as they enter the 2016 testing period, the more I fear that I will never be in that happy position. The information provided is endlessly interwoven in a labyrinthine manner worthy of Umberto Eco – the final blow being that it is temporary, since the latest information, when it was written, was only for 2016, and doubtless further mysterious stages are to follow in the pursuit of a flawless summative assessment system that can accurately measure progress, or the lack of it, year by year. A little light relief was provided by the fact that, despite the schools being weighed down by draconian instructions about how to conduct tests, the DfE failed to follow suit. Some hapless soul, several months before the test was to be taken, inadvertently put the real spelling test for May 2016 Key Stage 1 onto the website as an example of what the test might look like. This resulted in the Key Stage 1 spelling phonics and grammar tests being cancelled that year.

In an attempt to cut to the car chase, let's see what we can definitely state:

- A new national curriculum was published in 2014. For English, this was very detailed in relation to grammar and spelling, but broad-sweep in relation to reading, speaking, listening and writing, and provided little indication of what makes effective composition.

- Spelling and grammar tests for the end of both Key Stage 1 and 2 were introduced from 2014; the scope of the grammar test was extended for 2016 onwards.

- Statutory assessment arrangements changed for the summer of 2016 to align with the content and principles of the new national curriculum.

- From September 2015, levels were no longer to be used for statutory assessments. Although Attainment Targets remain in the national curriculum orders, they now refer explicitly to ensuring all pupils know, apply and understand the matters, skills and processes specified in the relevant programme of study.

This, of course, begs the question, if the levels are dead, then what have they been replaced with? It is at this moment that the plot thickens.

In March 2016, the Standards and Testing Agency issued a document to explain the changes called *Clarification: Key Stage 1 and 2 teacher assessment and moderation guidance*, which states:

> *As part of the national curriculum review, levels have been abolished. This is in part in response to concerns about the validity and reliability of levels and sub-levels. These concerns had an impact on pupils' learning, but also on the relationships between primary and secondary schools and the trust in their assessments. Levels have also been recognised as the driver of undue pace through the curriculum, which has led to gaps in pupils' knowledge.*

When you read this, you understand why suddenly the Government focus was all on breadth and depth, whereas before it seemed to be a race to prove you were level 6.

The reasons for getting rid of the levels are, on the surface, something that many teachers would agree with. The levels were supposed to be a summative measure of pupils' attainment at particular points in time – for example, end-of-year assessment – but in many schools they became the be all and end all of assessment, and so formative assessment was, in effect, abandoned, and the children endlessly assessed against summative targets. It was, sadly, all too common to see level ladders on the wall with children's names added as a constant reminder to those who weren't doing well that they were the bottom of the pile. Smug children would proudly announce themselves to be 5b and rest on their laurels. The levels system was contributing to a *fixed mindset*. Because every piece of work was graded summatively, teachers endlessly 'weighed the pig' and forgot that the important thing was to 'feed the pig'.

However, some would argue that it was not the levels that had created this counterproductive approach but rather the political situation within which the levels functioned. With so much national emphasis on measuring attainment and publishing league tables, it is not surprising that teachers obsessively worried about the final grades and kept assessing the children's work in the light of them.

Over time, teachers will get their heads round what the new scales mean, just as they finally got their heads round levels, but the tail will still wag the dog. As long as summative assessment determines the position of schools in the league tables, and hence the fate of schools and the likelihood of their being able to recruit good staff, this problem will not go away.

When this was written in May 2016, teachers in England were in the somewhat befuddling situation of knowing that the levels had been replaced by some sort of scales system and that these scales are pinned to a series of '*the pupil can*' statements that the children have to achieve in breadth and depth in a range of contexts to achieve higher grades. The logic behind scaled scores is, supposedly, that they will enable test results to be reported consistently year on year.

It's worth pausing here to think about how it would actually be possible to compare levels of writing accurately, given that there is a subjective element to what is effective. It is at this moment that the highly detailed focus on the grammar comes into play. It is possible to state categorically whether a child has or has not used fronted adverbials in a wide range of contexts; it is much harder to be able to say that the use of such structures has made the writing more effective. This, in effect, is the subtext: but let's return to the plot. Primary teachers were warned that these scales are only for summative assessment at the end of the key stages and that, in between, schools are free to decide on whatever assessment system best suits the children.

These statements from the *Interim teacher assessment framework at the end of key stage 2* sum up what is being attempted:

- *Teachers must base their teacher assessment judgement on a broad range of evidence from across the curriculum for each pupil.*

- *Individual pieces of work should be assessed according to a school's assessment policy and not against this interim framework.*

- *This statutory interim framework is to be used only to make a teacher assessment judgement at the end of the key stage following the completion of the Key Stage 2 curriculum. It is not intended to be used to track progress throughout the key stage.*

So you could say, ok, the national stuff is summative and the rest is for schools to decide and that is formative. But that would, in the case of Key Stage 2, leave four years before there is any summative assessment so, therefore, schools need to invent some sort of summative assessment for, say, the end of each year, plus formative assessment to guide the day-to-day direction of teaching. To have one national approach to summative assessment and then tell schools to knit their own for the bits in between the big test years seems strange indeed: it's bad enough coping with the complexities of one summative assessment system, let alone two.

In search of the expected standard

The assessment framework is divided into three stages for every section of the English curriculum:

- *Working towards the expected standard.*
- *Working at the expected standard.*
- *Working at greater depth within the expected standard.*

So, of course, everyone wanted to know what the expected standard was, but this remained a mystery until the first tests had been taken and the point on the scaled score that was found to be the 'expected standard' could be established. This may all be logical from the theoretical perspective of those trying to establish the new system, but it is very frustrating for teachers caught in the middle who are trying to implement it. The 2016 cohort was the first to reach the end of Key Stage 2, having studied sufficient content from the new national curriculum to be tested on it. So it was this group that were the guinea pigs for the new system.

The focus on depth is interesting. It is not all about racing ahead, but rather embedding and strengthening skills in a broad range of contexts. So, for writing at Key Stage 2, this greater depth stage means:

- *The pupil can write for a range of purposes and audiences: managing shifts between levels of formality through selecting vocabulary precisely and by manipulating grammatical structures.*
- *Selecting verb forms for meaning and effect.*
- *Using the full range of punctuation taught at Key Stage 2, including colons and semicolons, to mark the boundary between independent clauses, mostly correctly.*

Embedding skills, rather than rushing on in a skimpy manner, is eminently sensible. However, the last bullet point is entertaining because, as far as I can see, the full range of punctuation is included in the Key Stage 2 curriculum: you would not be able to race ahead here, even if you wanted to. Whether it is sensible to be expecting 11-year-olds to handle semicolons with depth and breadth is another matter.

To demonstrate that pupils have met the stated standard, teachers will need to have evidence that a pupil demonstrates consistent attainment of **all** the statements within the standard: in other words, you can no longer apply the best-fit approach which teachers had grown familiar with when applying the old levels. To reach the expected standard at the end of Key Stage 2 this means, among many other things, that you have to be able to spell most of the words on the Year 5 and 6 list correctly. There is no leeway for children with dyslexia. So, by this logic, F. Scott Fitzgerald, Jules Verne, Agatha Christie, George Bernard Shaw and W. B. Yeats would never have reached the expected level of an 11-year-old child, since all are said to have had dyslexia-related spelling problems.

A further dispiriting thing is that, unsurprisingly, the focus of the objectives is on skills and knowledge linked to spelling, punctuation, grammar and handwriting. This means that the teacher assessment exemplification documents have a clinical, naming-of-parts flavour. If you look at the Key Stage 2 exemplification, *Working at greater depth within the expected standard: Frankie*, you will see annotations like:

- *Fronted subordinate clause foregrounds.*

- *Expanded noun phrase (incorporating a preposition phrase) creates effective compressed description.*

- *Effective use of the past perfect passive form withholds the agent in order to build tension.*

No one when actually writing or reading thinks like this; this is the disembodied perspective of an academic linguist. It is as if someone wants to justify the obsessive focus on the naming of parts that has become the backbone of the national curriculum. But, of course, these features are measurable. Again the tail wags the dog. The focus is not on the quality of the writing but on the features that enable it to be assessed. Perhaps we are entering what could be described as the Lieutenant Scheisskopf syndrome, a minor character in *Catch-22*, who spends his nights wondering how he can improve his men's ability to march in straight lines:

> *Finishing last in three successive parades had given Lieutenant Scheisskopf an unsavoury reputation, and he considered every means of improvement, even nailing the men in each rank to a long two-by-four beam of seasoned oak to keep them in line. The plan was not feasible, for making a ninety degree turn would have been impossible without nickel-alloy swivels inserted in the small of every man's back, and Lieutenant Scheisskopf was not sanguine at all about obtaining that many nickel-alloy swivels from Quartermaster or enlisting the cooperation of the surgeons at the hospital.*

If you analyse the grammar test when it was first introduced in 2014, it was approximately 80% questions about how you might use grammar in practice and only 20% the arid naming of parts. The national curriculum was then amended so that obscure grammatical features, like the subjunctive, that were not identified as features to be tested in 2014, suddenly became part of the features to be tested from 2016. To make matters worse, the nature of the questions had been reversed so that, by 2016, 80% of the exemplar test materials focused on the naming of parts and only 20% were of the more useful, practical variety. Exactly why being able to identify the difference between the word *before*, when functioning as a conjunction as opposed to a preposition, is seen as being a useful skill defies all the teachers I've spoken to. Memorably, it was the question that Nick Gibb, Minister of State for Schools in England, failed to be able to answer when interviewed by the BBC. But, of course, it is a measurable skill.

Ironically, if binning the levels and replacing them with scales is partly about stopping teachers from teaching to the summative assessment statements of the test, probably the reverse will be true. Teachers will look at the annotations on the exemplar text and start thinking, 'Right, I've got to focus on teaching the children to identify and use the past perfect passive', rather than, 'I need to help them get the pattern of *Had he been seen?; Had she been standing there yesterday. . .* into their heads so they can use similar structures.' Moreover, the use of terms like *present perfect* and *past perfect* are disputed; some grammarians would argue that there is no such thing as a perfect tense in English, and that the term only fits languages with highly declined verbs like Latin. But let's move on.

If these were the success criteria you were given before completing a piece of writing:

 * use fronted subordinate clauses to foreground sentences;

 * use an expanded noun phrase (incorporating a preposition phrase) to create effective compressed description;

 * use the past perfect passive form to withhold the agent in order to build tension;

would they help you, or would they be counterproductive, leading perhaps to confusion and a sense of inadequacy and despair?

So how could it come about that such annotations have been given to us as the model of the way forward – the template for progress? I can only imagine that when these were put forward at a meeting by some grammatical specialist, everyone else was too daunted by the terminology or the desire to be able to measure things to say, 'Excuse me, but . . .'. Perhaps it was a case of the Emperor's New Clothes.

It is, of course, possible to translate such summative assessments into formative ones in what could be described as the Talk for Writing approach. In this way, the ingredients for what equals good are co-constructed with the class into toolkits and expressed in language the children understand with examples to help them translate understanding into practice. For example, the annotations above could be presented to the children in toolkit form something like this:

- Create effective tight description by helping the reader picture what is described and never wasting a word – e.g. *Squat toads with pulsating throats* . . .

- Build tension by using rhetorical questions that hide the person carrying out the action and make the reader wonder – e.g. *Had he been seen? Had the door been opened?*

But, sadly, the lure of the summative statements will possibly stand in the way of teachers doing this, not least because the curriculum has an imbalanced emphasis on grammar/spelling with little reference to the art of composition.

The remarkable story of the exclamation mark!

The surrealistic position that is reached when the need to be able to test things takes precedence over everything else is probably best summed up by the strange tale of how to use the exclamation mark. It is ironic, when the Government is berating schools for having allowed summative assessment to start to influence how things are taught, to see that they have started to change the rules about how to use exclamation marks to enable the use of the exclamation to be tested. We know someone lost perspective when whoever was responsible for issuing instructions about what is to be done allowed a statement like this to be made in 2015:

> **Sentences with different forms: exclamations**
>
> *For the purposes of the English grammar, punctuation and spelling test, an exclamation is required to start with What or How, e.g. What a lovely day! How exciting!*
>
> *A sentence that ends in an exclamation mark, but which does not have one of the grammatical patterns shown above, is not considered to be creditworthy as an exclamation (e.g. exclamatory statements, exclamatory imperatives, exclamatory interrogatives or interjections).*
>
> *4.5.2 of English grammar, punctuation and spelling test framework, national curriculum tests from 2016*

Even more depressingly, this document was revised in March 2016 to the text below, which makes it even more befuddling.

> *4.4.2 Sentences with different forms: exclamations*
>
> *An exclamation is a sentence that has a particular syntax. Exclamations begin with What or How and are usually demarcated by an exclamation mark e.g.*

- *What a lovely day it is!*

- *How exciting this term has been!*

A sentence that ends in an exclamation mark, but which does not have one of the grammatical patterns shown above, is not considered to be creditworthy as an exclamation (e.g. exclamatory statements, exclamatory imperatives, exclamatory interrogatives or interjections).

An exclamation mark is a punctuation mark that can end a statement, command or exclamation, or be placed after a phrase or single word (e.g. an interjection). An exclamation mark shows that a writer wants to indicate a certain effect, such as heightened emotion e.g. 'Be my friend!' (command) and will be considered creditworthy.

The eagle-eyed reader may have noticed that the initial *What . . .* example contained no verb, and thus is technically not a sentence – an oversight rectified by the later pedantic exemplification: *What a lovely day it is!* Only Little Red Riding Hood ever speaks in that way: 'What big ears you have!' Not surprisingly, teachers are disheartened by having to teach in such a counterproductive environment and worried about the negative effects on the children's learning.

How the Talk for Writing process can help

One very useful thing about the Talk for Writing process, in the midst of this sea of gloom, is that it bookends units with formative assessment through the cold to hot process (see pages 16–17) and thus provides schools with an excellent way of assessing progress formatively. This process establishes a baseline at the beginning of each unit pinpointing what the children already can do in relation to the skills about to be focused on, so that the unit can be adapted to build these skills step by step. The final independent work, at the end of the unit, can then be used to assess the progress made, and to help focus future work on embedding these skills across the curriculum. This offers the perfect simple solution to tracking progress formatively across the key stage. Look in the books and talk to the children and you will be able to see the progress. As long as the skills focused on are within the curriculum, then schools need look no further for a formative assessment system that not only encourages the teacher and the learner but also makes management learning walks much more meaningful. And, should Ofsted hove into sight, it is exactly what they are looking for. The Department for Education (DfE) is looking for teachers and children to take more ownership of individual strengths and weaknesses and how to improve: this is precisely what this process does.

Moreover, the underpinning features of the Talk for Writing approach are reflected within this broad-sweep curriculum. Look carefully at these extracts from the English Programmes of Study in the left-hand column:

Statutory requirements from the English Programme of Studies	*How Talk for Writing can help deliver these aspects of the curriculum*
• *By listening frequently to stories, poems and non-fiction that they cannot yet read for themselves, pupils begin to understand how written language can be structured in order, for example, to build surprise in narratives or to present facts in non-fiction.*	This is the central feature of Talk for Writing in the early years – by internalising a range of story and non-fiction patterns through imitation, children build up the pattern of storytelling, recounting, informing, etc. Through the innovation process, they can build on the stories and text that they have heard and create their own versions.
• *Through listening, pupils also start to learn how language sounds and increase their vocabulary and awareness of grammatical structures. In due course, they will be able to draw on such grammar in their own writing.*	This is precisely why warming up the text activities and the related model texts are so important. The teacher identifies the language patterns required to do the type of writing focused on and then devises a range of games to familiarise the children with the tune of this text so that the children can generate such grammatical structures themselves.
• *Explain and discuss their understanding of books, poems and other material, both those that they listen to and those that they read for themselves.*	This is encapsulated in the reading as a reader process that immediately follows the children being shown the text once they have internalised it. Open-ended, book-talk discussion plus vocabulary work ensure the children have fully comprehended what they have read and can increasingly infer from text. **Handout 5** (see Appendix 2 on **DVD 2**) provides a range of sentence stems to encourage classes to do this.
• *Pupils should learn about cause and effect in both narrative and non-fiction (for example, what has prompted a character's behaviour in a story; why certain dates are commemorated annually). 'Thinking aloud' when reading to pupils may help them to understand what skilled readers do.*	This again is fully explored within the Talk for Writing approach both through internalising the key cause and effect sentence signposts (see pages 165–167) and through book-talk techniques modelling how to talk about the purposes and effectiveness of text.

Statutory requirements from the English Programme of Studies	How Talk for Writing can help deliver these aspects of the curriculum
• Discussion should be demonstrated to pupils. They should be guided to participate in it and they should be helped to consider the opinions of others. They should receive feedback on their discussions.	Discussion and co-constructing understanding is key to the approach. Book-talk type discussion relies on the children being trained to listen to each other's ideas and adapt their thinking in the light of the contribution of others. The shared writing approach with its focus on what works also contributes to this.
Children should be taught to: . . . consider what they are going to write before beginning by: • planning or saying out loud what they are going to write about • writing down ideas and/or key words, including new vocabulary • encapsulating what they want to say, sentence by sentence • make simple additions, revisions and corrections to their own writing by: ✓ evaluating their writing with the teacher and other pupils ✓ re-reading to check that their writing makes sense and that verbs to indicate time are used correctly and consistently, including verbs in the continuous form ✓ proof-reading to check for errors in spelling, grammar and punctuation (for example, ends of sentences punctuated correctly) ✓ read aloud what they have written with appropriate intonation to make the meaning clear.	When you read through this, you assume that whoever wrote it was very aware of the Talk for Writing process. The bullet points take you through some of the key steps underpinning the process because it is all about getting the children to plan and talk the text before they write it. Then, once they have written it, they reflect on what they have written with a partner and improve it. The importance of regularly reading writing aloud to check how it sounds is modelled by the teacher so that the children start to automatically do this for flow, sense and accuracy. Correct intonation is also taught, not least at the imitation stage where children are not just taught to know the passage but are expected to be able to present it orally in a lively engaging manner that helps the listener understand what is being said.
• Pupils should understand, through being shown these, the skills and processes essential to writing: that is, thinking aloud as they collect ideas, drafting, and re-reading to check their meaning is clear.	Again, all this is modelled by the teacher and then practised by the children throughout the Talk for Writing process.

Statutory requirements from the English Programme of Studies	How Talk for Writing can help deliver these aspects of the curriculum
• The terms for discussing language should be embedded for pupils in the course of discussing their writing with them. Their attention should be drawn to the technical terms they need to learn.	This is central to the approach, but herein lies a significant difference. Yes, key grammatical terms should be taught and the grammar should be integrated into the writing process, not taught through disembodied worksheets. This last sentence is important: 'Their attention should be drawn to the technical terms they need to learn.' Indeed it should. However, we would differ in the range of terminology that is actually needed before the technical grammatical language presents a barrier rather than opening up understanding. But given the sad fact that the children are being tested on the naming of obscure grammatical features, as well as some that are of more practical use, as a compromise we must help the children be aware of these terms while not reducing the children's understanding of what equals effective writing to the naming of disembodied parts.
• They should also learn the conventions of different types of writing (for example, the greeting in letters, a diary written in the first person or the use of presentational devices such as numbering and headings in instructions).	Again, through imitation and innovation, Talk for Writing is structured to cover all these conventions in as engaging a way as possible.
• In using non-fiction, pupils should know what information they need to look for before they begin, and be clear about the task. They should be shown how to use contents pages and indexes to locate information.	The teacher models this for the children before giving them material to practise on so the class co-constructs understanding of how to access the information needed to complete a task.

Statutory requirements from the English Programme of Studies	How Talk for Writing can help deliver these aspects of the curriculum
• In Years 5 and 6, pupils' confidence, enjoyment and mastery of language should be extended through public speaking, performance and debate.	Talk for Writing puts this into practice, but would begin much earlier so the children would start performing text from the early years. The text map approach is an excellent way of giving children confidence when presenting, and can be adapted so that anytime they are required to stand up and perform formally they have turned what they want to say into a text map that they can picture in their heads. This is the perfect way to present information in an engaging manner because it helps the speaker remember the points they wish to make.

Key developments in Talk for Writing since 2011

Talk for Writing has developed significant breadth and depth since this book was first published. The depth has been achieved through teacher action research, most notably the Transforming Writing project; the breadth has been achieved through a growing understanding of the potential of the Talk for Writing approach to support learning of all subjects for students of all ages. Teachers have applied the approach from nursery to sixth-form level in a wide range of subject areas and found that it works. In addition, our attitude to what can be expected of children's handwriting by the end of reception, and why this matters, was transformed by a visit to St George's C of E Primary School in Battersea – see Appendix 4 on **DVD 2**.

Stage 1: The Transforming Writing project

The Transforming Writing project was set up in 2011 in partnership with the National Literacy Trust and funded by Esmée Fairburn. The principal aim of the project was to develop a powerful, well-researched and evaluated model of effective practice that underpins the teaching and learning of writing with formative assessment at its heart. The specific research questions were:

- Which teaching and learning approaches to formative assessment worked and why, and with which children in what contexts?

- Which skills and knowledge did the teachers need, and how were they best acquired?

- What substantive difference was made to children's confidence, engagement and articulation of their writing processes?

- How did collaborative talk support the children's development and the teacher's role?

Twelve schools, most of them in challenging areas and selected because of their existing strong understanding of the Talk for Writing process plus outstanding leadership, spent two years focusing on these questions. Project days provided regular input from us, plus the all-important chance to reflect on their learning and discuss their findings with other teachers before returning to school to further trial ideas.

You can read the full report of the evaluation of the project by Winchester University at www.literacytrust.org.uk/research/nlt_research/5714_transforming_ writing_final_evaluation_report

What difference did it make? The children's progress increased as a result of the modifications in the way the teachers planned and delivered lessons. The key changes were:

- Beginning a unit with a cold task to establish the particular expression skills that needed focusing on.

- Using this assessment to adapt the planning of the unit so that all the activities helped children build the skills they needed to make progress. This included establishing the key targets for all the class, as well as a range of different targets for different groups depending on attainment.

- Involving the children far more in discussing what worked so that the children developed an inner judge and could assess their own work and improve it in the light of their reflections.

- Using these discussions to co-construct toolkits of the key learning points – rather than providing lists of undigested success criteria.

- Making the learning highly visible by displaying work in progress on a washing line or working wall both to support the children's learning and to keep the teacher and TA focused.

- Using the assessment of writing at the innovation stage to identify common inaccuracies, misconceptions or weaknesses, and then offering the children a choice of 'mini-lessons' to select the feature they will focus on – see pages 42–43.

- Ending the unit with a hot task and giving time to allow the children, as well as the teacher, to reflect on their learning.

All of these learning points have been further refined since the project ended by being developed in practice in Talk for Writing schools. The training schools meet every term to reflect on progress and refine the approach. It is an ongoing learning journey. Chapter 2 outlines the Talk for Writing process and reflects the current stage of this learning journey in May 2016 when this revised edition was written. Visit www.talk4writing.com to keep informed of ongoing developments.

One thing that the journey has taught us is that it is counterproductive for teachers to devote endless hours to planning new units every year. It makes sense to establish some excellent units that deliver key objectives for every year and then the task of every teacher is to adapt those units to suit the needs of their class and refine them. In this way the school can resource each unit and time is spent on developing real teaching and learning.

Stage 2: Developing the approach across the curriculum

Since the Talk for Writing approach was developed from storytelling, and the Primary National Strategy, probably because it knew its days were numbered, was only interested in developing the approach as a support to fiction writing, it is not surprising that in primary schools there has been a tendency for people to focus on fiction. But when I first saw Pie imitating text in 2005, two thoughts came into my head:

- this is the perfect route for engaging and then involving parents who are perhaps not confident readers and writers themselves;

- this is the missing link from my attempts to establish a meaningful way of achieving literacy across the curriculum in secondary schools so that every teacher recognises that that it is their job to teach the tune of their subject rather than thinking that the English department does literacy and so it's down to them.

It is for this reason that we are concerned about the statement in the national curriculum that it's only the vocabulary that needs to be developed to meet the needs of other curriculum areas – see page 61.

Tuning into the language patterns of each subject area

Apart from the technical vocabulary, every subject has a set of phrases that help create the tune of that subject. Where subjects are closely related, they often share the same transferable sentence patterns. It's the particular phrasing that is important.

Look at these generic phrases:

- creates a mood of . . .

- gives the impression that . . .

- almost seems to suggest . . .

- evokes a mood of . . .

- echoes the sentiment . . .

As soon as you read them, you know that you have entered the subjective world of creative arts. This is the tune of English, art, music, drama; a scientist does not use such terms within their work.

Now try these:

- A short-term cause
- A long-term cause
- There is much evidence to suggest
- A key issue . . .
- Another possible cause is . . .
- Recent investigations have proven . . .
- One theory suggests . . .
- This has recently been reinterpreted as . . .

All of these phrases are linked to history, but they could also be found in science and medicine. These phrases signal a much more clinical, objective perspective. Now look at the precision of the highlighted sections of the model text for a science investigation below:

> **I am investigating what happens to** my heart **when** I take exercise.
>
> **My prediction, what I think will happen, is that** exercise will make my heart beat faster **because** the heart has to pump blood faster to enable me to do the exercise.
>
> **To carry out an investigation, you must compare two variables: two things that change or vary. For this investigation, I will compare** my heart rate when I am resting **and** when I am taking exercise.
>
> **However, it is important to make the test fair. To make this test fair, I must** time my heart for **exactly the same** amount of time **when** I am resting **as when** I am exercising. **It is essential that all the other conditions remain the same because, otherwise, I wouldn't know if it was the** exercise **or something else that was making the difference.**

There will have been nothing within the English non-fiction curriculum that will have prepared the children for such a pattern of text. It is therefore important to provide a model text for the key patterns of science expression (and other subjects across the curriculum that have a specific pattern that the children will not be familiar with). In this way, the children will be able to move from imitation to innovation to independent application. This is why expanding pupils' writing across the curriculum is not just a case of technical vocabulary as the new curriculum would have us believe. When teaching children how to write about history or science or whatever subject is being focused on, it will often be necessary to have a model text of what equals good and go through the same imitation to innovation to independent application. See pages 181–184 in the explanation chapter to see what this might mean for science investigations. Talk for Writing is all about getting the tune of the language of whatever subject is being focused on into the children's heads. Once they have that tune, they can read it when they see it, they can discuss it and refine their thoughts and develop ideas; they can, therefore, plan and write about it.

Retaining the content

Moreover, Talk for Writing does more than just help teachers to get the right pattern of language in pupils' heads so they can express the subject – it also helps the pupils retain the content.

If you think about it, there is no content in the teaching of English (not including literature) aside from expression. Look at the programme of study for English – the children are studying the expression of English. In all other subjects there is specific content within the programmes of study that has to be learned. The text maps developed by Talk for Writing were initially seen as a way of helping children get the language patterns in their heads by helping children recall the text being internalised.

Teachers who have adapted the approach to suit the needs of their subject have found that these text maps are also a brilliant way of helping pupils recall and retain information. As the pupils' linguistic skills develop, they can move beyond the imitating the text stage to being able to hear a model text read aloud, text map it, recall the language patterns as well as the content, and present the gist of the information coherently in spoken and written form. Secondary teachers and pupils across the curriculum – from science to business studies to PE to art – love it.

How the Talk for Writing process can be adapted to meet the needs of all subjects

Some years ago a primary teacher on a Talk for Writing joint-school project reported back that the younger classes loved the approach, but that the Year 5 children didn't. He implied that they needed something more sophisticated. Not knowing that he was the Year 5 teacher, I replied: 'That's not the children, that's the teacher.' He politely informed me that he was the Year 5 teacher. Everyone laughed, but the teacher had the courage to go away and try again and returned three months later with lots of evidence of how successful the approach had been right across the curriculum with his class. It is a question of adapting the approach to suit the needs both of the class and the different subjects.

The grid below relates the approach to the needs of any subject

The Talk for Writing process	How this relates to different subjects and age of pupils
Baseline assessment: Use a cold task/earlier work to enable teacher to assess the expression skills that are needed to enable pupils to progress	**Relevant to all subjects and all ages:** for practical subjects expression may focus on oral expression, rather than writing. For content-based subjects, the cold task may have to be an earlier piece of work related to a different topic, and therefore would only focus on expression. The cold task approach is also relevant to establishing what content the pupils have retained if they have covered some of the content of the topic earlier.
Hook to engage pupils	**Relevant to all subjects** but often easier at primary level. For example, the science curriculum at Key Stage 4 is very content heavy and therefore every lesson tends to have a different focus, so hooking people into learning is harder as there is so little time.
Warm up the tune of language used and context	**Relevant to all subjects and all ages** on a regular basis – for practical subjects this would probably be oral not written.
Provide a model text or process to help pupils grasp what they are trying to do (what = good for this particular unit of work)	**Relevant to all subjects and all ages:** for subjects like art and PE in primary and Key Stage 3 or maths for all key stages, this would usually be a process rather than a text.
Text map the model	**Relevant to all subjects and all ages:** moreover, text mapping supports the retention of content as well as the internalising of language patterns and can be done at a sophisticated as well as a very basic level.
Imitate the text or process	**Relevant to all subjects:** this helps pupils internalise the key language pattern as well as any steps they need to take and the related content. For older pupils, this may often be focusing on the gist of a text in Standard English, rather than word-for-word retelling.

The Talk for Writing process	How this relates to different subjects and age of pupils
Box up the structure of the text or process	**Relevant to all subjects and all ages:** boxing up helps pupils structure their writing appropriately for any subject; it also provides a frame for structuring any process or series of actions. It is a highly transferable way of helping pupils plan their learning in any subject. Advanced boxing up of the key content of a topic also provides an excellent basis for revision of a topic.
Co-construct learning including developing toolkit	**Relevant to all subjects and all ages:** helps pupils develop their own understanding so that their learning has depth. Toolkits provide a scaffold that, over time, will be internalised. It is important to build on these from year to year so that pupil understanding increases and to build in ways of internalising the process so that increasingly they can adapt their writing skills to any writing task for any audience.
Make the learning visible	**Relevant to all subjects and all ages:** helps pupils and teachers to remain focused.
Innovate on the model pattern	**Relevant to all subjects and all ages:** helps pupils understand how to apply their learning and develop an approach.
Evaluate own work followed by teacher assessment	**Relevant to all subjects and all ages:** key to pupils becoming in charge of their own learning and understanding what they need to do to improve.
Refine skills: focus on problems identified by assessment	**Relevant to all subjects and all ages:** without this, classes are in danger of just doing stuff, stuff and more stuff without building in the key steps for understanding, reflection and progress.
Independent application (hot task)	**Relevant to all subjects and all ages:** it is essential that pupils have the opportunity to develop the skills that they have learned to achieve breadth and depth of understanding so that they cease to have any reliance on model texts.
End of unit assessment	**Relevant to all subjects and all ages:** reflecting on progress is key to pupils becoming in charge of their own learning and understanding what they need to do to improve.

This means that Talk for Writing it is the perfect model for building literacy across the curriculum. The underpinning pattern of language can be established in English and built on as appropriate across the curriculum. Our experience is that in the development of this process secondary schools can learn from primary schools and vice versa.

Bibliography

Alexander, R., Rose, J. and Woodhead, C. (1992) *Curriculum Organisation and Classroom Practice in Primary Schools: A Discussion Paper* (known as the Report of the 'Three Wise Men'). London: DfES.

Andrews, R., Torgerson, C., Low, G., McGuinn, N. and Robinson, A. (2006) *Teaching and learning argumentative non-fiction writing for 7–14 year olds: A systematic review of the evidence of successful practice.* London: EPPI-Centre, Social Science Research Unit, Institute of Education, University of London. Download the full report from eppi.ioe.ac.uk

Beard, R. (1999) *The National Literacy Strategy: Review of Research and Other Related Evidence.* London: DfES. Download the full report from http://files.eric.ed.gov/fulltext/ED472219.pdf

Black, P. and Wiliam, D. (1998) Inside the Black Box . . . Raising Standards through Classroom Assessment. *Assessment in Education,* March: 7–74. Download the full article from http://www.rdc.udel.edu/wp-content/uploads/2015/04/InsideBlackBox.pdf

Brill, F. and Twist, L. (2013) *Where have all the levels gone? The importance of a shared understanding of assessment at a time of major policy change.* Slough: National Foundation for Educational Research. Download the full report from https://www.nfer.ac.uk/publications/99940/99940.pdf

Clarke, S. (2001) *Unlocking Formative Assessment.* London: Hodder & Stoughton.

Clarke, S. (2001) *Active Learning Through Formative Assessment.* London: Hodder Education.

Corbett, P. and Strong, J. (2016) *Talk for Writing in the Early Years.* London: McGraw-Hill, Open University Press.

Department for Education (2013) *English programmes of study: key stages 1 and 2.* London: DfE. Download the full report from https://www.gov.uk/government/uploads/system/uploads/attachment_data/file/335186/PRIMARY_national_curriculum_-_English_220714.pdf

Department for Education (2015) *2010 to 2015 government policy: school and college qualifications and curriculum.* London: DfE. Download the full paper from https://www.gov.uk/government/publications/2010-to-2015-government-policy-school-and-college-qualifications-and-curriculum/2010-to-2015-government-policy-school-and-college-qualifications-and-curriculum

English, E., Hargreaves, L. and Hislam, J. (2002) Pedagogical dilemmas in the National Literacy Strategy: primary teachers' perceptions, reflections and classroom behaviour. *Cambridge Journal of Education,* 31(1): 9–26.

English Review Group (2004) *The effect of grammar teaching (syntax) in English on 5 to 16 year olds' accuracy and quality in written composition.*

London: EPPI-Centre, Institute of Education, University of London. Download the report from eppi.ioe.ac.uk

Fisher, R., Lewis, M. and Davis, B. (2000) Progress and performance in National Literacy Strategy classrooms. *Journal of Research in Reading*, 23(3): 256–266.

Fisher, R., Lewis, M. and Davis, B. (2000) The implementation of the literacy hour in small rural schools. *Topic*, 24.

Fullan, M. (2003) *Watching and Learning: Final report of the external evaluation of England's National Literacy and Numeracy Strategies*. Toronto: Ontario Institute for Studies in Education, University of Toronto, reference DfES 0101/2003.

Gardner, K. and Lunzer, E. (1979) *The Effective Use of Reading*. London: Heinemann.

Halliday, M. and Hasan, R. (1985) *Language, Context and Text*: *Aspects of Language in a Social-Semiotic Perspective*. Oxford: Oxford University Press.

Hattie, J. (2008) *Visible Learning: A Synthesis of Over 800 Meta-Analyses Relating to Achievement*. New York: Routledge.

Hudson, R. (2001) Grammar teaching and writing skills: the research evidence. *Syntax in the Schools*, 17: 1–6. Download the full report from http://dickhudson. com/wp-content/uploads/2013/07/writing.rtf

Kirsch, I., de Jong, J., Lafontaine, D., McQueen, J., Mendelovits, J. and Monseur, C. (2002) *Reading for Change: Performance and engagement across countries: Results from PISA 2000*. Paris: Organisation for Economic Cooperation and Development.

Lewis, M. and Wray, D. (1994) *Exeter Extending Literacy Project*. Exeter: University of Exeter.

McIntosh, J. (2015) *Final report of the Commission on Assessment without Levels*. London: Standards & Testing Agency. Download the full report from https://www.gov.uk/government/uploads/system/uploads/attachment_data/file/483058/Commission_on_Assessment_Without_Levels_-_report.pdf

Mroz, M., Smith, F. and Hardman, F. (2000) The discourse of the literacy hour. *Cambridge Journal of Education*, 30(3): 379–390.

National Strategies (2000) *Grammar for Writing*. Download the paper from https://www.hamilton-trust.org.uk/system/files/page_files/grammar_for_writing.pdf

Ofsted (2002) *National Literacy Strategy: The first four years 1998–2002*. London: Ofsted. Download from http://dera.ioe.ac.uk/17512/7/Ofsted%20-%20national%20literacy%20strategy_Redacted.pdf

Palmer, S. (2003) *The Complete Skeleton Book*. Kirkby-in-Ashfield: TTS Group.

Plowden, B. (1967) *Report of the Central Advisory Council for Education (England) into Primary Education in England* (known as The Plowden Report). London: Department for Education. Download the full report from http://en.wikipedia.org/wiki/Plowden_report

Qualifications and Curriculum Development Agency (1998) *The Grammar Papers*. Coventry: QCDA. Download the paper from http://www.suehorner. com/resources/18_Part_1_Pages_1_to_12_The_grammar_papers_(1998).pdf

Rook, J., Loader, H. and McLaren, C. (2013) *Transforming Writing: Final Evaluation Report*. Winchester: Winchester University. Download the full report from http://www.literacytrust.org.uk/research/nlt_research/5714_transforming_ writing_final_evaluation_report

Rose, J. (2008) *Independent Review of the Primary Curriculum* (known as The Primary Review). Download the full report from http://www.educationengland. org.uk/documents/pdfs/2009-IRPC-final-report.pdf

Standards & Testing Agency (2015) *Interim teacher assessment frameworks at the end of key stage 1*. London: Standards & Testing Agency. Download the full report from https://www.gov.uk/government/uploads/system/uploads/ attachment_data/file/461547/Interim_teacher_assessment_frameworks_at_ the_end_of_key_stage_1_PDFA.pdf

Standards & Testing Agency (2015) *Interim teacher assessment frameworks at the end of key stage 2*. London: Standards & Testing Agency. Download the full report from https://www.gov.uk/government/uploads/system/uploads/ attachment_data/file/473675/Interim_teacher_assessment_frameworks_at_ the_end_of_key_stage_2_PDFA_V3.pdf

Standards & Testing Agency (2016) *English grammar, punctuation and spelling test framework: National curriculum tests from 2016: For test developers*. London: Standards & Testing Agency. Download the full report from https:// www.gov.uk/government/uploads/system/uploads/attachment_data/ file/510945/2016_KS2_EnglishGPS_framework_PDFA.pdf

Standards & Testing Agency (2016) *2016 teacher assessment exemplification: end of key stage 2. English writing: Working at greater depth within the expected standard: Frankie*. London: Standards & Testing Agency. Download the full guidance from https://www.gov.uk/government/uploads/system/ uploads/attachment_data/file/510910/STA-Ex2016-KS2-EW-FrankieNonAnn_ PDFA.pdf

Walker, M., Sainsbury, M., Worth, J., Bamforth, H., and Betts, H. (2015) *Phonics screening Check Evaluation: Final report*. Research report. Slough: National Foundation for Educational Research.

Recount

What is recount text?

Figure 4.1   A simple recount text map

Recount is one of the easier non-fiction text types because, since it focuses on telling what's happened, it has the same key ingredients as narrative and is thus comfortingly familiar. The difference is that, whereas narrative is fictional and thus made up, recount text should be a retelling of events that have actually happened: in the first person if it is a personal recount, and in the third person if recounting events that have happened to others. Perhaps not surprisingly, it is recount text that children and adults alike revert to if they are given a writing task that they feel they cannot do. After all, most of us spend a lot of our time recounting things that have happened to us, whether anyone wants to listen or not, and our recount triggers off another in listeners' minds. Like narrative, effective recount relies on the ability of the writer to relate events in an interesting manner that engages the reader.

Like most non-fiction, recount writing begins with an introduction that explains what the subject matter is about, often using the 'Who? What? Where? Why? and When?' approach to orientate the reader, crafted into some sort of 'hook' to encourage the reader to read on.

Ordering recount text is relatively straightforward because it is logical to retell events in chronological order. However, since the skill of recount writing lies in the ability to make the event sound interesting, this sometimes means breaking away from strict chronological order and always means thinking about just the right phrases to engage the reader. The 'and then' syndrome, succinctly described by Professor David Wray as the 'bed-to-bed style of writing', is the curse of recount. Consequently, children need to be taught how to link whatever they are recounting in an engaging way. If we are not careful, the over-drilling of children in time signposts to link their recounts, results in tedious writing that has never broken out of the initial 'first', 'next', 'after that' guidelines for very young children.

To write an effective recount, the author needs to have real knowledge about whatever happened and be interested in it, otherwise there will be little to say and what is said is likely to be deadly dull. This is why linking recount writing to real experiences, like class outings, is so important because then children actually know something in detail and want to communicate what they have experienced.

Typical ingredients of recount text

Audience	Someone who wants to know what happened.
Purpose	To retell a real event in an interesting and engaging way.
Typical structure	• A beginning, middle and end in chronological order. • Opening paragraph to hook and orientate the reader (often includes Who? What? Where? Why? When?). • Paragraphs often begin with a topic sentence.
Typical language features	• Past tense. • Time sentence signposts for coherence. • Specific and descriptive – often in style of information or explanation. • Direct speech.
Examples	• Trip to local museum. • Autobiography. • Newspaper article.

Choosing a recount writing topic

When it comes to recount writing, teachers are spoilt for choice because there are so many things that the children have experienced that can be the springboard for excellent writing. Personal feelings are an obvious source of inspiration: embarrassing moments, first day at school, being treated unfairly, most scary memory, favourite toy – the list is endless – can all lead to excellent writing as long as these memories and experiences are 'warmed up' so that the children are bursting with ideas and are being encouraged to select just the right words and phrases to make their memory come alive.

Apart from individual experiences, there are all the collective experiences like school events and outings that are the perfect focus for recount writing because the children have directly experienced what they are being asked to write about. And it's important to interrupt your planned schedule if, say, spectacular weather is occurring outside, so that the children can write their own experience of 'the great freeze' as it happens.

Role play is an invaluable tool for helping children understand the predicament of others across the curriculum in history, geography or RE. Topics like the evacuation of British cities in 1939 come alive when children are encouraged to put themselves in the shoes of an evacuee packing his or her little bag. They are then in a position to write moving recounts in role as an evacuee. Thus the recount skills introduced in literacy lessons can be honed across the curriculum.

Whatever focus you choose, remember the golden rule: the topic must engage the children so they have something that they really want to express. Without this essential foundation, their writing will be dull.

Audience and purpose

Always provide some sort of audience and purpose for whatever focus is chosen. It can be useful to get the children to draw a picture of someone who is typical of their audience to help them remember who they are writing for so they can pitch their writing accordingly.

Some key uses of recount writing skills across the curriculum

- All school events and trips (cross-curricular).

- First-hand experiences and sharing experiences – English, modern foreign languages (MFL) and personal, social and health education (PSHE).

- Relating significant discoveries/inventions, etc. (science and technology).

- Eyewitness accounts of key events or disasters (history, geography and RE).

- In-role personal experiences of human beings (history, geography, RE and PSHE).

- Accounts of key events (history, geography and RE).

Warming up the tune of the text

Figure 4.2   Making time signposts visual

It is worth thinking carefully about the tune of recount text and the topic selected: about the sentence signposts and structures that are typically used, as well as the information and vocabulary that the children will need when they come to write. Then devise daily games that will help the children internalise these patterns and the related information at the right level of difficulty for the class. The picture here shows reception children at Outwoods Edge Primary School in Loughborough constructing a visual timeline with key connecting phrases like *next*, linked to days of the week, as a concrete way of helping them understand one thing happening after another. Practising the tune of the text through talking, will enable the children to manipulate what they have to say effectively when they finally write it down. Recount writing lends itself to:

Tuning into the vocabulary games

- **Brain dumps**: For personal memory recounts, get the children to jot down all the words they associate with a particular memory. Try it cold and then get them silently to think through the event and then try again.

Tuning into sentence signpost games

Understanding the power of sentence signposts to link paragraphs, sentences and information within sentences is key to achieving cohesive text that flows logically and engagingly. Appendix 3 on **DVD 2** focuses on the grammar features of linking text and includes useful handouts: **Handout 6** is a list of a broad range of sentence signposts; **Handout 7** shows Pie demonstrating actions for the 14 key sentence signposts.

- **Spot the truth:** In pairs, one child has to come up with two true statements about themselves, plus one untrue statement, beginning with a temporal sentence signpost, for example:

  – 'Last year' / 'yesterday' / 'last week' . . .

  – 'A long time ago', . . .

  – 'When I was a toddler', . . .

The partner has to see if they can decide which is not true. The partner should be encouraged to use discursive sentence starters, often tentative, for example, 'I think that' . . . , 'I'm not sure' . . . , 'It seems unlikely' . . . , 'also' . . ., etc.

- **Using engaging sentence signposts:** Help the children recognise that endless standard time signposts or lists of precise dates to introduce facts can be confusing and dull. Provide them with interesting alternatives. Their task in groups is to decide which standard sentence starters or list of dates they could possibly replace with the alternative sentence starters to make the writing clearer and more engaging. Encourage the children to magpie useful words and phrases from this activity.

Tuning into the text games

- **Role play:** Get the children to enact aspects of the topic using a range of techniques like hot seating, visiting professor/minister, mobile phone conversations, mime, television interviews, news reporter interviews, etc.

- **What = 'good' for this sort of writing:** Write four different introductions to whatever recount you want the children to write, one of which is better than the rest. Include one example that is worthy but extremely dull, and one that has lost the plot (i.e. it is not a piece of recount writing but is persuasion or instruction). There should be no surface errors in any of the text – you want the children to focus on content and expression not surface error. Children select which is best, given the purpose, and suggest the ingredients that make it the best. This can be snowballed from pairs to fours to eights and then the whole class can establish their key ingredients for an effective introduction when writing a recount. Display these ingredients on the writing wall.

- **Anecdotes:** Unusual people, places or memorable events. Warm up the topic, for example, an embarrassing memory, by recounting something that made you very embarrassed that the children can relate to and then get them in pairs to tell their own memories to each other. You may want to get them to retell their memory focusing this time on making it as engaging as possible. You will probably find that the most engaging recounts use relatively few time signposts.

- **Swap the anecdote:** Once they have refined their anecdote telling, ask the children to retell a particular event to a partner. The partners then write their partners' anecdote in as entertaining way as they can.

- **Sequencing the text:** Find a good short exemplar of whatever sort of recount text you are focusing on and rearrange the paragraphs so that when it is cut into paragraphs the children cannot put it together again using the cut marks. In groups, the children have to sequence the text, read the sequenced text aloud to check it is coherent and, finally, be prepared to explain the order in which they have placed the text.

- **Warming up the content across the curriculum:** When applying what they've learned about recount writing to topics across the curriculum, provide the children with a number of facts on cards that are relevant to the event you want them to recount. Also include one or two bits of information that are not relevant. In pairs, the children have to discard the irrelevant information and place the rest in chronological order. They can also be asked to decide on what will be powerful information to provide the hook for the beginning and the amazing fact for the ending.

This activity can be developed further by asking the children to use symbols to represent the order of the information. Then, working in pairs with just the symbols to support them, see if they can recount the information to a partner introducing and linking the information in as interesting a way as possible. Get children to present some of the more effective presentations to the whole class and encourage the children to magpie good phrases that they might want to use when they write their recount.

A Year 1 example of model recount text

The key to the success of the Talk for Writing approach is its three stages: imitation, innovation and independent application, as explained in Chapter 2. If the teacher has a Key Stage 1 class, then they would want to develop a simple exemplar recount text, possibly around a school trip like the example below (see video clip 5 on **DVD 1**, for how to teach children to imitate this text). Remember, it's no use using this example if the children haven't actually had a trip to the Country Museum. Adapt it to somewhere they have visited to make it real for them.

Do not show the children the text at this stage. They are going to hear it and internalise it orally before they see it. With younger classes, you may want to colour code particular features of the model to help the children understand the central role of say topic sentences or sentence signposts in non-fiction text.

Now turn the text into a text map full of images and symbols to help the children recall the text. You may want to have one text map per paragraph and display it as a washing line. Talk the text for the children with actions making the children join in. Move from whole class retelling to groups and finally pairs so that ultimately everyone can retell the text on their own. You may want to refer to video clip 5 on **DVD 1** to remind you how to do this.

The worked example below explains how to ensure the children thoroughly internalise the text orally. Once they have done this, present the text that they have internalised to the children and start by reading it as a reader and then as a writer before moving on to the innovation stage.

Figure 4.3 Text map for *Our trip to the country museum*

Our trip to the Country Museum

Last week, we all went to the Country Museum.

First, we looked at the tractors. They had enormous wheels.

Next, we sat on the farm trailer and went for a bumpy ride.

After that, the farmer showed us the animals. We saw two different types.

1. The cows had sharp horns. They were waiting to be milked.

2. The sheep were with their babies.

Finally, we walked back to school. It was a great day.

Interestingly, as soon as you start to model how to embellish this simple recount text to add in a few more details about what was seen and what was interesting, you immediately start to move into information or explanation text (see video clip 7 on **DVD 1**). This is a timely reminder that there is very little 'pure' text and that from the earliest stages we have to make the children alert to the idea that the text has to work rather than follow a fixed template.

How to plan a recount unit in Talk for Writing style

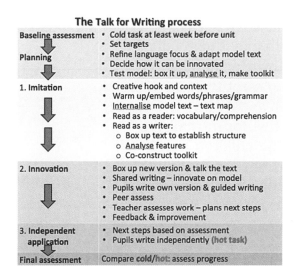

Figure 4.4   The Talk for Writing process

This image sums up the Talk for Writing process. If you have not already read Chapter 2, which explains this process in detail, you may find it useful to read that chapter before thinking about how the process can be applied to recount text. **Handout 1** is an expanded version of this process with more detail about the key essential features, as well as some optional suggestions that schools have found useful in helping children make progress. – see Appendix 2 on **DVD 2**.

Worked example for recount text

Below is a worked example of the three stages of the Talk for Writing approach, focusing on news article recount writing, bookended by the initial and final assessment to ensure formative assessment is at the heart of the planning, teaching and learning process.

Objective: To write interesting recount text (with a focus on newspaper articles).

Topic for imitation and innovation: News articles on *Little Red Riding Hood*.

Audience and purpose: Class display and presentation in assembly.

Baseline assessment and planning

Figure 4.5

For any unit of work on recount, you have first to think about what recount writing skills the class already possesses. As explained in Chapter 2, a good way of doing this is to set a **cold task**. This should be set at least a week before you begin to teach your unit so that you can alter your planning to suit the needs of the class. The pupils will need a familiar context (for example, select an entertaining classroom incident and ask the children to write an account of what happened in as entertaining a way as they can) so that they have something to write about that they know about and that interests them. Warm the topic up with a quick discussion but do not provide any teaching in how to write about this subject. If your model text is based on a story the children all know, then you can ask them to write a news article about it without giving them any help in how to write a news article. This is what one Year 1 child wrote for her article on *Little Red Riding Hood*:

> Once upon a time there lived a little girl. She had a red claok with a hood a pink dress And gleeming blue eyes. Everyobe cald her Little Red Riding Hood. One day her grany was poly Little Red Riding Hood had to give her some food and drink. She lived at the other side of the wood. But she dident see a wolf watching her from behind a tree. Then he jummt out.

From the above example, you can see that the child knows how to tell a story but has no idea how to structure and phrase a news article. Assessing this cold write will help you pinpoint what specific structure and skills to focus on in the unit to help all the children progress alongside helping you set a range of additional targets for children with different levels of attainment. This process also enables you to adapt the model text to ensure that it illustrates the features that suit the needs of the class, as illustrated by the model text below.

Local Gran wins through

Yesterday, local granny Mrs Berry, 80 years old, was awarded a golden frying pan at Fairyland Castle. This special ceremony celebrated her bravery after being attacked by a hungry wolf.

Last year, the gorgeous granny was eaten by a wolf but a quick-witted woodman cut open the wolf's tummy. Happily, granny gave him a hug and a kiss.

Granny told 'The Woodland Times' that she was delighted. 'I'm a lucky lady,' she said.

To understand the progress that can be achieved through this approach, see page 104 for what the child wrote for her hot task at the end of the unit.

Stage 1: Imitation

- Creative hook and context
- Warm up/embed words/phrases/grammar
- Internalise model text – text map
- Read as a reader: vocabulary/comprehension
- Read as a writer:
  - Box up text to establish structure
  - Analyse features
  - Co-construct toolkit

Figure 4.5a

The creative hook

Every unit needs a hook to ignite the children's interest. A Year 3 teacher, from Warren Farm Academy, Birmingham, decided that the very thing to engage children with recount text would be a trip to West Midlands Safari Park to visit 'The Land of the Living Dinosaurs'. Not only would the trip lend itself to recount

Figure 4.6   Children hooked by research on dinosaurs

but, at the Safari Park, the children could be engaged as palaeontologists searching for the prehistoric remains of dinosaurs in the sand in preparation for recount work in role as palaeontologists writing up their journals.

The focus of the recount work for this unit is Little Red Riding Hood, selected because it is a story that the class is already familiar with. To reignite the children's interest in the story, try any of the following:

- Mock up a front page of a local newspaper report about wolf sightings in the area.

- Create a class list of clues that might suggest that wolves are in the area, e.g. scratch marks, wolf prints in mud or snow, missing chickens or rabbits, strange howling at night . . .

- Hot-seat a few people who claim to have seen the wolf.

- Take the class on a walk during which various evidence is found, e.g. scratch marks, wolf prints, bits of red material . . .

Warming up the tune of news recounts

Games and activities devised to familiarise the children with the pattern of text and the context of the unit are key to success. As the games are played, flip-chart the vocabulary, sentence signposts and key sentence patterns that emerge and start to create a toolkit of useful ingredients for recount text to support the children's speaking and writing. Display these to make the learning visible and develop them throughout the unit. If the children have already been taught this text type in Talk for Writing style, build on their existing toolkit for recount. The corridors of Knowle Park, Bristol, are decorated with the key connecting phrases of the different text types accompanied by the comma that marks off the end of the phrase, where appropriate.

Tune the children into the style of news writing through reading news articles to them and providing newspapers (e.g. *First News* – www.firstnews.co.uk) for them to read. This might be done in quiet reading or as part of guided reading.

Figure 4.7   First, soon, next, after

Below are five warming-up-the-text activities to help the children become confident in the language of news articles. The order of these activities is important as the first and second help them to understand how news articles are laid out, structured and expressed, while the third helps them recall the content. The fourth scaffolds a news interview and the final activity provides the opportunity to talk some of the language of news articles in relation to the topic being focused on.

1   **Using real articles to tune into the text:** Provide copies of real newspapers (for example, *First News*) and focus on specific articles so children can see how real articles are laid out, structured and expressed. This would be a good opportunity to conduct a booktalk-style activity focusing on the nature of headlines. Through open-ended questioning (as outlined on pages 194–195) get the children to draw out the key features of headlines: short pithy hooks to attract the reader's eye.

2   **Using real articles to tune into the text:** Select an article for the children to sequence in pairs to help them understand how articles are structured *and* linked. Make certain it is a good exemplar of the *Who? What? Where? Why? When* opening paragraph.

3   **Role play to warm up the content:** Get the children to quickly recall in pairs or threes what happens in *Little Red Riding Hood.* Then in groups of five (the mother, Little Red Riding Hood, the wolf, granny and the woodcutter) ask them to mime the action.

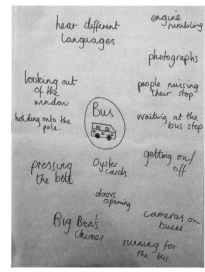

4   **Tuning into opening paragraphs:** As a class, list the possible questions when interviewing one of the characters from Little Red Riding Hood including When? Who? Where? What? Why?

Figure 4.8   Brainstorming vocabulary

5   **Tuning into the text and the content:** Model for the class how to conduct a news article interview with the wolf and then get the class, in pairs, to role play an interview with the woodcutter. You may also want to focus on some of the vocabulary that will be key to this recount. Figure 4.8, from Penn Wood, Slough, of a Year 2 recount of a day trip to London illustrates how the class were involved in brainstorming information about aspects of their trip so they would have detail to add to their recount.

Internalising the model text

Write a simple exemplar recount text (in this instance a newspaper article relating to *Little Red Riding Hood*) that contains the expected structure and language features appropriate to the level of the children but ensuring that that there is an edge of challenge. Now turn the text into a large class map. Since this text has several paragraphs, it lends itself to being displayed on a washing line on several sheets of flip-chart paper – one for each paragraph. Do not show the children the text at this stage. They are going to hear it and internalise it orally before they see it.

Figure 4.9   A washing-line text map for 'Local hero wins medal'

Make certain your text map offers the children the level of support they need. At Dashwood Academy in Banbury, a Year 3 text map of a letter of complaint (see images below) demarcates the sentences (in separate boxes), the punctuation (in red), and the paragraphs (one sheet per paragraph).

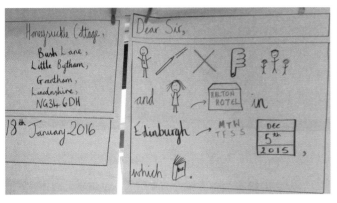

Figure 4.10   Text map for opening section of a letter of complaint

Figure 4.11   Washing-line text map showing the later paragraphs

To help learn the text, children should draw their own text maps. These may be annotated with anything that causes problems.

Retell the text in various different ways to help the children internalise the text:

- retell it silently;

- hold a race to see who can say it the quickest;

- in pairs say it sentence by sentence;

- prepare to present to children in another class.

Move from whole class retelling to groups and finally pairs so that ultimately everyone can retell the text on their own. You may want to refer to video clip 8 on **DVD 1** where Pie demonstrates how to do this.

1a) Reading as a reader

Don't show the children the text until after they have thoroughly internalised it orally. Once they have done this, present the text to them and start by reading it as a reader.

Local hero wins medal

Yesterday, local lumberjack hero Jim Stevenson, 32 years old, was awarded a medal at a special ceremony in the palace for his bravery in rescuing Little Red Riding Hood from the jaws of a terrifying wolf.

In December last year, sharp-witted Jim put his lumberjack skills to great use by tracking a vicious wolf he saw following a little girl in a red hood. He arrived at her grandmother's cottage **just in time** to save the little girl and her granny. Jim heroically fought off the wolf with his axe.

Jim told 'The Informer' that he was feeling very chipper about being awarded a medal: 'I never expected that. I only did what any ordinary person would have done. It was the proudest moment of my life,' he said.

With the wicked wolf now safely behind bars, we can all sleep more soundly in our beds. **But** little girls should still take Jim's advice and not walk alone in the woods.

They should be able to read it because they have internalised the language but that does not mean they have fully understood the meaning of the words. Help the children deepen their understanding of the text, becoming increasingly familiar with the structure and language patterns by using the following sorts of activities:

- Interview Little Red Riding Hood about her ordeal.

- Draw a map of Little Red Riding Hood's journey through the wood to her grandmother's.

- Describe to a friend in a phone call what happened.

- In the role as a local policeman, explain what action the police will be taking.

- Make a one-minute presentation, explaining how the lumberjack saved Little Red Riding Hood and her granny.

- Take each paragraph in turn and investigate closely in a range of different ways, e.g. highlight all the signposts and discuss what difference they make. Then look at the range of different sentence structures.

- Construct some tell-me style questions for the children to initially discuss in pairs to open up discussion on the text and ensure the children have understood what they are reading, for example:

  - Tell me why you think the article first tells us about Jim winning a medal and then tells us what he did to deserve it.

  - Tell me why you think Jim might feel proud.

  - Tell me why you think the article ends with a warning.

1b) Reading as a writer

Once the children have fully understood the text, you can then start reading it as a writer, identifying the language features that can be reused as well as analysing the techniques that the writer has used to make the writing effective.

Boxing up the text

The first thing for the children to think about when trying to understand how a text has been written is its structure, so show the children how to box up this news report. Ask them to count how many paragraphs there are. Box up the basic pattern with the children asking them to identify the focus of each paragraph, and then create a box for each paragraph, so that the underlying structure can clearly be seen. The more they are involved in co-constructing the structure, the more they will be able to understand it. See video clip 9 on boxing up recount text.

This boxed-up structure will also provide the basic plan for the teacher in the shared writing and for the children when they come to create their own news articles. You may want to inform the children that real journalists are trained to write articles using a similar planning grid.

Boxed-up planning for local hero wins medal

Heading for each section	Key points
Introduce story with news hook to grab reader's interest including: • Who? • What? • When? • Why? • Where? Note: This is usually one well-crafted long sentence	• lumberjack • received medal • yesterday • for rescuing girl from wolf • palace
More detail on key story	• happened last December • tracked wolf to grandmother's cottage • fought wolf with axe
Central character detail relating to story with quote	• how hero feels about award
Conclusion round off story	• immediate danger over • warning

Display your boxing up, so the children know how to plan their discussion writing.

- It is worth taking specific sentence patterns and amending (innovating) them to produce new sentences using the same underlying pattern. In this example, particularly stress the skill of dropping in extra information in the opening sentence in a journalistic manner, for example:

  – *Yesterday, local lumberjack hero Jim Stevenson, 32 years old, was awarded a medal at a special ceremony in the palace.*

- *Last week, national pole-vaulting hero Ali Khan, 22 years old, was awarded a medal at Buckingham Palace.*

- *Earlier today, have-a-go granny Mabel Roberts, 82 years old, was awarded a medal at Scotland Yard.*

- Take each paragraph in turn and investigate it closely in a range of different ways, e.g. highlight all the linking phrases and discuss what difference they make. Then look at the range of different sentence structures. What words or phrases are particularly effective. Are there any useful general phrases that could be magpied for other articles?

- **What links the paragraphs?:** Create a sorting activity by giving the children the same text cut up into paragraphs (remember to mix up the paragraphs before cutting it up so that the paragraphs can't be reassembled logically by the paper cuts). Ask the children to reassemble the text in the right order and identify the words or phrases that enable them to be certain that they have the text in the right order, e.g. *Yesterday; In December last year; With the wicked wolf now safely behind bars, . . .*

- **Identifying phrases to magpie**: Ask the children in pairs to highlight any phrases that might be useful when they come to write an article of their own, e.g. *Yesterday; x years old; in x last year; just in time to; heroically fought off.*

- **Identifying effective vocabulary:** Ask the children to identify the vocabulary that they think is most effective and be prepared to explain their choices, e.g. *local lumberjack hero; jaws of a terrifying wolf; sharp-witted; feeling very chipper; wicked wolf.*

- **Varying the length of sentences:** Ask the children to identify different lengths of sentences within the article and discuss the difference it makes. Note, in this one, Jim's quotes are in short sentences which make them sound realistic as well as contrasting with the longer sentences of most of the rest of the article.

- **Recognising the important role of pronouns in recount text:** Using pronouns appropriately is key to effective recount writing. If they are misused, you can't tell who is doing what to whom. First, ask the children to discuss where in the article pronouns could be used in place of names/ or vice versa and whether this would make the text better or worse. Then you could construct some sentences where pronouns have been misused to help children be aware of the problem and to encourage them to check pronouns carefully when writing. For example, in pairs, they could decide how many possible reinterpretations there are in these sentences and decide how they need to be written to make them have a clear meaning:

- He asked Jim and then he asked the policeman if they had seen another wolf and he said he had but he said he hadn't. Then, suddenly, he left.

- She looked at her friend and decided that she would do exactly what she wanted to do regardless of how many times she had been warned not to. She was always like that.

Support understanding by flip-charting and displaying useful words and phrases built up throughout the unit.

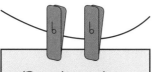
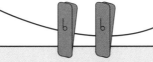
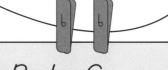

Poster A

In your introduction include

- Who?
- What?
- When?
- Why?
- Where?

Poster B

Guide your reader through the event

- Yesterday
- Last week
- In February last year
- It has just been announced

Poster C

Select powerful words

- brave
- plucky
- heroic
- public-spirited
- undaunted

The key 'writing ingredients' for success can be established through the reading-as-a-writer discussions. It is essential that the children co-construct these ingredients, otherwise they will be meaningless to them. These ingredients should be displayed as they will drive the shared, guided and independent writing, including self-/peer evaluation and feedback from the teacher. A useful method is to flip-chart each ingredient up as it is taught to help the children understand the significance of each ingredient. It is probably a good idea to keep the ingredients list as short as possible and back them up with a checklist that contains examples. Support the short

Figure 4.12   Making a toolkit visual through images not words

list with examples on the walls and in the children's journals from the activities they have taken part in. The Year 2 recount toolkit illustrated here from Penn Wood, Slough, is entirely visual, using symbols. It is also not hierarchical. The toolkit is displayed on the washing line and a copy stuck into each child's book. They then annotate the toolkit to explain what each symbol means.

Co-constructed toolkit for news articles

Plan it – order the information so it reads like an article	• Plan your article (box it up) remembering your audience. • Select interesting/entertaining events to engage your reader. • Begin with news hook to grab reader's interest: *Who? What? When? Why? Where?* (see poster A). • Round your story off e.g.: hint what could happen next.
Link it – make your article flow	• Link your ideas and check that it flows (see poster B). • Use pronouns to avoid repetition (*he, I, it*).
Express it – make your article sound interesting	• Use interesting varied language to keep your reader engaged (see poster C). • Check detail helps reader picture what happened, e.g. *Jim heroically fought off the wolf.* • Vary sentence lengths using short ones to make key points, e.g. *I never expected that.*
Check it	• Read your writing aloud. Make certain it flows, check it for accuracy, and improve it if it does not sound quite right. • Does it tell the reader what happened in an interesting and engaging way?

You may find it useful to watch clip 10 on how to co-construct a recount toolkit. Remind the class that you can include all the ingredients but still write a poor recount. They must remember to taste it (read it aloud to test if it works) to help guarantee quality writing.

Of course, such checklists should be matched to the stage the children are working at so that it might be less complex or more demanding. These can be used as a guide in the form of a 'response ladder' for evaluation, marking and feedback.

Stage 2: Innovation

2. Innovation
• Box up new version & talk the text
• Shared writing – innovate on model
• Pupils write own version & guided writing
• Peer assess
• Teacher assesses work – plans next steps
• Feedback & improvement

Figure 4.12a

Task: Write a news story giving the granny's view on the dreadful wolf attack in *Little Red Riding Hood.*

Audience and purpose: Class display and assembly presentation.

Now that the children have thoroughly internalised the pattern of news article language, they are in a position to innovate using this pattern and to write their own news story, this time giving the granny's view. Support this process through shared planning and shared writing alongside appropriately devised role play activities to further strengthen their familiarity with the structure and language patterns. See clip 9 on shared planning.

Use a similar boxed-up grid on a flip chart to act as a planner, to demonstrate to the children how to plan their article.

- Begin by getting the children to brainstorm a good heading for their article. Tell them that the words have to be as short and hard-hitting as possible as the headline is the key hook, but is given very little space.

- Then, in pairs, get them to role play interviewing granny in preparation for writing the article. Remind the reporters that they need to cover Who? What? When? Why and Where? in their opening paragraph so they must ask granny these questions and granny must invent appropriate answers. You may want to get them to draw the content for their opening paragraph.

- Using shared writing techniques (see **Handout 5** in appendix 2 on the **DVD**), work on planning the article, continually referring back to the original plan, using it as a basis for creating a boxed-up plan for the new version.

Boxed-up planning for granny article

Focus of each section	*Planning details for granny version*
Introduce Story with news hook to grab reader's interest including: – Who? – What? – When? – Why? – Where?	– Have-a-go gran beats wolf – Ethel Wainwright age 92 – Defended self and granddaughter from wolf – Last December – Self-defence – Cottage in wood near Nether Pudsey
More detail on key story:	– Wolf followed granddaughter Ellie (8) to cottage – Struck wolf on nose with walking stick – Lumberjack Jim Stevenson trapped wolf
Central character detail relating to story:	– Ethel recovering in Pudsey General Hospital – Grateful to Jim pleased hit wolf
End Round off story	– Local police congratulated Ethel – Warned young girls not to walk alone in wood

Shared writing

You can now, through shared writing, show them how to move from their plan to the actual writing. It helps to take this bit by bit, having the relevant paragraph from the original displayed on the interactive whiteboard, annotated and colour coded so that the language features stand out. Alongside this, display the plan you have just devised, plus the toolkit on the writing wall or washing line where you and the class can see it while you scribe the children's ideas on a flip chart. (The picture here shows a reception class's working wall at St Joseph's in Derby when they were recounting the mystery of Santa's missing sleigh.)

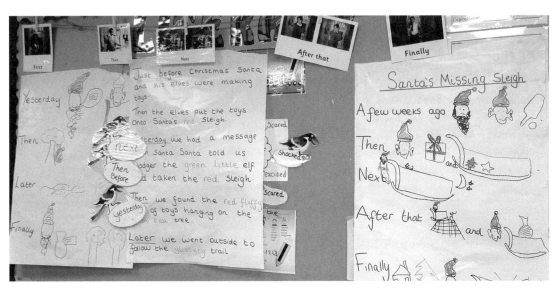

Figure 4.13   Working wall for recount work on Santa's missing sleigh

Through shared writing, turn each section into fluent writing, involving the children in making decisions, suggesting words and developing sentences. As you do this, get the children to 'magpie' good ideas by jotting them down in their writing journals. Encourage them to never dodge a good word by putting a dotted line under words that are hard to spell (e.g. granddaughter) demonstrating how to focus on composition at this stage rather than spending time now looking up the spelling. This can be done at the final draft stage. Keep reading the shared writing through (tasting it) to get the children into the habit of reading their sentences aloud to see if they sound right. You may want to build up the article paragraph by paragraph over a number of days, depending on the children's confidence. The process is quite simple:

- gather facts for the new paragraph;
- refer back to the original;
- turn the facts into similar sentences;
- keep rereading to maintain flow;
- 'test out' children's ideas to 'hear' whether they work;

- ask children to develop sentences in pairs or on mini-whiteboards;

- pace the writing over two or three days to ensure quality.

Ask the teaching assistant (or a pupil) to flip-chart key phrases and vocabulary to be turned into posters to support the writing.

Have a look at the useful phrases for shared writing sessions on **Handout 4** in Appendix 2 on **DVD 2** to build up your repertoire of ways to keep the class engaged.

Shared writing for Have-a-go gran beats wolf

Daring gran Ethel Wainwright (92 years old) was the hero of Nether Puddsey last week when she defended herself against a big bad wolf who viciously attacked her and her little granddaughter in her woodland home.

When the wicked wolf followed Ethel's eight-year-old granddaughter to the steps of her cottage, quick-witted Ethel grabbed her walking stick and dealt him a swift blow on the nose. The wolf was finally trapped by passing lumberjack Jim Stevens.

Ethel is now recovering from her ordeal in Pudsey General Hospital. 'I'm very grateful to that nice Mr Stevenson', she said, adding that she was thrilled to have given the wolf 'a good thwack on the nose'.

The local police, after congratulating Ethel Wainwright for her courage in confronting the wolf, issued a warning to young girls not to walk alone in the woods.

Once you have led the children through writing a class version of 'Have-a-go gran beats wolf', they are in a position to write their own versions and should be bursting with ideas for what to say and how to say it. Help them to fill in their boxed-up plan with their ideas for their version. Younger classes/less-confident children turn it into a text map and talk their text so by the time they come to write they know exactly what they want to say.

The children should write independently straight after the shared writing, gradually building their text over a number of days. Use guided writing to teach and support groups in a focused manner. More confident writers might be asked to write a longer article adding extra information and moving away from the model (see pages 37–40 for an explanation of how to do this).

Once the children have completed their writing they should be in the habit of sharing their writing with a partner. This should be an opportunity to test out their writing, hearing how it sounds when read aloud. A discussion can follow about what works and what might be done to improve any places where the writing does not flow or engage the reader. Refer back to the 'toolkit for recount text' above and use these to focus feedback. Remember, though, that while the children should have included the ingredients, the key factor will be whether the article engages the reader.

The writer now adapts aspects of their work in the light of their partner's comments, remembering that the final choice is the writer's. You may want to encourage them to write their own comment underneath their work focusing on what they think they have done well, how they have improved it, and what may still need improving. The teacher can then take the work in for assessment and write their comment so that it builds on the pupil's comment, creating a dialogue about the best way forward that can be continued in guided writing sessions.

When assessing the whole class's work, the teacher may find it useful to use a grid like the one below to help focus on what aspects of the writing particularly need improving if the children are to become skilled article writers.

Grid to help assess what needs teaching next

	Ingredients	*Have these ingredients been successfully implemented? Which features now need to be focused on?*
Plan it	• Can they plan articles (box it up)? • Can they devise punchy headings? • Can they begin with a news hook to grab reader's interest including: Who? What? When? Why? Where? • Can they add more engaging detail about the key story? • Can they include central character detail, including a quote? • Can they round off their stories well possibly with a warning of what could happen next?	
Link it	• Are they using topic sentences effectively to introduce paragraphs and guide the reader? • Can they link the text successfully with time signposts (*later on, after that*, etc.)?	
Express it	• Are they using interesting and varied words and phrases appropriately? • Can they use engaging language to help the reader picture what happened? • Are they using a variety of sentence structures?	

| **Check it** | • Is there evidence that they are reading their work aloud to see if it sounds good?
• Are they checking their spelling and punctuation? | |

Your marking should lead directly into your next piece of teaching including children editing their writing. Provide feedback on this work focusing on those areas that the children found most difficult and helping them understand how to edit their work effectively. A visualiser or iPad is a very useful piece of equipment to allow you to present exemplar work from the pupils immediately to the whole class to illustrate the improvements you are seeking.

Model for the children how to reflect on the effectiveness of writing. The more opportunities the children are given to talk about what works and what features make the writing engaging, the more they will be able to develop their own inner judge and craft and edit their own writing effectively. **Handout 5** is full of useful questions to help children reflect on what makes writing effective and discuss what works. If the teacher models this sort of reflection, the children will quickly pick up how to reflect on work. Focus on what makes the text engaging, not on the naming of parts.

On pages 177–178 is a list of possible problems that frequently appear in children's writing and the sort of work that may help rectify them.

One of the contributions that the Transforming Writing project made to the development of Talk for Writing was mini-lessons. This would be an excellent point within the unit to set up some mini-lessons so that pupils can focus on the areas that they need help with most (see pages 42–43).

Stage 3: Independent application

3. Independent application
• Next steps based on assessment
• Pupils write independently (hot task)

Figure 4.13a

Task: Write a news article on a topic of your choice using all the skills you have learned.

Audience and purpose: Class newspaper for distribution to other classes.

Once this redrafting has been assessed, the teacher is now in a good position to move to the third stage where there is more choice. The assessment will direct what has to be focused upon during shared and guided sessions.

Once again, model planning using a boxed-up grid as well as shared writing. You could be working on a class version perhaps about a recent school event and invite the children to write articles on a range of school events. A school sports day or summer fair would lend themselves to a range of news opportunities.

The children, working in pairs, could then role play interviews. After that, they could independently box-up their plan and, if necessary, turn it into icons and talk their text through. Younger or less confident pupils will then be able to compose their article more easily as they will have rehearsed the phrases and structure that they want to use. The level of support provided for the independent writing will depend on the needs of the class but, as explained on page 37–40, the teacher's job is to wean children from relying too heavily on the model. You may want to provide an exemplar text on the whiteboard and its related boxed-up planning on the washing line to remind children of the process. This work could be written on yellow paper to indicate it is the hot task, or a red sticker or tab be used so that the hot task can easily be identified.

Once the children have completed their work, ask them to read it through carefully and decide how to improve it. Then ask them to write their own comment on how well they have completed the task. This will help them reflect on their learning and increase their sense of responsibility for their learning.

End of unit assessment

Final assessment Compare cold/hot: assess progress

Figure 4.13b

The teacher now assesses the final piece of writing (the **hot task**) and looks back at the **cold task** to see what progress has been made. Below is a Year 1 child's hot task that you can compare with her cold task on page 89. Adding your comment to the child's comment helps to promote a dialogue about what needs to be done to improve the child's work. Again, when the work is handed back, focus on one or two areas that everyone needs to improve. This could be indicated by highlighting the areas selected in a particular colour – for example, green for growth. Provide some teaching relating to these areas and ask the children to immediately improve their work. Then ask them to reflect on their learning by looking back at the cold task and seeing what progress they have made.

Yesterday forest hero, Woodman, 29 years old, was awarded a golden axe at fairytale casel. This speshell seremony cellbrated his bravey in rescring pore little red riding hoods granny from the jaws of a hungry wolf.
Last sumer quwic wifed Woody put his choping scills to grat yous by cuting open the wolfs tummy. Graney happly jumpt out and gave him a bih hug and kiss!
Woodman told the forist times the he was apslootly dlitid to be awoded this axe. "Going to the fairy tale casel and rurseving this axe was the prawdest moment off my life"! Littlel red riding hood and grany all so atended the the party and we can exusvely ruport that they tiffly thankt the Woodman for saving there life.
With the hungry wolf to in barist to rurtun we can all sleep more sawndlly in are beds. But all forist crechers must take Woodman's advis an wotch out for wolfs.

Figure 4.13c   Child's hot task writing

The teacher is now in a position to decide which everyday language features will need focusing on in the next unit of work, as well as logging any recount features that will need strengthening when the class next revisits news article writing.

Mastering the approach across the curriculum

Objective: Be able to use recount text as appropriate across the curriculum.

Teachers sometimes ask children to write news accounts relating to a wide range of topics like natural disasters or historical events, and this is often presented as a fun activity. But, if the teacher hasn't taught the children the skills of news article writing, then this is just making the writing even more daunting as it adds extra complexity. The text the children produce may look like an article from a distance if it has a headline and is laid out in columns but, as soon as you read the text, the sense that it is a news article collapses and the writer will recognise that their work does not sound right. However, if in English lessons the children have internalised the tune of news article writing, then they can apply it to any topic.

Applying their recount writing skills across the curriculum in a range of contexts will provide the depth and breadth that is essential if the children are to achieve mastery of the skills that underpin effective recount writing.

Fortunately, recount is one of the easiest text types to embed across the curriculum as it is used in many subjects. For example, it is an excellent writing activity following a role play to help pupils understand the situations of others in subjects like geography, RE and history. Some of the greatest stories of human endeavour are linked to science or technology. Again the children can research and recount what led inventors to develop their ideas or scientists to investigate their hypotheses.

Once a unit on recount writing has been taught, then places across the curriculum should be found where the children can practise their recount writing skills. For example, simple recount skills of the *Our trip to ...* variety will be taught in English in reception. These skills can be applied in other subjects as illustrated by

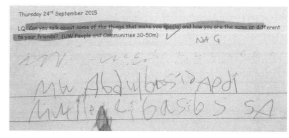

Figure 4.14 Reception cold task for recount

Abdullah, a reception child at St Matthew's Primary in Nechells, Birmingham. At the beginning of the school year, when asked to write about the things that make him similar or different to his friends, you can just about decipher his name, but it is hard to know what he was trying to express. But, by March of his reception year, he could recount simple events as part of his work within People and Communities. Of course, such progress would not have been possible if he had

not learned about recount in his English lessons and also been systematically taught how to form his letters clearly so that his handwriting is legible. See Appendix 4 for guidance on how to do this.

By Year 3, children will be capable of much more sophisticated recount of real experiences linked to the curriculum. In history, Year 3 pupils at Warren Farm Academy, Birmingham, visited a safari park as part of their work on dinosaurs.

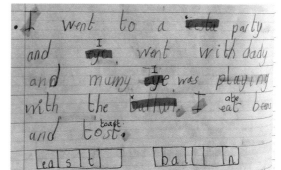

Figure 4.15 Reception hot task for recount

This provided a perfect opportunity to refine their recount skills and model how most real recount text also includes information, as this extract from their shared writing of the outing shows:

First, we stopped to look at the timeline, which illustrated the history of life on earth. The timeline began with the formation of the moon 4.5 billion years ago. Furthermore, we were able to locate when the first mammals appeared on earth

(210 million years ago) and the time when dinosaurs became extinct (66 million years ago).

Then we walked around the exhibit stopping to research facts about the different dinosaurs. The dinosaurs moved in different ways and each one had their own cries. Walking through we saw real life fossils of dinosaur eggs, a Tyrannosaurs' tooth and even coprolites!

At the end of the exhibit, we were able to be palaeontologists and search for fossils in the sand. We uncovered many prehistoric remains and tried to identify which part of the dinosaur they had once belonged to.

Moreover, subjects like history provide an excellent context in which to embed skills of gathering and selecting information that are often essential preparation for recount writing. As part of their work on evacuees, Year 4 pupils at Warren Farm Academy, Birmingham, visited old people's homes to interview people about their wartime experiences and created spider maps of key information relating to individuals who had been evacuated as children, as illustrated here. This unit of work culminated in an inspiring afternoon parents' event – see pages 255–256.

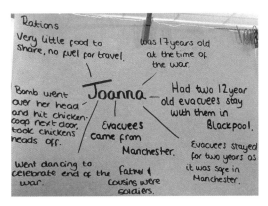

Figure 4.16   An evacuee's memories

If you look at the model text for an older class from another school of a child recounting their thoughts as they prepare to be evacuated, you will see a wide range of tenses being used: we have come a long way from the plain *first, next, after that* signposts of simple recount text.

Recount is also the text type that is most taught when teaching a foreign language, since it is the closest one to everyday conversation. Many schools have found the Talk for Writing approach is perfect for adapting to the needs of whichever modern language is being taught as the underlying principles are the same. Story, recount and instructions are the perfect way of getting language into the children's heads in any language and building confidence in speaking and writing. The typical ingredients of story are also the typical ingredients of recount so the one supports the other. You will probably recognise the text map on page 107 as representing *The Hungry Caterpillar*, but in

Packing Up

This Friday I am being evacuated to the countryside with my teacher and my classmates. At this very moment, I feel excited about visiting the countryside however on Friday I know that I have to leave my family and friends and I will be broken hearted. As I am leaving for such a long time, I must remember to take:

• my teddy bear

Figure 4.17   Model text for an evacuee's letter

this case it is *La Chenille Qui Avait Très Faim.* See video clip 14 on **DVD 1** to see how the Talk for Writing approach has been adapted by ilanguages.com to support the teaching of other languages. Selby CP School in North Yorkshire uses the Talk for Writing approach to get the children (in this case Year 3) speaking and writing in French.

Figure 4.18   Text map for Year 3 French

Video clip 11 on **DVD 1** shows Jonny from Adswood Primary School in Stockport teaching history to his Year 2 class. You will recognise how he has used a text map of model text recounting some key events within the Gunpowder Plot to help the children

internalise the facts as well as the pattern of the language so that they can act out the event. Note how he uses phrases like *However, one or more of* and *We know that* to distinguish the facts from the interpretation of the facts. History is not a question of recounting facts, but more a recognition that past events will be interpreted differently depending on the perspective of the writer, and that we need to be tentative and discursive in how we express things that have not been proved. Video clip 12 shows how text mapping and actions help children recall historical facts while clip 14 shows year 1 children imitating recount text about how plants grow.

Through adapting their recount writing skills to the needs of real contexts and purposes across the curriculum, children will embed and extend their skills. This will encourage the child's growing confidence as a young writer developing a flexible toolkit of writing skills that can be applied to any writing task.

A note on hybrid text

Though it is possible to write pure recount text, in real life such text is rare. Normally, as explained throughout this chapter, an engaging recount will include passages of information and/or explanation relating to whatever is being recounted as illustrated in the shared recount writing on video clip 5 on the **DVD**. In fact, it is quite likely that most good non-fiction writing will include some recount text: for example, an engaging cookery book, although being fundamentally instructions, is liable to include some recount of when the writer first came across a recipe. Equally, a good travel writer recounts their journey in such a way that the reader not only learns what happened on the journey but is provided with lots of engaging information about what was seen, and may be persuaded to make such a trip themselves.

CHAPTER 5

Instructions

What is an instruction text?

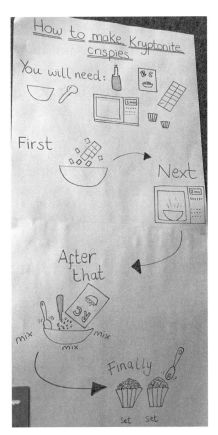

Figure 5.1 An instruction text map

Instructional language is very familiar to most children as they are usually instructed from birth – 'Sit down', 'Drink this', 'Don't do that!' It tends to be a common form of language used both at home and in school. This means that instructional language patterns have usually become internalised early on. Indeed, anyone listening to young children play will soon notice how they try to 'boss' each other about!

In some ways, instructions might appear, at first glance, to be easy enough to write. However, anyone who has tried to fill in a tax form, assemble a flatpack table or start up a computer will know that it is actually quite hard to communicate what needs to be done in a simple and clear manner that can easily be followed. Instructions in the real world are usually accompanied by helpful images, showing what needs to be done. This visual aspect is important in children's own writing. In today's world of technology, writing is so much more than the written word, for computers allow us to use images, diagrams, video clips and audio voice-overs. Being able to control and make good use of all of these aspects of communication should become part of a child's repertoire as a writer.

Instructions often begin with a succinct opening – that explains to the reader why they need to follow the instructions. Depending on the context, this might tempt the reader into trying out the instructions or setting the scene in some other way. There is then a section that lists what will be needed, in order of usage. After that, there is a chunk of writing which explains what to do, in order. This often appears as a list with diagrams. Sometimes, instructions end with a final section that may add in an extra tip, word of warning, reminder or crucial point.

To write effective instructions, the writer has to be an expert on the topic. In other words, the children have to have carried out the instructions themselves so that they have a clear idea of what steps need to be taken – and in what order. To be really successful at writing instructions, the writer has to have a strong sense of sympathy with the reader, to be able to judge whether what they have written is sufficiently clear, organised and crisp. Good instructions are easy to follow and get the job done!

Typical features of instructions

Audience	Someone who needs to know how to do something.
Purpose	To inform the reader about how to accomplish something in as clear a way as possible.
Typical structure	• Opening that explains what the instructions are for and why they might be necessary. • List of what is needed in order of use. • List of steps to be taken in chronological order. • Often uses diagrams. • Ending – that adds in any extra points, reminders, warnings or encouragement to the reader.
Typical language features	• Temporal signposts to organise the steps taken, e.g. 'first', 'next', 'after that', 'then', 'so', 'finally'. • Steps to be taken: organised by numbers, letters of the alphabet or bullet points. • Fairly formal as the reader may be unknown. • Use of short sentences to make the writing very clear and easy to follow. • Use of 'bossy' words (imperatives), e.g. 'turn', 'push', 'click', 'stir', etc. • Subject specific and technical vocabulary. • Commas used when writing a list of ingredients or tools. Possible use of colon before a list, e.g. What you need: a spade, bucket and trowel.
Examples	• How to make a pizza topping. • How to invade a walled city. • How to keep ourselves warm. • How to work the computer. • How to keep an alien happy.

Choosing a topic for instructional writing

Many teachers use 'real' topics for instruction writing. For instance, it seems very obvious that if you are working on *The Gingerbread Man*, then the children should make gingerbread biscuits and should write a set of instructions so that others

Figure 5.2 Writing instructions to the wolf

can also make biscuits. The picture here shows reception children at Selby Community Primary, North Yorkshire, writing instructions to the wolf from the *Three Little Pigs* to keep away from their cardboard house. There may be other topics that arise in the classroom that are genuinely needed such as 'how to work the computer' or 'how to set out the tables for lunch'.

While these more functional sets of instructions are important, because in real life these will be the sort of instructions that they may well need (recipes, directions, domestic needs), they may lack excitement. Many teachers have found that more imaginary topics benefit because they allow the children to become engaged creatively while developing their use of key language structures at the same time. 'How to Tame a Unicorn', 'How to Defeat a Dalek' or 'How to Make a Home for a Borrower' have considerable child appeal.

Audience and purpose

A strong sense of the needs of the audience is vital to writing successful instructions. Can they be followed? Do the instructions work? Anyone who has asked for directions will know how hard it is to direct someone. Some people give too much detail while others miss out vital landmarks. It is a considerable skill to turn a complex procedure into simple and clear instructions for a novice.

Think up interesting audiences to help the children. Publish instructions in scrapbooks, as posters, on the school website. Try using response partners from other classes or online blogs who can give feedback on the clarity, accuracy and ease of use of the instructions. Split the class in half so that both sides write different instructions and then pair the children up so that they can offer a more genuine sense of audience.

Some key uses of instruction writing skills across the curriculum

- How to put on a toga.

- How the Vikings crossed the seas.

- How to grow a tomato plant.

- How to stay healthy.

- How to build a tissue-paper, hot-air balloon.

- How to build a cola-can dragster.

- How to keep the rabbit fed and watered.

- How to make a simple finger puppet.

- How to make a mosaic.

- How to make a clay 'coil pot'.

- How to divide a large number by a fraction.

Warming up the distinctive features of instruction text

It is worth thinking carefully about the vocabulary, sentence structures and information that the children will need when they come to write instructions. Daily games help children internalise the patterns so that when talking or writing, they are able to manipulate what they have to say effectively. Instruction writing lends itself to games that involve giving orders to the class or other classes. Try using PowerPoint, digital cameras or audio recorders such as 'easi-speak' to capture and communicate instructions. The use of ICT is usually a great motivator and means the children can stand back from what they have been doing and consider 'what works'. Practising the tune of the text through talking the text, will enable the children to manipulate what they have to say effectively, and select just the right words, phrases and sentence patterns when they finally write it down. The examples below as well as those on Clip 15 can all be adapted to suit a wide range of ages. Instruction writing lends itself to activities like these:

Tuning into the subject: vocabulary games

- A key aspect of writing instructions will be the judicious handling of very precise adjectives and adverbs. In this sort of writing an adjective will only be used when it is needed – e.g. press the **red** button. Provide the children with a set of instructions in which the adjectives and adverbs are overdone and ask them to trim it back to what is necessary. For example:

  Calmly and steadily, press the sky-blue button until the beautiful, yellow and lemon-coloured dish flickers in a shimmering glitter of colour.

- Another important part of instructional writing is to handle the imperative or 'bossy' verbs. Play games where children have to give instructions to someone else in the class. I have had many amusing occasions watching children trying to instruct a partner in how to put on a jumper or how to walk to the door. Or try asking them to instruct someone on how to draw a noughts and crosses grid without the use of a diagram. The partner has to follow the instructions word for word!

Tuning into the signposts games

- In the main, instructions use temporal signposts to make sure that the key steps are placed in the right order. Play a game of 'drawing instructions', in which the children are paired. Partner A instructs Partner B in how to draw something simple such as the outline shape of a house. Partner B has to follow the instructions – compare end results!

Tuning into the sentence games

- Play 'crazy instructions' using time signposts. The children write or say a rapid set of instructions, directing a hobgoblin in 'How to cook a rainbow' (it is helpful to know that the colours needed are red, orange, yellow, green, blue, violet and indigo), for example:

  - First, squeeze the sap from a red apple and store it in a scalding, scarlet pepper.

  - Next, stir in the sunset's sweet delight.

  - After that, whisk in the yolk of the simple sun.

  - Then, take the grass from a football pitch and let the mixture simmer.

  - Once this is well cooked, add a section of the sky's sheer blue.

  - Now, sprinkle over the top a thistle's royal purple feathers.

  - Finally, add the bruised juice of a blackberry.

  - Stir the ingredients and enjoy your tasty rainbow – ideally served with cloud pudding.

Tip: to help children who have English as a new language, colour code temporal sentence signposts in the order that they usually appear.

Tuning into the text games

- Work in small groups, to design a simple playground game. Create instructions. Present the new game to the class, explaining how the game is played. Can the others follow the instructions?

- Children love designing new games. Provide materials for them to design a new board game. They then have to create a set of instructions and present the game, explaining how it is played.

What = 'good' for this sort of writing

'Compare' – write some different instructional sentences or sections about the same subject so the children can consider which works best. Discuss what makes it effective. Which is the weakest? Why? What advice would you give to the weaker writer? Use this activity to draw up a wall chart entitled, 'What you need to do to write an effective set of instructions.' Try comparing these for a start:

After that, turn the scarlet handle, as crimson as blood, to the right.

After that, turn the red handle to one side.

After that, turn the handle to make the large wheel start moving.

Warming up the specific content

- Draw the basic ingredients and make sure these are in order.

- Mime the instructions in a group with each child miming the next step.

- Draw the steps.

- Discuss who might be interested in reading the instructions and list ways to 'hook' the reader in.

- Discuss any extra ideas or points that might need to be added at the end.

Sequencing the text

Provide the class with a jumbled set of instructions. This could be a whole text or different sections. The activity focuses on the overall organisation of a text. Try using this set of instructions about creating a superhero/superheroine:

How to make Hawkboy

✂ -

Once you have become Hawkboy, be careful to stay away from cages and anyone with scissors or hedge clippers.

✂ -

Final Note:

✂ -

Have you ever wanted to escape at a moment's notice? Do you want to soar high above the clouds? If so, follow these instructions and you too could become 'Hawkboy'.

✂ -

What you need:

✂ -

After that, take the grip from a vice and use this for your claws.

✂ -

Finally, trap the speed of a jet engine as it breaks the sound barrier and drink this carefully.

✂ -

Once this has been done, enter a hospital and borrow their X-ray vision to complete your senses.

✂ -

Next, capture a giant squid and attach its beak to your face.

✂ -

First, take the feathers of the Phoenix and stick them to your body.

✂ -

What you do:

✂ -

the feathers of the Phoenix, the beak of a giant squid, the grip of a vice, the vision from an X-ray machine, and the speed of a jet.

Figure 5.3   How to make Hawkboy

How to plan an instruction unit in Talk for Writing style

The Talk for Writing process

Baseline assessment	• Cold task at least week before unit • Set targets
Planning	• Refine language focus & adapt model text • Decide how it can be innovated • Test model: box it up, analyse it, make toolkit

1. Imitation	• Creative hook and context
	• Warm up/embed words/phrases/grammar
	• Internalise model text – text map
	• Read as a reader: vocabulary/comprehension
	• Read as a writer:
	   o Box up text to establish structure
	   o Analyse features
	   o Co-construct toolkit

2. Innovation	• Box up new version & talk the text • Shared writing – innovate on model • Pupils write own version & guided writing • Peer assess • Teacher assesses work – plans next steps • Feedback & improvement
3. Independent application	• Next steps based on assessment • Pupils write independently (hot task)
Final assessment	Compare cold/hot: assess progress

Figure 5.4   The Talk for Writing process

This image sums up the Talk for Writing process. If you have not already read Chapter 2, which explains this process in detail, you may find it useful to read that chapter before thinking about how the process can be applied to any text type.

Worked example for instruction text

Below is a worked example of the three stages of the Talk for Writing approach bookended by the initial and final assessment to ensure formative assessment is at the heart of the planning, teaching and learning process.

Objective: To write effective instructions.

Topic for imitation and innovation: To write instructions on 'how to trap a mythical creature'. **Imitation** – 'how to trap a stone giant'; **innovation** – 'how to trap a water goblin'; **independent choice** – children select any other mythical creature to trap.

Audience and purpose: Posters or a TV programme about trapping mythical creatures. Class assembly to inform others about basic giant-, troll- or goblin-trapping methods.

Baseline assessment and planning

For any unit of work on instructions you have to first to think about what instruction writing skills the class already possesses. As explained in Chapter 2, a good way of doing this is to set a **cold task**. This should be set at least a week before you begin to teach your unit so that you can alter your planning to suit the needs of the class. The pupils will need a familiar context (for example, ask them to give instructions about how to turn their teacher into a toad, as illustrated here by a pupil from Mrs Lynch's class at Montgomery Academy in Birmingham) so that they have something to write about that they know about and that interests them. Warm the topic up with a quick discussion but do not provide any teaching in how to write about this subject. You can see the progress this child made by looking at his hot write, page 129, at the end of this chapter.

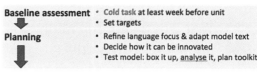

Figure 5.5

Figure 5.6   Cold task for instructions

Assessing this cold write will help you pinpoint what specific skills to focus on in the unit to help all the children progress. Also, set a range of additional targets for children with different levels of attainment. This process also enables you to adapt the model text to ensure that it illustrates the features that suit the needs of the class. Remember to plan the toolkit you will co-construct with the class.

Stage 1: Imitation

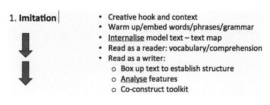

Figure 5.7

The creative hook

The topic throughout this unit is trapping mythical creatures, which is guaranteed to engage classes. It also lends itself to great images and role play.

- Mock up the local newspaper so it appears that a giant has been sighted.

- Leave a giant footprint to be found.

- A giant letter or message arrives in the classroom.

- Hot-seat a member of staff who is certain that she has seen a giant.

- This idea might accompany such a wonderful book as Roald Dahl's *The BFG* or Ted Hughes' *The Iron Man*.

- Year 2 or 3 children might well learn 'Jack and the Beanstalk'. Older pupils might be learning the story of 'Odysseus and the Cyclops'.

Warming up the tune of explanation

Games and activities devised to familiarise the children with the typical language pattern of instructions and the context of the unit are key to success. As the games are played, flip-chart the vocabulary, sentence signposts and key sentence patterns that emerge and start to create a toolkit of useful ingredients for instruction text to support the children's speaking and writing. Display these to make the learning visible and develop them throughout the unit. If the children have already been taught this text type in Talk for Writing style, build on their existing toolkit for instructions.

Tune the children into the style of writing through reading to them as well as providing examples of instructional writing about a range of subjects for independent reading. This might be done in quiet reading or as part of guided reading. An exciting read to have available would be any of the books such as *Dragonology* and others in the series.

To catch the children's interest, the book *The Secret Histories of Giants* by Professor Ari Berk, published by Templar Publishing in 2008, would be a useful support. This contains such intriguing facts as 'What's inside a giant's sack?', a recipe book entitled, *Simple Fare for Great Folk*, as well as information such as giants at work, giant fashion, famous giants from around the world – and there is also a good set of instructions on how to play 'quoits'.

- **Never-heard-the-word grids:** Devise a Never-heard-the-word grid to introduce the technical or tricky vocabulary related to the instruction topic selected. See pages 197–198 for an example of how to do this.

- **Muddled instructions:** Provide a set of instructions that are muddled up. The children have to reorganise them as fast as possible, e.g.

  - Top the peanut butter with slices of chopped banana.

  - Press the two slices together and cut in half.

  - Enjoy eating.

  - Add on a thin coating of peanut butter.

  - Spread the butter thinly on both pieces.

  - Take two slices of bread.

Role play

- In role as spies, leave secret instructions – e.g. 'How to steal the secret planes'.

- Role-play, in pairs, giving instructions to an alien – for instance: how to boil an egg, how to walk to school, how to multiply two large numbers, how to eat an orange.

- Role-play being Jamie Oliver and mime demonstrating a simple recipe!

- Role-play being a judge on *X Factor* or some other such game show and instruct a dreadful participant in what they need to do in order to improve. Provide the challenge for each pupil – e.g. you have just seen an appalling magical act. Instruct the so-called magician in how to pull a rabbit from a hat.

- In role as a minor god or goddess, instruct Perseus in how to capture Medusa's head without being frozen to stone.

Internalising the model text

Having warmed up the tune of instructions, the children can now start to focus on imitating an instruction text. Use a simple but interesting version of a set of instructions that contains the expected structure and features appropriate to the level of the children so that there is an edge of challenge. Do not show the children the text at this stage. They are going to hear it and internalise it orally with just a text map to support them before they see it. (The simple instruction text map pictured here was for a reception class at Dashwood Primary, Banbury.)

Turn this into a large class map or washing line with a page for each section as illustrated below. Learn as a class with actions or divide up so that groups can learn a section and then teach each other. Move from whole class retelling to groups and finally pairs so that ultimately everyone can retell the text. Learn the text

Figure 5.8   A simple instruction text map

with a view to performing it at an assembly. This set of instructions would be ideal for Year 2 or 3 children. (See the **DVD** instruction section for how to use a washing line to help children imitate text. Note that the text being learned is very similar to the text below.)

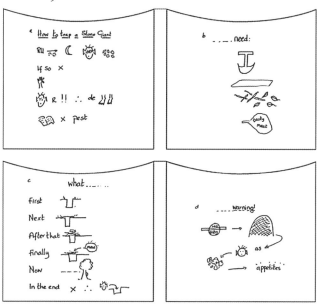

Figure 5.9   Washing-line text map for *How to trap a stone giant*

Retell the text in various different ways to help the children internalise the text, for example:

- chant as a circle or class;

- mime the text making it obvious how to carry out the instructions;

- tell as a pair or trio, word for word or chunk by chunk;

- hold a race to see who can say it the quickest;

- prepare to present instructions to children in another class.

To help learn the text orally, children should draw their own mini washing lines or text maps. These may be annotated with anything that causes problems and personalised to make it easier to remember.

1a) Reading as a reader

Once the children have thoroughly internalised the text orally, present the text that they have internalised to them and start by reading it as a reader.

How to trap a stone giant

Are you kept awake at night by the sound of a stone giant crunching rocks? If so, do not despair. Help is at hand. Stone giants are dangerous and therefore must be defeated. Read these instructions and soon you too will be rid of this terrible pest.

What you need: a magical spade, a brown sheet, some leaves and sticks plus a large lump of tasty meat.

What you do:

- First, dig a deep pit.

- Next, cover the pit with a brown sheet.

- After that, scatter on the leaves and sticks.

- Finally, place the large lump of meat on top.

- Now, tiptoe behind a tree and wait.

- In the end, the stone giant will not be able to resist the temptation and will, therefore, fall into the pit.

A final note of warning

Do not enter a stone giant's cave as there may be baby giants chewing on pebbles and they have BIG appetites.

Lead the children through each section, discussing how the writer draws the reader in, then state clearly what is needed and what has to be done. The children should be able to read it because they have internalised the language, but that does not mean they have fully understood the meaning of the words. Deepen their understanding so that they become increasingly familiar with the structure and language patterns of instructions by using the following sorts of activities:

- **Interview on *News Round*** with a tame mountain giant on advice for capturing dangerous giants.

- **Phone in with the Minister for Giants** who explains how to trap a stone giant.

- **Have you understood?** Construct some questions for the children to initially discuss in pairs to open up discussion on the text and ensure the children have understood what they are reading:

    - Explain why you think the instructions begin by asking if you are kept awake at night by the sound of a stone giant crunching rocks.

    - Can you think of a reason why the list of ingredients is listed before the actual instructions begin?

    - Why do you think the stone giant will eventually fall into the pit?

- **Play the alternative words game:** List some of the tricky words from the text and ask the children in pairs if they can come up with alternative words or phrases that mean the same thing. For example:

despair	spade	temptation
defeated	pit	appetite
pest	resist	

1b) Reading as a writer

Once the children have fully understood the text, you can then start reading it as a writer, identifying how it has been structured and the language features that can be reused, as well as analysing the techniques used to make the writing effective. See Clip 16 which explains how this is the bridge into writing.

Boxing up the text

The first thing for the children to think about when trying to understand how a text has been written is its structure, so show the children how to box up this text. Normally that would mean counting the paragraphs and creating a boxed-up version with one box for each paragraph. Instructions are often written in paragraphs with a clump of bullet points, like this model text, so it is a question of boxing up the paragraphs and the bullet point instruction clumps and deciding why it has been presented in the order it has been presented.

Box up the basic pattern with the children asking them to tell you what different sections there are so that the underlying structure of the instructions can clearly be seen. The more they see you creating the structure in front of them, the more they will be able to understand it. This boxed-up plan will provide the basic structure for the children when they come to create their own versions.

Boxed-up planning for 'How to trap a stone giant'

Heading for each section	*Key points*
Introduce what the instructions will help you do with a hook	Trap a stone giant. Are you kept awake . . .?
List of ingredients	*What you need:*
What to do	*First, dig a deep ditch . . .*
End Final – point, reminder, word of warning or encouragement to reader	*Do not enter a stone giant's cave. . .*

Now help the children identify language features that can be reused as well as discussing the techniques that the writer uses. It is worth taking specific sentence patterns and innovating on them to produce new sentences using the same underlying pattern, e.g.

- *Are you kept awake at night by the sound of a stone giant crunching rocks?*
- Are you fed up with unicorns trampling over your roses?
- Are you tired of goblins stealing your knives and forks?
- Do you ever wonder if you will be able to tame your local dragon?
- Do you have a house goblin problem?
- Have you ever wished that the forests were rid of trolls?
- Have you been robbed by a thieving cyclops?

The key 'writing ingredients' should be displayed as they will drive the shared, guided and independent writing, including self-/peer evaluation and feedback from the teacher. It is also very important that the children are involved in creating the list of writing ingredients, using their own language so that they can understand what the list means.

Support understanding by flip-charting and displaying useful words and phrases built up throughout the instruction text activities.

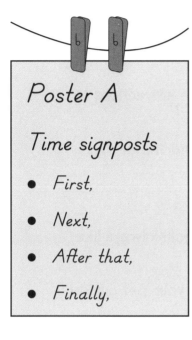

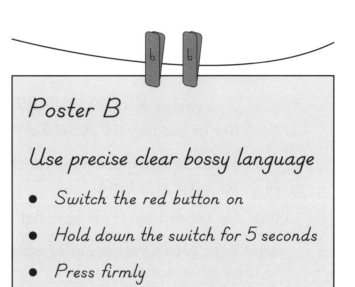

Poster A

Time signposts

- First,
- Next,
- After that,
- Finally,

Poster B

Use precise clear bossy language

- Switch the red button on
- Hold down the switch for 5 seconds
- Press firmly
- Fold the paper in half
- Turn to the right

With older children, broaden the scope of their writing toolkits by looking at other sets of instructions so that they can see a range of different ways in which they might be written. For instance, try adding to their repertoire by looking at this set of instructions which is closely related by theme, but pitched at a more challenging level:

How to look after a pet dragon

Have you ever wanted to keep a unique pet? If so, just visit the local dragon orphanage and select your very own baby dragon. You will never be bored.

However, a pet dragon is not easy to care for and you will need to follow these instructions. If not, you may find that your baby dragon becomes a fiery nuisance!

What you need: a dragon whistle, a collar, plenty of food and a dragon's den.

What you do:

Your pet dragon will roam freely. However, if you use a dragon whistle it will come whenever you call. Dragons have very good hearing so, even if your pet has flown into a distant valley, it will hear your whistle and fly to you.

If you need to make sure that your dragon stays near you, then a good collar is a necessity. Even young dragons can be very strong, so the collar should be made of the finest dwarf metal. A collar will be essential if you intend to put your dragon in for a 'Best Baby Dragon Competition'.

Dragon mealtimes can be scary, so follow these instructions to the letter or you may be scorched!

First, collect dragon food such as mice, rats and the bodies of other lesser creatures.

Next, lay the dragon feast on a flat rock.

After that, provide a bucket of water as dragons always like to drink after eating.

Finally, retire to a safe distance before letting your pet out for its dinner.

Remember that a hungry dragon may well mistake you for its next meal, so a disguise is essential.

Keep your pet lodged in a simple dragon's den. These have to be custom-made and can be purchased at your local Dragons R'Us' store. They should be made of fireproof material. At first you may keep a very young dragon in the house but, as it grows larger, you will have to find an outdoor spot as a sleeping dragon will snore loudly. They have also been known to cause house fires accidentally.

A final note of warning

Dragons are not just for birthdays – they are for a lifetime. As your pet matures, it will be able to communicate with you telepathically. It will protect you from danger and, of course, a trained dragon will allow its owner to ride on it as it flies. Many owners treat their dragons by polishing their scales with the juice of sun flames and feed them titbits such as cloud berries.

One final word of caution: dragons cannot help hoarding. It will always be their instinct to collect and hide anything bright, shiny or valuable. This means that you must hide away anything that glitters.

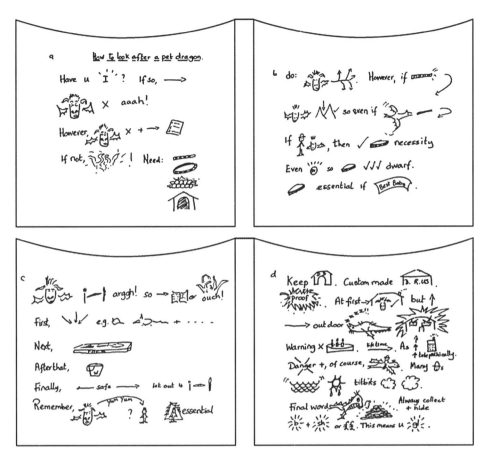

Figure 5.10   Washing-line text map for *How to look after a pet dragon*

The key writing ingredients for success, which we call a toolkit, can be established through these activities. It is essential that the children co-construct these ingredients, otherwise they will be meaningless to them. The toolkit of ingredients should be displayed as it will drive the shared, guided and independent writing, including self-/peer evaluation and feedback from the teacher. A useful method is to flip-chart each ingredient up on the toolkit as it is taught to help the children understand the significance of each ingredient. It is a good idea to keep the ingredients list as short as possible and back them up with a checklist that contains examples (see below). Support the short list with examples on the walls and in the children's journals from the activities they have taken part in. By the end of the innovation stage, the ingredients toolkit may look something like this:

Instruction writing toolkit

Plan it – order your instructions by boxing them up step by step	• Explain clearly what the instructions are about and hook your reader: *How to trap . . . Are you kept awake . . .?* • List the ingredients in the order that they will be used. • List the steps in the order in which they need to be carried out. *First, Next, After that . . .* • End with a final comment, point, warning or reminder. *Do not enter . . .*

Link it – join your ideas effectively	• Use time signposts, numbers, letters or bullet points to list the steps in order and introduce the list with a colon:
	
	  – *First, Next, After that, Finally;*
	  – *1. 2. 3., etc;*
	  – *A. B. C., etc.*

Express it – make your instructions clear	• Use interesting language and vary sentences in the opening to tantalise the reader and make them want to read more, e.g. *Do not despair. Help is at hand.* • Keep sentences in the steps section brief and clear, e.g. *First, dig a deep pit.* • Use descriptive language only when it is needed, e.g. *red button, turn to the right, press firmly.* • Try talking to the reader and making the instructions sound easy, e.g. *Now tiptoe . . .* • Use technical language where necessary, e.g. *pit.*
Check it	• Read your instructions aloud. Check for accuracy and improve it if it doesn't sound quite right.

Of course, such checklists should be matched to the stage the children are working at so that it might be less complex or more demanding. These can be used as a guide in the form of a 'response ladder' for evaluation, marking and feedback. If the children have been taught previously in Talk for Writing style, then their existing toolkit for this type of writing should be amended to build in progress.

Remind the class that you can include all the ingredients but still write a poor set of instructions. They must remember to taste it (read it aloud to test if it works) to help guarantee quality writing. Does it work? Would these instructions be easy to follow?

By this point the children should not only be expert 'giant trappers' but also very familiar with the overall pattern of instruction writing and its various language features – they will have heard, spoken, read, discussed and played with the sentence types till they have begun to become part of their linguistic repertoire. It would be ideal to end this stage with some sort of enthusiastic performance to other classes or invite the parents in at the end of the day and get them to join in.

Stage 2: Innovation

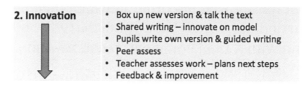

Figure 5.11

The good news is that the local stone giant has been trapped. However, a water goblin has moved into the area. Use the boxed-up grid on a flip chart to act as a planner as this will clearly show the basic organisation of a set of instructions. To support the innovation stage, your washing line or working wall should contain the original model, the boxed-up planning, toolkit and word bank to support the children's learning and help keep you focused.

Start by getting the children to work in pairs, discussing their ideas for trapping the goblin. Have several pairs present their ideas and decide which would make the most effective trap. These ideas can be drawn and then spoken. Then work together as a class on shared planning altering your boxed-up planning to fit

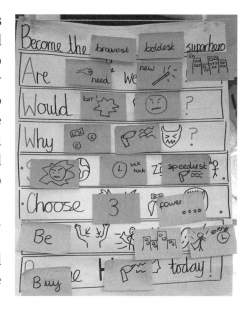

Figure 5.12   Using Post-it notes to innovate on the model

the new creature that is to be trapped. This can be done by adding another column into your boxed-up plan or by using Post-it notes to show the changes on the original map, as illustrated here. This prepares the children before moving into shared writing. (A word of warning: Post-it notes have an irritating habit of falling off, especially in hot weather.)

In shared writing, work on developing the chosen method for trapping such a slippery creature! Continually refer back to the original, using it as a basis for creating the new version.

Use the grid to display basic ideas for trapping the water goblin. It helps if you keep the original model clearly displayed so that you can keep referring back to it. You are about to lead the children through writing a class version of 'How to trap a water goblin'. This is followed by the children writing their own versions.

Boxed-up planning for 'How to trap a water goblin'

Heading for each section	Key details
Title	• The ideal method for trapping pesky goblins . . .
Introduction – 'hook' the reader so that they want to read the instructions. Explain clearly what the instructions will help the reader be able to do.	• Would you know what to do if a goblin moves . . .? • On the increase • A must-have read
List of 'ingredients'	• Use tempting food • Goblins very greedy • Net made of dwarf steel
The steps to take	• Food in large box • Drop net onto goblin
Final point, reminder, word of warning or encouragement to the reader.	• Goblins bite – be careful! • Can hide easily, change colour!

You can now, through shared writing, show the children how to move from their plan to the actual writing. It helps to take this bit by bit, having the relevant paragraph from the original displayed on the interactive whiteboard, colour-coded so that the language features stand out. Alongside this, display the plan you have just devised on the writing wall or washing line where you and the class can see it while you scribe the children's ideas on a flip chart.

Through shared writing, turn each section into fluent writing, involving the children in making decisions, suggesting words and developing sentences. As you do this, get the children to 'magpie' good ideas by jotting them down in their writing journals. Encourage them to never dodge a good word by putting a dotted line under words that are hard to spell (e.g. *dangerous*) demonstrating how to focus on composition at this stage, rather than spending time now looking up the spelling. This can be done at the final draft stage. Keep reading the shared writing through to get the children into the habit of reading their sentences aloud to see if they sound right. The process is quite simple:

- Gather facts for the new instructions.

- Refer back to the original.

- Turn the facts into similar sentences.

- Underline or highlight key features, like sentence signposts.

- Keep rereading to maintain flow.

- 'Test out' children's ideas to 'hear' whether they work.

- Ask children to develop sentences in pairs or on mini-whiteboards.

- Ask the TA (or a pupil) to flip-chart key phrases and vocabulary to be turned into posters to support the writing.

There are two useful handouts on shared writing in Appendix 2, on **DVD 2**: **Handout 3** – *The art of shared writing*, lists the key ingredients that contribute towards successful shared writing; **Handout 4** lists useful phrases to use when doing shared writing.

The Ideal Method for Capturing any Variety of Goblin

Would you know what to do if a goblin moved into your house? Are you prepared for a goblin invasion? These pesky creatures are on the increase in your local area! These instructions are therefore a 'must-have' read because any day now you could find yourself targeted by these bothersome pests.

What you will need to rid yourself of any type of goblin: tempting food, a large sturdy box with a good lock and a net made of fine dwarf steel.

What you should do:

a. *Gather as much stale food as possible.*

b. *Place this inside the sturdy box.*

c. *Make sure that the lid will easily close and you have a strong padlock.*

d. *Now dangle the net above the box and wait.*

e. *In the end, the goblin will not be able to resist the temptation of so much disgusting food.*

f. *Once it has climbed into the box, slam the lid shut and close the padlock.*

g. *Wrap the box up in the net.*

h. *Finally, use the local dragon postal express to send your captive goblin to another part of the world.*

Important note: goblins like to eat sour lemons, mouldy cheese, rotten eggs, stale bread, out-of-date milk and meat where flies have laid their eggs.

A word of warning to anyone considering trapping a goblin. These are very tricky creatures and can give a nasty nip. Their capture is almost impossible because many varieties can change colour like a chameleon and have the ability to hide almost anywhere. This makes them hard to spot. However, their one weakness is that they are very greedy.

You will notice in the example above that the class has moved on from the original model by adding extra ideas.

The children should write independently straight after the shared writing, gradually building their text over a number of days if needed. Use guided writing to teach and support groups in a focused manner. More confident writers might be asked to add extra sections, for instance, by explaining how something works. In this way, the instructions begin to become more of a hybrid text.

After writing, the children should work as response partners, reading their writing to each other, considering what has been effective and what might be improved. Refer back to the instruction toolkit that was co-constructed from the annotation activity and use these to focus feedback. Remember, though, that while the children may have included the ingredients, the key factor will be whether the instructions would work and be easy to follow.

Your marking should lead directly into your next piece of teaching. Provide feedback on this work focusing on those areas that the children found most difficult and helping them understand how to edit their work effectively. A visualiser or iPad is a very useful piece of equipment that allows you to present exemplar work from the pupils immediately to the whole class to illustrate the improvements you are seeking.

Model for the children how to reflect on the effectiveness of writing. The more opportunities the children are given to talk about what works and what features make the writing engaging, the more they will be able to develop their own inner judge and craft and edit their own writing effectively. **Handout 5** is full of useful questions to help children reflect on what makes writing effective and discuss what works. If the teacher models this sort of reflection, the children will quickly pick up how to reflect on work. Focus on what makes the text engaging, not on the naming of parts.

On pages 177–178 is a list of possible problems and the sort of work that may help rectify them. One of the contributions that the Transforming Writing project made to the development of Talk for Writing was mini-lessons. This would be an excellent point within the unit to set up some mini-lessons so that pupils can focus on the areas that they need help with most (see pages 42–43).

This is also a good time to bring in examples of real instruction text, good and bad, to get the children to discuss why they are good or how they could be improved. For example, ask the children what is wrong with the text shown here.

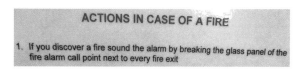

Figure 5.13   Improve this instruction

Draw out from the children that inserting the missing comma after the first clause would help – without it the sentence is very hard to understand. Then discuss whether this clause is necessary at all. In an emergency, the less you have to read before carrying out the appropriate action, the better. Providing trimming down activities, at the right level for the age of the class, would be a useful activity.

Stage 3: Independent application

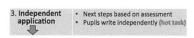

Figure 5.13a

Once the children's writing has been assessed, the teacher is now in a good position to move to the third stage where there will be more choice for the children. The assessment will direct what has to be focused upon during shared and guided sessions and inform the children about what they need to concentrate on.

The most obvious idea is to let the children choose a different mythological creature to write about, designing their own method for trapping. To do this, they should ideally research their creature. A useful book for this would be *Monsterology* or *Arthur Spiderwick's Field Guide* by Tony DiTerlizzi and Holly Black (Simon and Schuster, 2005) which has a full array of different creatures from boggarts to elves.

Make sure that the shared writing focuses on specific aspects that the children have found difficult – picked up from marking (assessing) their previous writing. This means that your marking leads directly into the next piece of teaching. Once again, model planning using a boxed-up grid as well as the actual writing. You will be working on a class version, perhaps, 'How to tame a leprechaun', while the children will all be writing about different sorts of imaginary creatures.

Other ideas for instruction writing on this theme might include:

- How to feed a baby mermaid.
- How to find a lost baby dragon.
- How to communicate with a forest sprite.
- How to stop your pet dwarf from escaping.
- How to teach a dragon to fly.

- How to tame a troll.
- How to ride a phoenix.
- Caring for a dragon's teeth.
- How to keep a unicorn happy.
- How to keep an ogre amused.

End of unit assessment

Final assessment   Compare cold/hot: assess progress

Figure 5.14

The teacher now assesses the final piece of writing (the **hot task**) and looks back at the **cold task** to see what progress has been made. If you look back to the cold task pictures on page 115, you will be able to see the progress that Ghulam has made within the unit. The teacher's comment refers back to the child's targets and helps keep him motivated to improve.

Again, when the work is handed back, focus on one or two areas that everyone needs to improve. This could be indicated by highlighting the areas selected in a particular colour, for example, *green for growth*. Provide some teaching relating to these areas and ask the children to immediately improve their work. Then ask them to reflect on their learning by looking back at the cold task and seeing what progress they have made.

The teacher is now in a position to decide which everyday language features will need focusing on in the next unit of work as well as logging any instruction features that will need strengthening when the class applies instruction writing across the curriculum.

Encouraging real independence, creativity and invention

If children are to become effective creative writers who enjoy writing, they will need the motivation that comes from being able to choose your own topic and writing about it as you choose. At the end of the unit, it is a good idea to plan in free writing opportunities when the children know in advance that they will have the freedom to write in the way they select about what interests them.

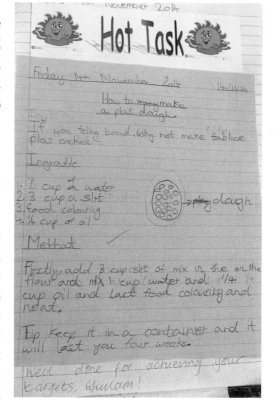

Figure 5.15   Hot task

Mastering the approach across the curriculum

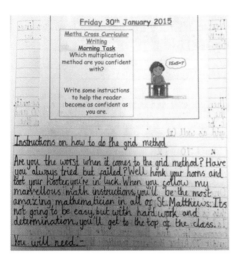

Figure 5.16   Instructional writing in maths

Instructional writing is crucial as part of a writer's repertoire because it will often be needed in real life. Being able to communicate instructions clearly and effectively is key to many aspects of the curriculum, especially when children are talking about how they set about solving problems in maths or technology. So it can make an excellent focus for work in literacy or be part of a maths or technology unit in its own right. Here is the beginning of a delightful piece of instruction writing for maths from a Year 6 pupil at St Matthew's, Birmingham.

Many teachers have found it useful to run a three-stage unit of work on instructions, as described here, using imaginary creatures. This can be followed immediately by further work on instructions based on something real found in the rest of the curriculum or school life. The class could move straight into innovation in this case as they should have already internalised the key language patterns of instruction.

Figure 5.17   Testing if the instructions work

Once a thorough unit on instruction writing has been taught, then places across the curriculum should be found so that the text type can be revisited and the language features embedded as part of the child's repertoire as a young writer. This embedding of the skills in a range of contexts to provide depth and breadth is essential if the children are to achieve mastery of the skills that underpin effective instruction writing. The Talk for Writing process can be adapted to meet the needs of any class. At the Harbour Centre in Staines, which is now a Talk for Writing Training Centre, the children are all Key Stage 2 SEND. The centre developed an instruction unit based on *The Three Little Pigs* and built understanding for the children through role play and practical activities to give and follow instructions. They linked the unit to D&T and science - the children designed and built their own model houses and then testing whether they could be blown down by the hairdryer 'wolf'. Clip 17 shows how a pupil has internalised maths instructions.

A note on hybrid text

In real life, instructions are often one of the only 'pure' text types. However, some do have extra pieces of information and explanation. Recipe writers may add in their memories of where they were when they found a recipe, describe the dish in a mouthwatering way to persuade you to make it, or embellish with extra explanation or information about where recipes come from.

CHAPTER 6

Information

What is information text?

The Primary National Strategy chose to call information text 'non-chronological report' to distinguish between newspaper reports – which are usually a form of recount – and 'reports' that tell the reader information about something. Not only is it a bit of a mouthful, but it's not a term anyone would ever use in real life. Good information writing 'informs' someone in an interesting manner, so we are using the term 'information' instead.

Typically, information is rather like entries in an encyclopaedia. It generalises about a subject, providing the reader with information

Figure 6.1   Boy writing from a book

about the topic. The skill of information writing lies in the ability to make the subject sound fascinating yet, at the same time, to provide accurate information.

Like all non-fiction, information text begins with an introduction that explains what the subject matter is about, hopefully with some sort of 'hook' to encourage the reader to read on. Generally, the facts are 'clumped' together into sections or paragraphs. These might have subheadings or use topic sentences. Each section provides relevant information. Usually, this is generalised so that the writer talks about 'most' sharks rather than a specific shark. The facts are generally written about in the present tense – for example, 'sharks are found around the world'. The report often ends with a final section that may address the reader, relating the subject matter in some way to the reader's life: 'So the truth is that most sharks are harmless and you may never come across one when swimming.'

To write an effective report, the author needs to be an expert in the subject, otherwise the information will be meagre. This is why many schools have found that a return to a 'topic' approach has improved children's non-fiction writing – because they actually know something in depth and want to communicate what they have discovered. While the author has to be an 'expert', the reader will be someone who wants to find out about the topic. Of course, the clever writer will be able to intrigue and interest readers who may not have realised that they are about to be interested!

Objective: To write engaging information text.

Typical ingredients of information text

Audience	• Someone who is interested in the topic. • Someone who enjoys information.
Purpose	• To inform the reader about the topic, describing its characteristics in an engaging and interesting way.
Typical structure	• Opening that introduces the reader to the subject. • Chunks of information, logically organised, possibly with subheadings, information boxes, lists, bullet points, diagrams and images. • Paragraphs usually begin with a topic sentence. • Ending – that makes a final 'amazing' point or relates the subject to the reader.
Typical language features	• Generalisers such as – *most, many, some, a few, the majority.* • Sentence signposts to add information – *furthermore, also, moreover, additionally.* • Subject-specific and technical vocabulary. • Often in the present tense and third person, e.g. *whales are large.* • Usually fairly formal, especially if written for an unknown reader. • Detail and description, including comparisons.
Examples	• Natural world: *sharks, dinosaurs, butterflies, flowers,* etc. • Places – *our school, India, river deltas,* etc. • People – *life in the Caribbean, living in the desert,* etc. • Objects – *racing cars, mobile phones,* etc. • Hobbies – *football, dance,* etc.

Choosing an information topic

Children love information and there is no shortage of subjects that work well as topics for writing information text. Boys usually pass through a stage when they love collecting objects or facts, often making lengthy lists. I remember one of my brothers listing the distances from earth to each planet. As a child, I wanted to know everything about the Romans. I drew and labelled pictures of Roman soldiers, made lists and, when I was older, I walked along Hadrian's Wall. This natural desire to collect, organise and gather knowledge can be capitalised on, especially when a topic is alighted upon that grabs the children's imagination.

Indeed, many teachers have found that 'imaginary' subjects make a useful starting point. For instance, the class might create a *Dragon Hunter's Guide to Dragons of the British Isles*. This would contain information about different types of dragons. Having read *The Chronicles of Spiderwick*, others have written 'field guides' with reports on different types of fairies, goblins, elves, dwarves, mermaids, aliens, unicorns and giants. Of course, children love this element of playfulness and in some ways it makes the writing easier because the information can be invented. This allows the child to focus on the language patterns.

Teachers have found that moving from such 'imaginary' topics into writing about 'real' subjects works well as the children transfer their ability to structure a report and write in the appropriate voice. In terms of 'real' subjects, animals make an ideal focus for children, especially if this can be tied into a visit to a wildlife park, a visitor bringing animals into the classroom or even keeping an animal. To write well, the children will need to have some first-hand experience and to have researched their subject.

Audience and purpose

Always provide some sort of audience and purpose for whatever focus is chosen. Children should become used to making presentations to their class, other classes and the whole school in which they talk about what they have discovered about their topic. This might also include publishing booklets, making fact posters or using the internet to inform other schools.

Some key uses of report writing skills across the curriculum

- Relevant to all topic work.
- What the Romans ate (history).
- Victorian school report (history).
- Where we live (geography).
- Key facts about earthquakes and volcanoes (geography).
- Information about minibeasts (science).
- The human skeleton (science).
- Pets and how to care for them (science).
- Wheeled vehicles (technology).
- Information about religious ceremonies (RE).
- Van Gogh (art).

Warming up the distinctive features of information text

It is worth thinking carefully about the vocabulary, sentence structures and information that the children will need when they come to write. Daily games help children internalise the patterns and information so that when talking or writing they are able to manipulate what they have to say effectively. Information writing lends itself to games that involve 'reporting' to the class or other classes. This may involve making mini-programmes using the digital camera and preparing PowerPoint presentations. This use of ICT guarantees increased engagement. Children can present information about hobbies, sports, pets, holiday destinations, cars, football teams – anything that they are crazy about! Tapping into the current children's fad is a handy way into report writing. My son passed through a stage when he was the world expert on Pokemon cards – an ideal topic for a class presentation at the time.

As the games are played, flip-chart the vocabulary, sentence signposts and key sentence patterns that emerge and start to create a toolkit of useful ingredients for information text to support the children's speaking and writing. Display these to make the learning visible and develop them throughout the unit. If the children have already been taught information text in Talk for Writing style, build on their existing toolkit for information text.

Tuning into the subject: vocabulary games

- **Never-heard-the-word grids:** Devise a Never-heard-the-word grid to introduce the technical vocabulary related to the information topic selected. See pages 197–198 for an example of how to do this.

- **Sorting games:** Identify key subject or technical vocabulary needed for the topic and provide a list. Beside this, provide a list of definitions. The game is to rapidly and successfully match the terminology to the right definitions. This is best presented as a card-sorting game, to be completed in pairs, where the children have to match each word with its definition as this maximises discussion about the vocabulary. For example:

Key words	Definitions
incisors	chisel-edged teeth at the front of the mouth that can cut
jaw	the part of the skull that holds the teeth
enamel	hard coating covering an object for protection or decoration
gum	fleshy tissue that covers the jawbone around the base of teeth
molars	teeth that can grind

Tuning into the signposts and generalisers games

- Understanding the power of sentence signposts to link paragraphs, sentences and information within sentences is key to achieving cohesive text that flows logically and engagingly. Appendix 3 (see **DVD 2**) focuses on the grammar features of linking text and includes useful handouts: **Handout 6** is a list of a broad range of sentence signposts; **Handout 7** shows Pie demonstrating actions for the 14 key sentence signposts.

- 'Join' – select different linking phrases and practise using them to join two short sentences to make one. For example:

  - They hide in trees. They are not often seen.

  - <u>Because</u> they hide in trees, they are not often seen.

  - Dragons are not often seen <u>because</u> they hide in trees.

- 'Add on' – provide a list of adverbial signposts that allow the addition of more facts. Play a game which involves rapid invention, using the same pattern. For example:

  - Additionally, unicorns are very rare.

  - Additionally, unicorns are white.

  - Additionally, unicorns can be seen at night.

  - Additionally, unicorns have long tails.

- 'The majority' – choose a generaliser (a word that can be used to sum up information) and create sentences rapidly about different animals, using the same structure. For example:

  - The majority of elephants are large.

  - The majority of mosquitoes are tiny.

  - The majority of emus run fast.

  - The majority of tigers are scary.

Tuning into the sentence games

- Provide a topic sentence. The children have to jot down what they think the paragraph will include.

- Provide the first half of a sentence for the children to complete, for example: 'Despite being enormous, the African elephant . . .'.

- Provide a few key words that have to be turned into a sentence, for example: 'unicorns', 'rarely', 'seen', 'because', 'forest'.

Sentences of three

- Provide the children with an example of what a typical sentence of three in an information text might look like, for example: *The Triceratops can be easily identified by its large skull, colourful neck frill and the three horns that protrude from its face.*

- Then give the children some information to practise such sentences with in pairs, for example: *Tyrannosaurus Rex; huge head; forward-pointing eyes; blood-curdling roar.*

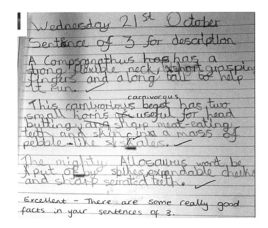

Figure 6.2   Practising sentences of 3

The picture above from Warren Farm Academy, Birmingham, shows that Year 3 children can successfully do this once they have a pattern to imitate.

Tuning into the text games

- The teacher models a simple report, giving basic facts about their family, for example: 'The Corbetts are a small variety of human being'.

- Children talk for 'just one minute' about a subject that they know about, for example: a sport, hobby, place, interest, game, TV programme.

- Children read and select an interesting paragraph from a report of their choice – in groups they prepare an oral presentation, using actions and a text map to teach the rest of the class their chosen paragraph. This could involve the whole class in learning different mini reports.

Role play

- Hot-seat, interview or hold TV news bulletins about different subjects. Give the children cards showing the linking phrases, generalisers and technical language that has to be used.

- Role-play being an expert on a subject on a radio 'phone-in'.

- Pretend to be 'Professor Know-it-all' and give a talk on the subject.

- Create a mini blog about a familiar subject.

What = 'good' for this sort of writing

- **'Compare'** – write three different information paragraphs about the same subject so the children can consider which works best. Discuss what makes it effective. Which is the weakest? Why? What advice would you give to the weaker writer? Use this activity to draw up a wall chart entitled, 'What you need to do to write information interestingly'. Try comparing these three paragraphs as a start:

1. The main attraction for visitors to Stroud on a Saturday is the Farmers' Market. This is held every Saturday and people from miles around come to buy different things. There are all sorts of stalls and lots of people who sell things. It's great.

2. If you have ever been bored on a Saturday, why not visit the Stroud Farmers' Market? This is held in the town centre with over 50 stalls. Here you will find many organic food stands, local craft sellers as well as local people selling a whole range of produce. The market is very popular and enjoyable to visit.

3. The best thing about Stroud on a Saturday is the Farmers' Market. There is always plenty of hustle and bustle as it is very popular. Local farmers and gardeners sell honey, homemade cheeses, and wines as well as bread and meat. There are stalls of vegetables that come fresh from the ground. Craftsmen sell pottery, jewellery and a range of homespun clothing and bags. Furthermore, there is a small café for those who get tired and need a refreshing drink of stimulating carrot juice!

Warming up the specific content

 List specific questions about the subject – what would we be interested in finding out about? Use these to guide the enquiry and to determine paragraph headings.

 Bullet point information and organise into boxes.

● Use colours to highlight the best facts.

Sequencing the text

Provide the class with information that has been jumbled up, with each section or sentence on a separate piece of card. The activity focuses on being able to re-sequence and then explain decisions for where each piece has been placed, identifying the clues and links. For instance:

The Storm Unicorn

✄ –

The last known sighting of a Storm Unicorn was in 1673 by a man called Dr Dapper who claimed that he saw one while walking in the woods. The most amazing thing about Storm Unicorns is that if you meet one, it can bring you great luck. For this reason, many people still hope to catch a glimpse of this most beautiful and fiery creature.

✄ –

Like the Common Unicorn, the Storm Unicorn lives in forests. They are very shy and therefore are not often seen. During the daytime, they sleep under bushes or curled up amongst ferns. At night, the Storm Unicorn emerges and, if you are lucky, can be seen by moonlit pools. They are easy to detect because they make a low rumbling sound as they breathe.

✂ –

Storm Unicorns have a fairly limited diet. In the main, they live on leaves, grass and other forms of vegetation. However, they can also be tempted with apples. Additionally, some like to eat nuts. Be careful when you are near a Storm Unicorn because their bodies can give off an electric shock!

✂ –

The Storm Unicorn is a type of unicorn that has become very rare.

✂ –

Unfortunately, because Storm Unicorns have magic in their horns, this has meant that they have been hunted almost to extinction. Their horns are ground down to a paste that can then be used to enchant even the cruellest of tyrants. Over the years, so many Storm Unicorns have been killed that they have learned to stay away from mankind.

✂ –

Storm Unicorns have the body of a horse and a long horn. The horn is usually of a spiral shape and sticks out from the middle of its head. Most Common Unicorns are a beautiful ebony colour with flashes of gold and silver that look like lightning. As a Storm Unicorn moves, it sends out showers of tiny, electric splinters.

✂ –

Look at the Information section of **DVD 1** for a range of additional warming up activities relating to information text as well as how to apply the three-stage approach to information text. It also includes useful additional material on how to clump information effectively.

How to plan an information unit in Talk for Writing style

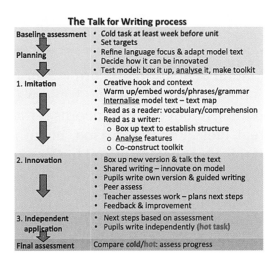

Figure 6.3   The Talk for Writing process

This image sums up the Talk for Writing process. If you have not already read Chapter 2, which explains this process in detail, you will find it useful to read that chapter before thinking about how the process can be applied to information text.

Worked example for information text

Below is a worked example of the three stages of the Talk for Writing approach bookended by the initial and final assessments to ensure formative assessment is at the heart of the planning, teaching and learning process.

Objective: To write information text that fascinates the reader.

Topic for imitation and innovation: To write reports about different dragon species for the *Dragon Hunter's Guide to Dragons of the British Isles*. **Imitation** – The Manchester Ridge-back; **innovation** – The Storm Dragon; **independent choice** – children invent their own dragon species to write about.

Audience and purpose: Class display and a class guide to dragons for the school library. Class assembly about 'The Storm Dragon'.

Baseline assessment and planning

Figure 6.4

For any unit of work on information text you have to think first about what information writing skills the class already possesses. As explained in Chapter 2, a good way of doing this is to set a **cold task**. This should be set at least a week before you begin to teach your unit so that you can alter your planning to suit the needs of the class. The pupils will need a familiar context (for example, if there are foxes living in the school grounds and the children have already done some work on foxes they could write an information text about foxes). In this way, they have something to write about that they know about and that interests them. Warm the topic up with a quick discussion but do not provide any teaching in how to write about this subject. Assessing this cold write will help you pinpoint what specific skills to focus on in the unit to help all the children progress, alongside helping you set a range of additional targets for children with different levels of attainment. This process also enables you to adapt the model text to ensure that it illustrates the features that suit the needs of the class.

For example, if this Year 1 child's cold writing on bats were typical of the class:

Bats Han up side down.

Bats like new homes.

Bats like to eat inses.

the teacher would know what features need to be the focus of the unit and would create or adapt a model text that illustrates how to:

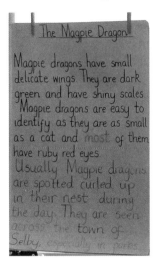

- structure information text;

- hook the reader;

- extend sentences from simple to compound;

- include interesting, relevant detail;

- broaden vocabulary.

If you look at this simple model text written by a teacher in Selby Community Primary, North Yorkshire, you can see how the sentences have been carefully crafted to model the way information text generalises information and introduces comparisons to help the reader picture what is being described.

Figure 6.5 Simple model for information text

Stage 1: Imitation

1. **Imitation**
- Creative hook and context
- Warm up/embed words/phrases/grammar
- Internalise model text – text map
- Read as a reader: vocabulary/comprehension
- Read as a writer:
  o Box up text to establish structure
  o Analyse features
  o Co-construct toolkit

Figure 6.6

The creative hook

The topic for this unit is dragons, which is always a winner with children. Since dragons seem to feature in myths across the world, it is something all children can relate to and, of course, it is easy to find great images to illustrate it. The warming-up activities below include many that will help hook the children's interest.

Warming up the text type and the content

Tune the children into the style of writing through reading to them as well as providing examples of information writing about a range of subjects for independent reading. This might be done in quiet reading or as part of guided reading. An exciting read to have available would be *Dragonology*.

To catch the children's interest try any of the following:

- Mock up a front page report from a local newspaper about dragon sightings in the area.

- Create a class list of clues that might suggest that dragons are in the area, for example scratch marks, dragon prints in mud, missing cats and dogs, scorch marks, burnt bushes, empty arcades, maidens tied to stakes, dragon dung . . .

- Hot-seat a few people who claim to have seen the dragons.

- Find useful clips on YouTube, e.g. three news clips showing dragon sightings in Louisville (just type *Dragons sighted in skies over Louisville* into www. YouTube.com).

- Take the class on a walk during which various evidence is found, for example scratch marks, dragon prints, dragon shell . . .

Internalising the model text

Having warmed up the tune of information text and the topic, the children can now start to focus on imitating an information text. Use a simple but interesting version of a report that contains the expected structure and features appropriate to the level of the children so that there is an edge of challenge. Do not show the children the text at this stage. They are going to hear it and internalise it orally before they see it.

Turn the text into a large class map. Since this text has several paragraphs, it lends itself to being displayed on several sheets of flip-chart paper (one for each paragraph) and displayed on a washing line. The illustration here is from St Joseph's, Derby, showing paragraph 3 on habitat.

Figure 6.7   Text map using one flip-chart sheet per paragraph

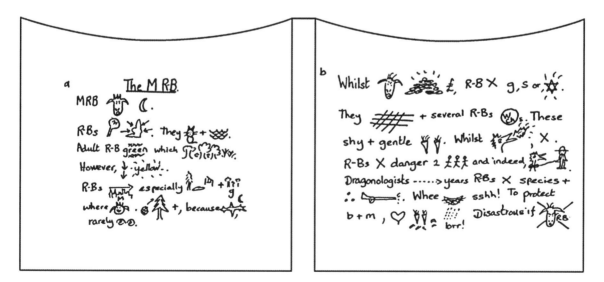

Figure 6.8   Washing-line text map for the Manchester Ridge-back

Learn as a class with actions or divide up so that groups can learn a section and then teach each other. Move from whole-class retelling to groups and finally pairs so that ultimately everyone can retell the text. You may want to refer to pages 21–22 and section 6 of the **DVD** to remind you how to do this. Learn the text with a view to performing it at an assembly.

To help learn the text orally, children should draw their own mini washing lines or text maps. These may be annotated with anything that causes problems and personalised.

Retell the text in various different ways to help the children internalise the text, for example:

- chant as a class;
- present in a circle;
- mime the text;
- tell as a pair or trio;
- hold a race to see who can say it the quickest;
- in pairs say it sentence by sentence;
- prepare to present to children in another class.

1a) Reading as a reader

Once the children have thoroughly internalised the text orally, present the text that they have internalised to the children and start by reading it as a reader.

The Manchester Ridge-back

The Manchester Ridge-back is a rare form of dragon that is only seen at night.

Ridge-backs are easy to identify as they are the smallest dragon in the British Isles. They are the size of a cat and covered in shiny scales. The adult Ridge-back is a dark green colour which enables it to hide in trees and tall grass. However, juveniles are born with a yellowish tinge.

Ridge-backs are found across the city of Manchester especially in parks and gardens where they feel safest. They nest in fir trees and, because they only fly at night, are very rarely seen.

While most dragons are renowned for hoarding treasure, the Ridge-back shows no interest in gold, silver or any valuable stones. They are only interested in playing chess and several Ridge-backs have become world champions. These shy and gentle creatures are vegetarians. While their breath is warm, they do not breathe fire. Ridge-backs present no danger to humans and, indeed, some have been tamed as household pets.

Dragonologists have been concerned for many years that Ridge-backs might be mistaken for other species and, therefore, become hunted. Where nests have been discovered, their location is kept secret. To protect these mysterious and beautiful creatures, all dragon lovers should make sure that vegetable peelings are left out during snowy weather. It would be disastrous if another species of dragon became extinct.

Pie Corbett, Dragon Seeker

They should be able to read the text because they have internalised the language, but that does not mean they have fully understood the meaning of the words. Help the children deepen their understanding of the text, becoming increasingly familiar with the structure and language patterns, by using the following sorts of activities:

- Interview on 'Dragon Watch' with 'Professor Know-it-all' who is interviewed about 'The Manchester Ridge-back dragon' – what they look like, where they are found, etc.

- Take each paragraph in turn and investigate closely in a range of different ways, for example:

  - Draw and label the dragon.

  - Describe to a friend in a phone call what it looks like.

  - In role as a dragon seeker, explain where such dragons are found.

  - Draw a map to show typical location and hideouts.

  - In role as a 'dragon pet shop owner', describe how to look after a pet Ridge-back.

  - Make a one-minute presentation, explaining why these dragons should be protected.

- Play the alternative words game. List some of the tricky words from the text and ask the children, in pairs, if they can come up with alternative words or phrases that mean the same thing. For example:

rare	enables	concerned
form	juveniles	location
identify	renowned	extinct
scales	vegetarians	

- Construct some 'Tell-me' style questions for the children to initially discuss in pairs to open up discussion on the text and ensure the children have understood what they are reading:

  - Tell me why you think the opening paragraph is so short.

  - Tell me how you would be able to identify a Manchester Ridge-back.

– Tell me why you are not likely to ever see a Manchester Ridge-back.

– Tell me how the habits of these dragons differ from normal dragons.

See video clip 18 on how drama and games can aid comprehension.

1b) Reading as a writer

Once the children have fully understood the text, you can then start reading it as a writer, identifying the language features that can be reused as well as analysing the techniques that the writer has used to make the writing effective.

Boxing up the text

Box up the basic pattern so that children can easily see the underlying structure.

This text has been divided into five paragraphs so the boxed-up version will have five rows – one row for each paragraph.

Box up the basic pattern with the children, asking them to tell you what is the focus of each paragraph so that they understand how the text has been constructed and its underlying structure can clearly be seen. The more they see you creating this in front of them, the more they will be able to understand it. This boxed-up plan will also provide the basic plan for the children when they come to create their own explanation text.

Boxed-up planning for 'The Manchester Ridge-back'

Heading for each section	*Key points*
Introduce what it is – definition	*The Manchester Ridge-back is a . . .*
What it looks like – description	*Ridge-backs are easy to identify . . .*
Where it is found – habitat/location	*Ridge-backs are found . . .*
What it is best known for – key aspect or concern	*While most dragons are renowned for . . .*
Conclusion important or amazing fact/point	*Dragonologists have been concerned for many years that . . .*

Reading as a writer, identify language features that can be reused as well as discussing the techniques that the writer uses. It is worth taking specific sentence patterns and innovating on them to produce new sentences using the same underlying pattern. For example:

- The Manchester Ridge-back is a rare form of dragon that is only seen at night.

- The Stroud Lesser-spotted Dragon is a well-known species that makes a good pet for young children.

- The Dover Blue is an almost extinct variety of dragon that lives on the white cliffs above the English Channel.

- The Tameside Rock Dragon is a common variety of dragon that is renowned for being hard to find.

Support understanding by flip-charting and displaying useful words and phrases, building these up throughout the information text activities.

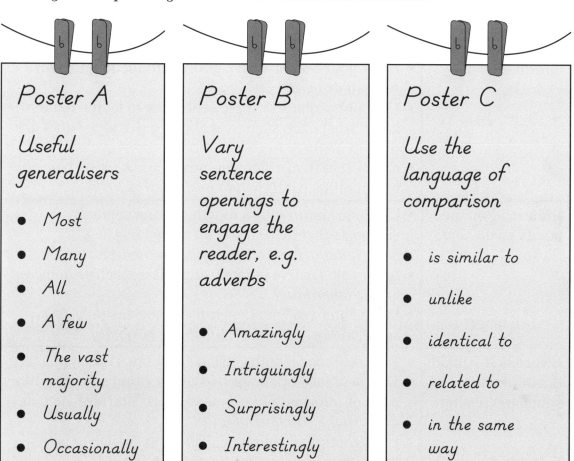

Poster A

Useful generalisers

- Most
- Many
- All
- A few
- The vast majority
- Usually
- Occasionally

Poster B

Vary sentence openings to engage the reader, e.g. adverbs

- Amazingly
- Intriguingly
- Surprisingly
- Interestingly

Poster C

Use the language of comparison

- is similar to
- unlike
- identical to
- related to
- in the same way

The key 'writing ingredients' for success can be established through the reading-as-a-writer discussions. It is essential that the children co-construct these ingredients, otherwise they will be meaningless to them. A useful method is to flip-chart each ingredient as it is taught and discussed throughout the unit to help the children understand the significance of each ingredient. These ingredients should be displayed as they will drive the shared, guided and independent writing, including self-peer evaluation and feedback from the teacher. The toolkit for information writing illustrated here is for a Year 6 class in Knowle Park Primary, Bristol. The toolkit would have been co-constructed from memory by the class during the unit as the pupils are well on the way to having

Figure 6.9 Information toolkit

internalised this toolkit. It is probably a good idea to keep the ingredients list as short as possible and back it up with a checklist that contains examples (see below). Support the short list with examples on the walls and in the children's journals from the activities they have taken part in.

By the end of the innovation stage, the information toolkit may look something like this:

Information toolkit

Plan it – order the information logically	• Box up your points in logical order. • Hook your reader with a good introduction, e.g. *rare form of dragon.* • Use subheadings or topic sentences to let the reader know what each section is about, e.g. *Ridge-backs are easy to identify as . . .* • End with a final comment, possibly a striking piece of information, e.g. *It would be disastrous if . . .*
Link it – join the points so the text flows	• Link your information together using sentence signposts that help to add on more facts, e.g. *additionally, furthermore, also, moreover.* • Add in alternative points using words such as *however, on the other hand.* • Link sentences with generalisers such as *they, it, some, many, a few, lots, most, the majority.*
Express it – make the information sound interesting	• Vary sentence lengths, using short ones for emphasis. • Vary sentence openings to avoid writing sounding like a list of information, e.g. use adverb 'starters' such as *amazingly, intriguingly.* • Use descriptive language, including similes to paint the picture, e.g. *covered in shiny scales.* • Use the language of comparison, such as *is similar to, unlike, identical to, related to.* • Use technical language, explaining it if necessary.
Check it	• Read your writing aloud. • Make certain it flows, check it for accuracy and improve it wherever it does not sound quite right.

Remind the class that you can include all the ingredients but still write a poor report. They must remember to 'taste it' (read it aloud to test if it works) to help guarantee quality writing.

Of course, such checklists should be matched to the stage the children are working at, so they might be less complex or more demanding. These can be used as a guide for evaluation, marking and feedback.

By this point, the children should not only be experts about the Manchester Ridge-back Dragon but also very familiar with the overall pattern of the text and the various language features – they will have heard, spoken, read, discussed and played with the sentence types until they have begun to become part of their linguistic repertoire. It would be ideal to end this stage with some sort of enthusiastic performance to other classes and, with younger classes, inviting the parents in at the end of the day and getting them to join in. As well as giving information, dragon dances, music, masks, poems and stories all leap to mind as a useful adjunct.

Stage 2: Innovation

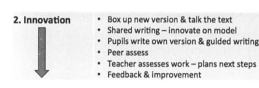

2. Innovation
- Box up new version & talk the text
- Shared writing – innovate on model
- Pupils write own version & guided writing
- Peer assess
- Teacher assesses work – plans next steps
- Feedback & improvement

Figure 6.10

An invitation arrives in class, asking the children to contribute entries to *The Dragon Hunter's Guide*. Use the boxed-up grid on a flip chart to act as a planner. In shared writing, work on developing an entry for the guide, continually referring back to the original, using it as a basis for creating the new version. It helps to take this bit by bit, having the relevant paragraph from the original displayed on the interactive whiteboard, annotated so that the language features stand out, while you scribe the children's ideas on a flip chart. The difficulty of the text has to be built up progressively across the years so that, year on year, the children's ability to craft effective information text increases. The picture here shows shared writing of information text about whales with a small reception class group at Maidwell Primary School in Northamptonshire.

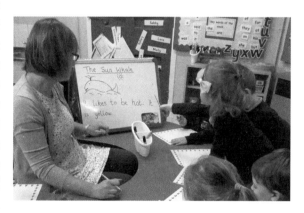

Figure 6.11 Shared writing with reception-age children

For the dragon example, begin by inventing a name for the dragon, e.g. Thunder Dragon. Now generate information, using a range of different strategies. See video clip 19 on brainstorming ideas for innovation. Log information onto the boxed-up planning grid. You could:

- describe a Thunder Dragon to your partner;
- draw and label a Thunder Dragon;
- interview a Thunder Dragon expert about its habits;
- sketch a map or picture and identify where such dragons are found;
- hold news bulletin describing key reason Thunder Dragons well known;
- hold a mini debate about whether Thunder Dragons should be hunted – this could be in the form of *Any Questions*, using a panel of 'dragonologists', taking questions from the class.

Use the grid to display information about the 'Thunder Dragon'. It helps if you keep the original model clearly displayed so that you can keep referring back to it. Look at video clip 20 where Pie illustrates how to use boxing up to plan an innovation of the original model.

Boxed-up plan for the innovation

Heading for each section	Key ideas (brainstormed)
Introduce What it is – definition	Thunder Dragon – much feared
What it looks like – description	Enormous Dark colours Emits lightning Makes thunderous sounds
Where it is found – habitat/location	Exist throughout world Mountains Lives in caves Flies in clouds
What it is best known for – key aspect or concern	Blamed for creating storms Often flies over sea Sailors tame them
Conclusion important or amazing fact/point	Not harmful Needs protecting

Use shared writing to turn each section into fluent writing, involving the children in making decisions, suggesting words and developing sentences. This can be done paragraph by paragraph over a number of days, depending on the children's confidence. The process is quite simple:

- Gather facts for the new paragraph.
- Refer back to the original.
- Turn the facts into similar sentences.
- Keep rereading to maintain flow.
- 'Test out' children's ideas to 'hear' whether they work.
- Ask children to develop sentences in pairs or on mini-whiteboards.
- Pace the writing over two or three days to ensure quality.
- Ask the teaching assistant (or a child) to flip-chart key phrases and vocabulary to be turned into posters to support the writing.

Handouts 4 and **5** (appendix 2, **DVD 2**) are useful supports for shared writing; one lists the ingredients that make it work; the other lists useful teacher phrases.

Video clip 21 on **DVD 1** shows Pie demonstrating how to make shared writing effective through interaction.

Shared writing for 'The Thunder Dragon'

The Thunder Dragon is an unusual variety of dragon that is much feared by many people across the world.

It is easy to recognise because they are the largest variety that exists. Thunder Dragons are as large as buses and covered in black and grey scales. The adults make a thunderous roar when flying and send out brilliant, white shafts of lightning from their eyes. This can be terrifying to see. However, juveniles can only squeak and breathe sparks.

While most dragons are only found in particular regions, the Thunder Dragon lives across the world, especially in mountainous regions where they can hide in caves. They fly in clouds so that no one can see them because they are afraid of being attacked.

Thunder dragons are renowned for creating storms both on land and at sea. However, the truth is that despite their frightening appearance and behaviour, the Thunder Dragon is actually a gentle beast and much misunderstood. In order to avoid being attacked, many fly over the oceans. Some sailors have tamed these dragons as they can make very loyal pets. Unexpectedly, they are only interested in living a quiet life and enjoy playing riddling games and crosswords.

Dragonologists have been worried for years that the Thunder Dragon might be hunted to extinction. There is no doubt that it needs protection. If you are lucky enough to know where one lives, do not tell anyone else as there are Dragon Hunters who get paid well for their leathery hides.

You will notice in the example above that the class hugged very closely to the original. This can provide great support for the less confident writer. However, care must be taken to wean children off too much reliance on the model through progressively illustrating how to extend the approach. See pages 37–40 for advice on how to do this.

Figure 6.12   Using the writing wall to illustrate key features

Use shared writing to focus on the features that the class needs to strengthen in order to write more independently. The picture above from the working wall in the Year 5/6 class at Maidwell Primary, Northampton, shows how the teacher was using her working wall to illustrate features that she would demonstrate through the shared writing. Next to her list of useful sentence signposts to introduce new information in an engaging way into information text, she has illustrated the technique with some full sentence examples. The children need to hear, say and see how these sentences work so that they can confidently replicate such structures in their own work.

Another useful technique, illustrated here from information shared writing with a younger class, is to make a deliberate mistake for the children to correct. The

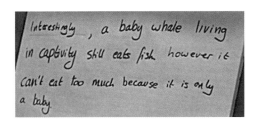

Figure 6.13   Make deliberate mistakes for the children to correct

word *however* seems to cause punctuation problems. Whenever the word *however* is used to introduce a change of direction, it must begin a new sentence and be immediately followed by a comma, as it is functioning as a fronted adverbial. If it is functioning as an aside, then the sentence could have been written like this: *Interestingly, a baby whale living in captivity still eats fish, but it can't eat too much, however, because it is only a baby.* It is only by reading such sentences out loud and hearing and discussing the differences that the children will be able to tune their ears and eyes into understanding how to punctuate text to guide the reader through the intended meaning. See Appendix 3 on **DVD 2** for more support on this.

You may have noticed that the children of all different ages at Maidwell are working on the same text type and the same theme – whales – as the lessons took place at the same time, but the level of difficulty of the model text and the activities throughout the units are designed to build in progression. This is a good way of ensuring that progression occurs and it is easy to monitor.

The children should write independently straight after the shared writing, gradually building their text over a number of days. Guided writing is key to teaching and supporting groups in a focused manner at the level they require. More confident writers might be asked to write more paragraphs, adding extra information. For instance, reports could be developed further by explaining how a dragon's fire-breathing mechanism works or debating whether they should be hunted or safeguarded in specialist dragon parks. This allows the better writers to tackle a more hybrid text, including explanation and discussion, which is typical of information text in real life.

After writing, the children should work as response partners, reading their writing to each other, considering what has been effective and what might be improved. Refer back to the 'writing ingredients' and 'checklist' that were listed from the annotation activity and use these to focus feedback. Remember, though, that while the children should have included the ingredients, the key factor will be whether the information informs, interests and engages the reader.

When assessing the work of the whole class, the teacher may find it useful to use a grid like the one below to help focus on what aspects of the writing particularly need improving if the children are to become skilled writers of explanations.

Grid to help assess what needs teaching next

Ingredients	Have these ingredients been successfully implemented? Which features now need to be focused on?
Plan it • Can they plan their information (box it up)? • Can they hook their reader by introducing the information in an interesting way? • Can they present the information in a logical order? • Can they round the information off with an engaging conclusion?	
Link it • Can they use topic sentences to guide the reader through the information? • Can they link the text together using signposts to add more facts or signal alternative points?	
Express it • Can they use generalisers to sum up information? • Can they vary sentence lengths, using short ones for emphasis? • Can they use descriptive language including similes to paint the picture? • Can they use the language of comparison? • Can they use language that will interest the reader? • Can they use technical language appropriately?	
Check it • Is there evidence that they are reading their work aloud to see if it sounds good? • Are they improving their work following the peer assessment? • Are they checking their spelling and punctuation?	

Of course, such checklists should be matched to the stage the children are working at, so they might be made less complex or more demanding. These can be used as a guide for evaluation, marking and feedback. Remember, though,

Polish this paragraph

first sighting was triceratops there is no mistakin this dinosaur whith three huge horns sticking out of its hed and this colourful bony frill around its neck. The latter look like a ruff worn by a Elizabethan gentleman I expect we shall see a lot more these stocky plant eaters they live in big herds I believe.

What tips would you give to this writer?

Figure 6.14   Faulty text that needs improving

Figure 6.15   Modelling editing through shared writing

that while the children may have included the ingredients, the key factor will be whether the information would work and be easy to follow.

Your marking should lead directly into your next piece of teaching. Provide feedback on this work, focusing on those areas that the children found most difficult and helping them understand how to edit their work effectively. A visualiser or iPad is a very useful piece of equipment that allows you to present exemplar work from the pupils immediately to the whole class to illustrate the improvements you are seeking. Or you can mock up a paragraph full of the type of errors that have arisen, as illustrated here from Warren Farm's work on dinosaurs, so that the children work in pairs discussing what needs to be done before deciding as a class on the best advice to give the writer.

Such activities provide excellent opportunities to model for the children how to reflect on the effectiveness of writing. The more opportunities the children are given to talk about what works and what features make the writing engaging, the more they will be able to develop their own inner judge and craft and edit their own writing effectively. The picture here shows the Year 5/6 teacher at Maidwell, Northamptonshire, showing children how to edit their writing. **Handout 5** in appendix 2 on **DVD 2** is full of useful questions to help children reflect on what makes writing effective and discuss what works. If the teacher models this sort of reflection, the children will quickly pick up how to reflect on work. Focus on what makes the text engaging, not on the naming of parts. Also see Clip 26 on advanced shared writing.

One of the contributions that the Transforming Writing project made to the development of Talk for Writing was mini-lessons. This would be an excellent point within the unit to set up some mini-lessons so that pupils can focus on the areas that they need help with most (see pages 42–43).

Stage 3: Independent application

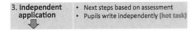

| 3. Independent application | • Next steps based on assessment |
| | • Pupils write independently (hot task) |

Figure 6.16

Once the children's writing has been assessed, the teacher is in a good position to move to the third stage, where there will be more choice for the children. The assessment will direct what has to be concentrated on during shared and guided sessions and inform the children about what they need to focus on.

This is also a good opportunity to introduce a wider range of information models, and focus on particular sentence patterns to help the children develop their independent information writing skills. It is particularly useful if these can be sourced from real information text relating to the area the children live in, like this text from a notice on the hill above Clifton Suspension Bridge in Bristol:

You are standing in the middle of an Iron Age hillfort. Had you stood here 2000 years ago, you would have been surrounded on three sides by a wooden stockade on top of an earth rampart.

Use this to practise these sorts of sentence patterns:

- *You are sitting in the middle of x school. Had you sat here 100 years ago, you would have been surrounded by the walls of the chocolate factory that used to be on this site.*

- *You are standing in the middle of the new shopping mall. Had you stood here ten years ago, you would have been surrounded by trees and grass.*

Now, *The Dragon Hunter's Guide* could be extended. The children might invent different types of dragon such as Sun Dragons, Moss Dragons, Cloud Dragons, Mountain Dragons or even Long-tailed Mouse Dragons. Everyone could draw and label their own creation. This might be followed by children discussing what the dragons eat, where they live, their habits and what makes their type of dragon special.

Such drawing and talk helps the children to generate information as well as orally rehearse the sort of thing that they will write. Time spent preparing in this way will make the writing richer and more interesting. This idea could be broadened by the children writing about different sorts of imaginary or mythical creatures such as goblins, dwarves, unicorns, minotaurs and so forth.

Make sure that the shared work focuses on specific aspects that the children have found difficult – picked up from marking (assessing) their previous writing. This means that your marking leads directly into the next piece of teaching. Once again, model planning using a boxed-up grid as well as the actual writing. You will be working on a class version perhaps about 'The Greater Ormskirk Water Dragon' while the children will all be writing about different sorts of dragon or other imaginary creatures.

The different reports can then be made into a class book, organised alphabetically. Entries might be enhanced by boxes with key facts, glossaries and diagrams. An ideal model for this work would be to look at the popular book, *Dragonology* (from Templar Publishing, who also publish *Working with Dragons* as well as *Tracking and Training Dragons* – check out their website for video clips: www.dragonology.com).

See Clips 22, 23, 24 & 25

Many teachers have found it useful to run a three-stage unit of work as described above using imaginary creatures. This can be followed immediately by further work based on something real such as an animal. The class could move straight into innovation in this case as they should have already internalised the key language patterns. The innovation might focus everyone on finding out about foxes. This would involve research, perhaps using library books and the internet, as well as interviewing someone local who is knowledgeable about foxes. Shared and guided writing must still be used in order to maximise the opportunities for teaching.

For independent application, the children might move on to select their own creature to investigate – in groups, pairs or individually. Once again, shared and guided writing must be used to focus teaching in order to ensure progress so that the children increasingly move away from the models and write independently.

End of unit assessment

Final assessment   Compare cold/hot: assess progress

Figure 6.17

The teacher now assesses the final piece of writing (the **hot task**) and looks back at the cold task to see what progress has been made. If you have asked the children to write a comment on how well they think they have completed the work, then adding your comment to the child's comment helps to promote the dialogue about what needs to be done to improve the child's work.

Again, when the work is handed back, focus on one or two areas that everyone needs to improve. This could be indicated by highlighting the areas selected in a particular colour, for example *green for growth*. Provide some teaching relating to these areas and ask the children to immediately improve their work. Then ask them to reflect on their learning by looking back at the cold task and seeing what progress they have made.

The teacher is now in a position to decide which everyday language features will need focusing on in the next unit of work, as well as to log any information text features that will need strengthening when the class next revisits information writing when applying it across the curriculum.

Mastering the approach across the curriculum

Information report writing is crucial as part of a young writer's repertoire because it will often be needed when writing across the curriculum. Being able to communicate information clearly and interestingly is key to all aspects of the curriculum. Furthermore, it also introduces the idea of writing in a generalised way rather than the particular. This way of thinking becomes essential as children develop from the particular to the more abstract. It is the difference between:

‘Sparkle Dragon lives in a cave and she is very shy.’

(Katie – aged 7)

and

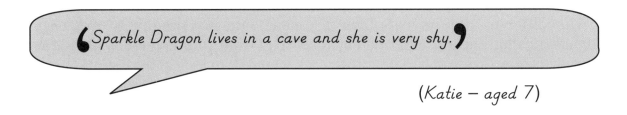

‘Kite Dragons have the extraordinary ability to sleep during flight and generally make their homes inside clouds.’

(Malcom – aged 11)

Once a unit on information writing has been taught, then places should be found for it across the curriculum. This embedding of the skills in a range of contexts to provide depth and breadth is essential if the children are to achieve mastery of the skills that underpin effective information writing. Finding opportunities to develop skills across the curriculum is particularly valuable because it helps the children put their understanding of what they have learned into action for a range of audiences and purposes.

Figure 6.18 A text map on Space

Information text is perfect for practising across the curriculum from an early age. Here is one of six text maps that a reception class in Selby Community Primary School, North Yorkshire, used to internalise not just information about the universe in which we live, but also to begin to embed the typical language patterns of information text that they had learned in their English lessons. The children then took the maps home and, as pictured here, practised talking the text, to the delight of their parents. Read more about this in Chapter 11 on involving parents and see Clip 27.

A Year 3 history topic on dinosaurs at Warren Farm Academy, Birmingham, provided lots of scope for embedding non-fiction writing skills across the curriculum. Below you can see children involved in sorting information about dinosaurs into fact and fiction, a very important skill when selecting accurate information to use, especially in an age when there is so much information on the web that has not been through any sort of editing process. The picture on the next page shows pupils from West St Leonard's Academy in East Sussex presenting information about Henry VIII from a text map.

Figure 6.19 Reception pupil talking about the Universe

All cross-curricular topics will include information and, as part of that, there will be technical terms that need to be understood and integrated into the language that the children can speak, read and write with confidence. An excellent way of doing this is to use Never-heard-the-word grids, as explained on pages 197–198 and illustrated by Figure 6.22. The example illustrated here is from a Design and technology unit for Year 6 at St Matthew's C of E Primary in Birmingham. Here, the pupil has steadily built up his comprehension until he has

Figure 6.20 Sorting information into fact or fiction

Figure 6.21   Pupils presenting information about Henry VIII from a text map

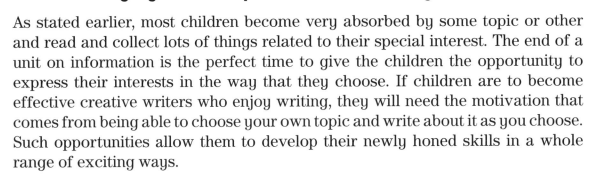

Figure 6.22   Never-heard-the-word grid for design and technology

good definitions of all the words. Such approaches are an excellent way of building pupils' vocabulary which will help them cope with the reading test. In Clips 28 and 29, you can see Pie boxing up information from the pupils' knowledge about Queen Victoria, followed by shared writing. These are very useful clips for staff training.

Encouraging real independence, creativity and invention

As stated earlier, most children become very absorbed by some topic or other and read and collect lots of things related to their special interest. The end of a unit on information is the perfect time to give the children the opportunity to express their interests in the way that they choose. If children are to become effective creative writers who enjoy writing, they will need the motivation that comes from being able to choose your own topic and write about it as you choose. Such opportunities allow them to develop their newly honed skills in a whole range of exciting ways.

A note on hybrid text

Though it is possible to write pure information text, in real life such text is rare. Normally, an engaging information text will include passages of explanation relating to the topic because, for example, when you inform a reader that an eagle has a hooked beak and claws, it is only logical to throw in an explanation of why this is. If you pick up any good information text about somewhere you are visiting, that text is liable to include instructions on how to get there, persuasion text about the best places to go to, recount about some historical events and explanation about the significance of some of the features to be seen. As the children's understanding of information writing progresses, it is a good idea to encourage them to include features of other text types within it, as appropriate.

CHAPTER 7

Explanation

What is explanation text?

Explanation text is any text that explains actions, ideas or processes to the reader. It is probably the most difficult of the text types as you have to be able to understand something very well to be able to explain it clearly. It is also the one that adults tend to dodge most, so good oral exemplars are thin on the ground. When children ask 'Why?', it is tempting to reply 'Because I say so' or 'Because it is'. Of course, such responses can be explained by exhaustion or desperation, but often part of the real reason is that we don't actually know why. It's not easy to answer all the questions listed in Yew Tree Community School's display about light. To make matters worse, explanation is easily confused with instructions – instructions tell you how to make or do something, while explanation tells you why something happens or how it works. And if that wasn't enough, when it comes to explaining real-life events, explanation verges into discursive

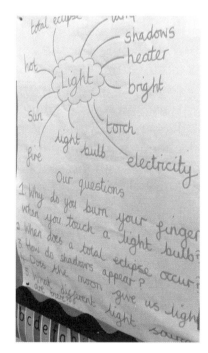

Figure 7.1 Poster about understanding light

writing as there are often many possible alternative causes that are not necessarily linked and may be subjective.

The confusion caused by explanation can perhaps best be illustrated by the fact that in everyday speech the word 'explain' can be used to indicate four different sorts of text type, as illustrated below:

- Explain how I get to the station from here (instructions).
- Explain the causes of the First World War (discursive).
- Explain what you witnessed at the station last night (recount).
- Explain why rain falls (explanation).

No wonder explanation can be hard. However, being able to explain clearly is a particularly valuable skill because it is at the heart of learning. Involving the children in being able to explain what they are learning to others is the best way of helping them retain information. Doubtless, most of us will have experienced that terrible moment when you are explaining something to a class and realise that you do not know what you are talking about. The best thing to do in such circumstances is to suddenly invent a spelling test to give you some time to change tack. But the experience lets you know that you have to think more about the topic so you can explain it clearly. The more we involve the children in explaining-to-others activities within our teaching repertoire, the more children will understand and recall what they have learned.

Like most non-fiction, explanation writing begins with an introduction to inform the reader of what the writer is explaining. This is often presented as a 'hook' to encourage the reader to want to learn more.

Ordering explanation text is based on the logic of whatever is being explained. Much explanation is chronological and thus can be ordered in 'this leads to this, which leads to this' mode. However, some explanation is cyclical, like the rain cycle, in which case, although the order is still basically chronological, you end up back where you started once you've completed the cycle. Another type is reversible, like the tide; again you end up back where you started. Finally, there is multi-causal explanation that, as mentioned above, often shades into tentative discursive writing of the 'on the other hand', 'this could possibly be explained by' variety and is ordered logically.

To write an effective piece of explanation, the author needs to have an excellent understanding of what they are explaining, an interest in the topic and a clear picture of the audience who wants to understand what is being explained.

Typical features of explanation text

Audience	Someone who wants to understand a process or an event.
Purpose	To help someone understand a process or why something is, or has happened.
Typical structure	• Series of logical – often chronological – explanatory steps. • Paragraphs usually beginning with a topic sentence. • Often illustrated by diagrams to aid understanding.
Typical language features	• Formal language. • Present tense. • Causal sentence signposts to link explanation. • Generalisation. • Tentative language to refer to unproven theories. • Detail to help understand points – often in form of information. • Technical vocabulary.
Examples	• How does a bicycle pump work? • Why does it get colder when you go up a mountain? • How did the Egyptians build the pyramids?

Choosing something to explain

This is tricky as the children need to have sufficient knowledge of whatever they are being asked to explain to be able to explain it. The best way, as usual, is to come up with something that the children are interested in – but with explanation this too is hard because, all of a sudden, mobile phones cannot be on the list. The teacher, let alone the children, probably hasn't the faintest idea how mobile phones work and, if they did, it would be too complex.

The simplest place to start is obviously personal experience, but even here care is needed. Explaining why you are late for school is relatively easy as there can be concrete reasons for this: not having an alarm clock, not liking to get out of bed, etc. Explaining why you like strawberries is much harder. 'Because I do' is the instant response and beyond that you are entering the language of evaluation, which is complex.

One good solution is to choose awe-inspiring aspects of the natural world like thunder and lightning, tornadoes, volcanoes or earthquakes, as long as you can keep the concept simple. And, of course, this could come in handy. The 10-year-old girl on Maikhao beach in Phuket, in 2004, who remembered from her geography lessons that the sea suddenly retreats just before a tsunami strikes (and explained this to her parents, who then cleared the beach of the people running to see where the sea was going) is an excellent example of how understanding how things work can be most useful.

An invaluable book for the science curriculum is Bill Bryson's *A Really Short History of Nearly Everything*. This book has great examples of how to write recount, information and, most of all, explanation text in a way that really engages the audience. For technology, or English, Roger McGough and Chris Riddell's *Until I Met Dudley* is superb. As the introduction to the book explains, 'Dudley, the techno wizard dog, takes children from the furthest realms of fantasy into the fascinating world of technology, to discover the workings of familiar machines.' These engaging texts are excellent for basing explanation units on.

Whatever focus you choose, remember the golden rule: the topic must engage the children so they have something that they really want to explain. Without this essential foundation, their explanation is liable to be both inadequate and tedious.

Audience and purpose

Always provide some sort of audience and purpose for whatever focus is chosen. It can be useful to get the children to draw a picture of someone who is typical of the audience to help them remember who they are writing for and to pitch their writing accordingly.

Some key uses of explanation writing skills across the curriculum

- Explaining why certain values and beliefs are held (RE and PSHE).
- Explaining how something works (technology and maths).
- Explaining why things happen (science, geography and RE).

- Explaining why characters / people behave in certain ways (English and RE).

- Explaining what motivates people (English, science, history, geography, RE, etc.).

Warming up the tune of explanation text

To help children write effective explanation text, time must be spent helping them to understand what language features give explanation its particular flavour so that they can begin to recognise these techniques when they hear or see them and start using them in their speaking and writing. What are the language patterns and sentence signposts, or the vocabulary, that are typical of explanation writing? For any work on explanation writing, daily games need to be devised that will help the children familiarise themselves with the pattern of explanation writing and the types of vocabulary that go with it. These activities which co-construct understanding of what explanation writing is like are an essential step in helping children master writing skills.

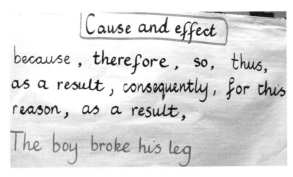

Figure 7.2   Displaying causal language

As the games are played, flip-chart the vocabulary, sentence signposts and key sentence patterns that emerge and start to create a toolkit of useful ingredients for explanation text to support the children's speaking and writing. Display these to make the learning visible and develop them throughout the unit, as illustrated here from Montgomery Primary, Birmingham. If the children have already been taught this text type in Talk for Writing style, build on their existing toolkit for explanation.

Practising the tune of the text through talking will enable the children to manipulate what they have to say effectively, selecting just the right words, phrases and sentence patterns when they finally write it down. The examples below can all be adapted to suit a wide range of ages. Explanation writing lends itself to:

Tuning into causal language games

- **The explanation game:** In pairs, swapping roles, and using phrases like 'because', 'as a result of this' or 'therefore', explain any one of the following in as creative a way as you like (the important thing here is not to let lack of knowledge get in the way of practising the language of explanation):

  - Why bananas are curly.

  - Why trees have bark.

  - Why dogs bark.

- Why rainbows don't wobble in the wind.

- Why the moon changes shape.

- Why it gets colder when you go up a mountain.

   Sequencing the text: Find a good short exemplar of whatever sort of explanation text you are focusing on and rearrange the paragraphs. Make sure that, when the text is cut up into paragraphs, the children cannot put it together again using the cut marks. In groups, the children have to sequence the text, then read the sequenced text aloud (to check it is coherent) and finally be prepared to explain the order in which they have placed the text. You may want to highlight the sentence signposts.

Example: Why vaccinations work

> **At a later time**, you might be infected with a harmful form of the micro-organism. **Because** your white cells have already learned how to defeat these germs, they can quickly detect the germs **and** make the antibodies to attack them.

> The harmful micro-organisms are, **therefore**, killed **before** they can make you ill.

> **This allows** your white blood cells to detect this type of micro-organism **and** learn how to make antibodies to attack and kill it.

> **When** you have a vaccination, the doctor injects a weak or dead form of particular micro-organisms into your blood.

Extension: Warming up understanding of the process

In groups of six, mime/act out how vaccinations work so that a 9-year-old audience could understand. (Ground rules: no physical contact – all attacks and defences must be mimed.)
   Two people are the micro-organisms invading the body.
   Four people are the white blood cells.

Tuning into explanation text games

   Role play – the investigation game: Invent an investigation scenario based on whatever story or novel you are focusing on. For example: the police are investigating a complaint made by the three bears against Goldilocks. Roles: Goldilocks, three bears, one or two policemen. Explain that in groups of five or six they must:

- use lots of how and why questions to find out what happened;

- use as many different explaining words as possible;

- stick to the story or come up with some more unusual versions, but remember that the purpose is to explain, not to recount.

The policeman might start by asking Goldilocks: 'Why did you go into the three bears' house?'

- **The evidence game:** Provide the children with two statements explaining whatever theme you want to focus on (one of which is false). Then provide the children with information relating to the topic which could be used to support or oppose either of the statements. The children have to gather their evidence and then present evidence to support their conclusion.

This activity can be strengthened by asking the children to decide what order they want to present their points in and then getting them to draw a symbol to represent each point in order. Working in pairs, with just the symbols to support them, they present their explanation to their partner, introducing and linking their explanation appropriately. Get children to present some of the more effective explanations to the whole class and encourage the children to magpie good phrases that they might want to use when they write their explanations.

How to plan an explanation unit in Talk for Writing style

This image sums up the Talk for Writing process. If you have not already read Chapter 2, which explains this process in detail, you will find it useful to read that chapter before thinking about how the process can be applied to explanation text.

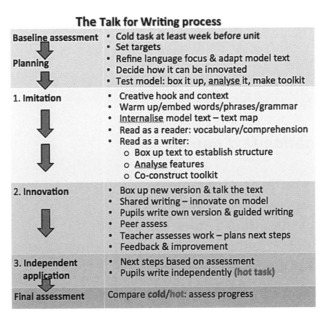

Figure 7.3   The Talk for Writing process

Worked example for explanation text

Below is a worked example of the three stages of the Talk for Writing approach bookended by the initial and final assessments to ensure formative assessment is at the heart of the planning, teaching and learning process.

Objective: To write clear, interesting explanation text.

Topic for all stages: Why have some animals become extinct, focusing on dragons (imitation), dinosaurs (innovation), then other species (independent application).

Baseline assessment and planning

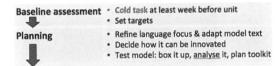

Figure 7.4

For any unit of work on explanation you have to think first about what explanation writing skills the class already possesses. As explained in Chapter 2, a good way of doing this is to set a **cold task**. This should be set at least a week before you begin to teach your unit so that you can alter your planning to suit the needs of the class. The pupils will need a familiar context (for example, if the area has recently been flooded, you could ask the children to explain why the area flooded) so that they have something to write about that they know about and that interests them. Warm the topic up with a quick discussion but do not provide any teaching in how to write about this subject. This will help you pinpoint what specific skills to focus on in the unit to help the children progress. Assess this work and decide what language features to focus on within the unit as well as setting targets for children with different levels of attainment. This will also enable you to adapt the model text to ensure that it illustrates the features that suit the needs of the class.

See chapter 2, pages 15–17 for an example of how this cold writing helps the teacher decide the language features to focus on. The model text should be based on something that the children have done, know about and have experienced or might be interested in learning about. If you look at the text map here from Front Lawn Primary in Havant, and then look at the model text on dragons in this chapter and its text map, you will see that the teachers have adapted the model text from this chapter and simplified it so that the language is at the appropriate level for Year 1, substituting explaining why witches can fly for explaining why dragons became extinct.

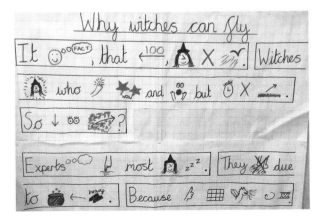

Figure 7.5   Text map for *Why witches can fly*

Stage 1: Imitation

The creative hook

1. Imitation
- Creative hook and context
- Warm up/embed words/phrases/grammar
- Internalise model text – text map
- Read as a reader: vocabulary/comprehension
- Read as a writer:
  - Box up text to establish structure
  - Analyse features
  - Co-construct toolkit

Figure 7.6

The innovation focus for this unit is explaining why dinosaurs died out. Dinosaurs never seem to fail to interest children. A few grand dinosaur images should do the trick. You may want to recreate the image below from Royal Tyrrell Museum, Drumheller, Canada, so that the children can measure themselves against the hind leg of a stegosaurus.

Warming up the tune of explanation

Tune the children into the style of explanation writing through reading explanation texts to them and providing simple explanation texts for them to read.

Below are five warming-up-the-text activities to help the children become confident in the language of explanation. The order of these activities is important as the first introduces them to the trickier language of the unit; the second provides them with some of the explanation phrases they will need; the third scaffolds the use of this language; the fourth provides an opportunity for them to start talking the language of explanation; and the fifth provides the opportunity to talk the language of explanation in relation to the topic being focused on.

1. Never-heard-the-word grids

Devise a Never-heard-the-word grid to introduce the difficult vocabulary in the unit. For this unit the words selected might be:

Figure 7.7   The appeal of dinosaurs

extinct	moorlands	bounty hunters
roam/roamed	vital	scales
fiery	camouflage	destroy
experts	visible	flee/fled
remote		

See page 197 for an explanation of how never-heard-the-word grids work.

2. Magpieing the language of explanation from real text

Provide copies of simple explanation text from children's websites and get children to identify all the causal sentence signposts within it. Encourage the children to magpie useful vocabulary from this activity.

3. Cloze procedure targeting causal language

Fill in the gaps with the language of explanation – for example, causal sentence signposts like 'because' or 'as a result'. How many alternative words or phrases can you think up for each gap?

Why Anthony was often in detention
Anthony found it impossible to stick to deadlines and, _____, he was always late for school. His _____ were many and varied. Sometimes he said it was _____ his alarm failed to go off or that it was _____ his sister refused to come out of the bathroom. Another favourite _____ was that he was finishing his homework or walking the dog. _____ he was often in detention.

Draw out the language below and encourage the children to magpie useful vocabulary from this activity:

- as a result / consequently / therefore / subsequently;

- reasons / excuses / explanations;

- was caused by, resulted from;

- because / owing to the fact that / due to the fact that.

4. Role play to tune into the language of explanation: Sorry Miss, it's all the dog's fault

In pairs, swapping roles between pupil and teacher, the pupil works out a linked series of events which resulted in:

- being late for school;

- not doing homework;

- not having the correct uniform on.

The teacher should work out a reply explaining why the excuses are not acceptable. Encourage the children to use causal sentence signposts such as 'so', 'because', 'as a result', 'consequently', 'this causes', 'the reason that', 'this results in', 'therefore', 'when', 'since . . .'. The children magpie useful linking phrases from this activity.
   Extension to embed the language: This could be followed up by role-playing a telephone call from the teacher to a parent of the child explaining why the child

is being kept in detention for not obeying key school rules. Role-play phone calls work best if the children sit back to back. Not being able to see the person you are talking to makes it easier to stay in role.

5. Role play to tune the children into the language of explanation and the focus

First, give the children one minute to brainstorm all the fanciful reasons they can think of for why dragons became extinct. Next, to get the children talking in explanation mode, model for them being a visiting professor of Dragonology who has come to explain what caused dragons to become extinct and then ask them, in pairs, to be the professor.

Internalising the model text

Having warmed up the tune of explanation and the topic, the children can now start to focus on imitating an explanation text. Write a simple exemplar text (in this instance a short explanation of why dragons are extinct) that contains the typical structure and language features of explanation text, appropriate to the level of the children but ensuring an edge of challenge.

Do not show the children the text at this stage. They are going to hear it and internalise it orally before they see it.

Now turn the text into a text map to help the children recall it. You may want to have one text map per paragraph and display it as a washing line. Talk the text for the children with actions, getting the children to join in. Move from whole-class retelling to groups and finally pairs, so that ultimately everyone can retell the text on their own. You may want to refer to video clip 5 on **DVD 1** to help you do this.

Figure 7.8   Text map for *Why dragons are extinct*

To help learn the text, children should draw their own text maps or mini washing lines (one card for each paragraph). These may be annotated to support anything that causes problems.

Retell the text in various different ways to help the children internalise the text (see video clip 37 on **DVD 2** to see how to do this). For example:

- retell it silently;

- hold race to see who can say it quickest;

- in pairs, say it sentence by sentence;

- prepare to present to another class.

The picture shows pupils from Front Lawn, Havant, presenting explanation with the help of a text map.

Figure 7.8a   Text map supporting pupils' presentation

1a) Reading as a reader

Once the children have thoroughly internalised the text orally, show the model text and start reading it as a reader. With younger classes you may want to colour code particular features of the model to help the children understand the central role of, say, topic sentences or sentence signposts in non-fiction text. With older children, you may want to leave this until after they have analysed the text themselves and co-construct the colour coding with the class.

Why dragons are extinct

It is a well-known fact that, up until a few hundred years ago, dragons roamed England terrorising villages with their fiery breath and capturing maidens. So, why are they now extinct?

Experts think that the main reason is the rise and rise of football. Because so many England fans started wearing the colours of St George, the dragons fled to remote moorlands.

Unfortunately, the very cold weather of the moorlands meant that the dragons' favourite green foods (gooseberries, cabbage and spinach) refused to grow. These plants were not only vital for the dragons' health but also for their colour which provided camouflage in the woods. Slowly, the green dragons turned purple, caused by eating too much heather.

It is this colour change that led to their final extinction. Once the heather had died away in the autumn, the dragons could no longer hide because their purple scales made them easily visible. This enabled local bounty hunters to hunt and destroy them.

So that is why the only dragons you see in England today are in pictures, books or films.

They should be able to read it because they have learned it orally word for word, but that may not mean they have fully understood the meaning. The more you have used actions and alternative words to help them understand the meaning, the more they will understand.

Help the children deepen their understanding of the text, becoming increasingly familiar with the structure and language patterns, by using the following sorts of activities:

- **Interview on 'Dragon Watch'** with 'Professor Know-it-all' who is interviewed about why dragons have died out.

- **Take each paragraph in turn** and investigate closely in a range of different ways, for example:

  – describe to a friend over the phone why the dragons died out;

  – in role as an England supporter, explain how you hadn't meant to harm the dragons;

  – make a one-minute presentation, explaining why the dragons should have been protected.

- **Play the alternative words game:** List some of the tricky words from the text (as listed on page 164) and ask the children in pairs if they can come up with alternative words or phrases that mean the same thing.

- **Construct some questions** for the children to initially discuss in pairs to open up discussion on the text and ensure they have understood what they are reading:

  – Why do you think the explanation begins with a description of dragons in England a few hundred years ago?

  – What main explanation is given for why dragons have died out in England?

  – Why was it such a problem that the moorlands were cold?

  – Why did eating heather turn out to be a disaster for dragons?

1b) Reading as a writer

Once the children have fully understood the text, you can then start reading it as a writer, to create a toolkit identifying the language features that can be reused as well as analysing the techniques that the writer has used to make the writing effective.

Boxing up the text

Now box up the text so that the underlying structure can clearly be seen. This text has been divided into five paragraphs so the boxed-up version will have five rows – one row for each paragraph.

Box up the basic pattern with the children, asking them to tell you what is the focus of each paragraph so that they understand how the text has been structured and its underlying structure can clearly be seen. The more they are involved in co-constructing the structure, the more they will be able to understand it.

This boxed-up structure will also provide the basic plan for the children when they come to create their own explanation text.

Boxed-up planning for 'Why dragons are extinct'

Heading for each section	Key points
Introduce what is being explained and hook	• Dragons – why are they extinct?
Key reason why wiped out	• Popularity of football – wearing flag of St George • Dragons fled to moorlands
Which led to a)	• Colder weather meant dragons' food didn't grow • Green food also vital for dragon camouflage • Ate heather – turned purple
Which led to b)	• Purple colour meant easily seen • Hunters shot them
Conclusion rounding off	• Now only seen in books, etc.

Display this boxed-up plan because it will provide the basic structure for the shared writing innovation and the children's work when they come to create their own versions.

Now help the children identify language features that can be reused as well as discussing the techniques that the writer uses. In this example, help the children identify the explanation phrases and techniques used and add them to the explanation toolkit if they are not already there.

It is worth taking specific sentence patterns and innovating on them to produce new sentences using the same underlying pattern – for example:

- *Experts think that the main reason is* the rise and rise of football.
- *Experts think that the main reason is* the use of pesticides.
- *Scientists argue that the main cause is* the change of habitat.
- *Scientists argue that the main cause is* climate change.
- *Local residents believe that the key reason is that no one wants* a dragon in their back yard.
- *Local residents believe that the key reason is that no one wants* a supermarket in the area.

Ask the children in pairs to highlight all the causal sentence signposts used in the text to build up the explanation and help link it together. Add new examples to your causal signposts poster: *the main reason*; *because*; *meant that*; *caused by*; *That led to*; *This enables*; *So that is why*.

Identify any other sort of general phrasing that might be useful for explanation text:

- *. . . not only . . . but also . . .;*
- *It is this . . .;*
- *Once the . . .;*
- *could no longer.*

Challenge the children to see if they can use some of these phrases to explain different things, for example why people should not eat too much sugar or why dragons will not make good pets. Support understanding by flip-charting and displaying useful words and phrases, building these up throughout the explanation text activities.

Poster A

Useful time signposts for chronological explanation

- At first,
- Before
- During
- After
- At an earlier time,
- At a later time,
- Finally,

Poster B

Useful causal signposts for explanation

- When . . .
- Because . . .
- So . . .
- Since . . .
- Therefore, . . .
- This allows . . .
- This enables . . .
- . . . was caused by . . .
- Consequently, . . .
- . . . resulted from . . .
- Owing to the fact that . . .
- This can be explained by . . .
- Another reason why . . .

The key 'writing ingredients' for success can be established through the reading-as-a-writer discussions. It is essential that the children co-construct these ingredients, otherwise they will be meaningless to them. A useful method is to flip-chart each ingredient as it is taught and discussed throughout the unit to help the children understand the significance of each ingredient. These ingredients should be displayed as they will drive the shared, guided and independent writing, including self-peer evaluation and feedback from the teacher. It is probably a good idea to keep the ingredients list as short as possible and back it up with a checklist that contains examples (see below). Support the short list with examples on the walls and in the children's journals from the activities they have taken part in.

By the end of the innovation stage, the ingredients flip chart may look something like this:

Explanation toolkit

Plan it – order your points logically	• Box up the content. • Begin with a hook, e.g. a rhetorical question to interest the reader: *So why are they . . .?* • Build up your explanation from paragraph to paragraph: *This led to this, led to this, led to this.* • End with a final comment, possibly an interesting piece of information about why this explanation matters: *So that is why . . .*
Link it – join your ideas effectively	• Use topic sentences to introduce each key point: *Experts think that the main reason is the rise and rise of football.* • Link your explanation together using causal signposts that express how one thing leads to another: *the main reason is; because; caused by* (see poster B).
Express it – make your writing sound good	• Vary sentence openings to avoid writing sounding like a dull list, e.g. use adverb starters (*Unfortunately*) mixed with statements (*Experts think . . .*). • Use descriptive language to illustrate key points and help the reader build a picture of what is being explained: *remote moorlands; their purple scales made them clearly visible.* • Use technical language, explaining what it means where necessary: *camouflage; bounty hunters.* • Use different types of sentences to help engage the reader, using short sentences for emphasis and complex sentences for explanation: *So why are they now extinct? It is this colour change that led to their final extinction.*
Check it	• Read your writing aloud: check that it flows and is accurate, and improve it wherever it does not sound quite right.

Remind the class that you can include all the ingredients but still write a poor explanation. They must remember to taste it (read it aloud to test if it works) to help guarantee quality writing.

Of course, such checklists should be matched to the stage the children are working at, so they might be less complex or more demanding. These can be used as a guide for evaluation, marking and feedback.

Stage 2: Innovation

2. Innovation
• Box up new version & talk the text
• Shared writing – innovate on model
• Pupils write own version & guided writing
• Peer assess
• Teacher assesses work – plans next steps
• Feedback & improvement

Figure 7.9

Task: Write an explanation of why dinosaurs became extinct.

Audience and purpose: Pupils and families: Class and school display.

Now that the children have thoroughly internalised the pattern of explanation text, they are in a position to innovate on this pattern and write an explanation themselves, this time explaining why dinosaurs became extinct. Provide a purpose for this, which could be for classroom or school display. Support this process through shared planning and shared writing alongside appropriately devised role-play activities to further strengthen the children's familiarity with the structure and language patterns.

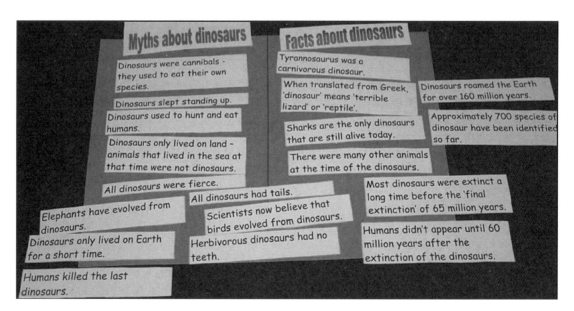

Figure 7.10   Sorting activity to establish what is fact and what is fiction

Because the focus is moving from a fictional explanation to real explanation, the children will first have to be provided with facts and theories about why the dinosaurs died out. Sorting activities are an engaging way of doing this, as illustrated here by an activity for Year 3 children at Warren Farm Academy in Birmingham.

Use a similar 'boxed-up grid' on a flip chart to act as a planner, to demonstrate to the children how to plan their explanation.

- Begin by getting the children to brainstorm some possible reasons why dinosaurs became extinct.

- Then, in pairs, get them to role-play being Professor Know-it-all who can explain precisely why dinosaurs became extinct.

- Using shared writing techniques, work on planning the explanation, continually referring back to the original plan, using it as a basis for creating a plan for the new version.

Boxed-up planning for 'Why did dinosaurs become extinct?'

Heading of each section	*Key points*
Introduce: what is being explained with a hook	• Why dinosaurs became extinct • No certain explanation • Asteroid theory supported by best evidence
Key reason why wiped out	• Massive asteroid collided with earth – destroyed dinosaurs • Evidence – fossil records abruptly end
Which led to a)	• Collision caused dust – no sun – massive climate change
Which led to b)	• Dinosaurs not coping with cold and no food
Conclusion: rounding off	• Died out +50% of all animals

You can now, through shared writing, show them how to move from their plan to the actual writing. It helps to take this bit by bit, having the relevant paragraph from the original displayed on the interactive whiteboard, annotated and colour coded so that the language features stand out. Alongside this, display the plan you have just devised on the writing wall (where you and the class can see it) while you scribe the children's ideas on a flip chart.

Through shared writing, turn each section into fluent writing, involving the children in making decisions, suggesting words and developing sentences. As you do this, get the children to 'magpie' good ideas by jotting them down in their writing journals. Encourage them to push, push, push for the best word and never to dodge a good word, by putting a dotted line under words that are hard to spell (for example, asteroid). This demonstrates how to focus on composition at this stage rather than spending time now looking up the spelling, which can be done at the final draft stage. Taste it – keep reading the shared writing through to encourage the children to get into the habit of reading their writing aloud to see if it sounds right.

You may want to build up the article paragraph by paragraph over a number of days, depending on the children's confidence level. The underlying process is quite simple:

- Gather facts for the new paragraph on your boxed-up plan.

- Refer back to the original.

- Turn the facts into similar sentences.

- Underline or highlight key features, like sentence signposts.

- Keep rereading to maintain flow.

- 'Test out' children's ideas to 'hear' whether they work.

- Ask children to develop sentences in pairs or on mini-whiteboards.

- Pace the writing over two or three days to ensure quality.

- Use the teaching assistant (or a pupil) to flip-chart key phrases and vocabulary to be turned into posters to support the writing.

There are two useful handouts on shared writing in Appendix 2 (see **DVD 2**): **Handout 3** – *The art of shared writing* lists the key ingredients that contribute towards successful shared writing; **Handout 4** lists useful phrases to use when doing shared writing.

Shared writing for why dinosaurs became extinct

It is, in fact, not known for certain why the dinosaurs became extinct. There are several interesting theories. <u>However</u>, the one supported by the most convincing evidence is the asteroid theory.

<u>Around 65 million years ago</u>, a large asteroid or comet collided with earth <u>and</u> it is this that is believed to have destroyed the dinosaurs. <u>This startling conclusion</u> is supported by the fact <u>that</u> their fossil records did not gradually die out across the centuries <u>but</u> abruptly disappeared.

This massive collision <u>caused</u> so much dust to rise into the air <u>that</u> the sun was unable to shine through. The whole earth was plunged into a dim haze, <u>which</u> <u>resulted</u> in a sudden dramatic change of climate.

Dinosaurs were ill equipped to cope with such a drop in temperature <u>and</u>, to make matters worse, their main sources of food were wiped out.

<u>Suddenly</u>, dinosaurs became extinct <u>along with</u> an estimated 50% of all other animal species.

During this shared writing, emphasise that now we are dealing with facts and therefore it's important to be tentative about anything that is not proved. Get the children to identify the tentative language that has been used in the shared writing (*It is, in fact, not known . . .; supported by the most convincing evidence; supported by the fact that . . .; it is believed that . . .*). Add this feature and the examples to the toolkit for explanation writing. If we are not careful, school teaches children to think that only the right answers are important and thus children shy away from being tentative and

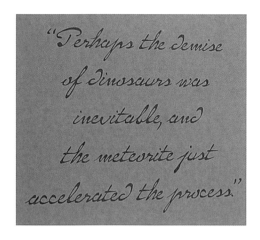

Figure 7.11 A good model of tentative expression

considering other possibilities. They shy away from real thought. Through modelling tentative responses, we can help the children recognise that acknowledging that you are not certain about something is a good thing; it is particularly important in explanation text as the causes of everything are often not known. Provide additional model texts related to your topic that illustrate tentative language, such as this example from the Royal Tyrrell Museum, Canada. Discuss with the children the difference the word *perhaps* makes to the meaning of the sentence.

Once you have led the children through writing a class version of 'Why did dinosaurs become extinct?', they are in a position to write their own versions and should be bursting with ideas for what to say and how to say it. Dinosaurs is a topic that many children will know lots about so they may want to focus on a different theory about why they died out, but steer the children away from the theories that have no scientific evidence to back them up, as fundamentalist websites are full of these!

The children should write independently straight after the shared writing, gradually building their text over a number of days. Use guided writing to teach and support groups in a focused manner. More confident writers might be asked to write a more complex explanation including extra information and moving away from the model (see pages 37–40 for an explanation of how to do this).

Once the children have completed their work, they should be in the habit of sharing their writing with a partner. This should be an opportunity to 'test out' their writing, hearing how it sounds when read aloud. A discussion can follow about what works and what might be done to improve any places where the writing does not flow or engage the reader. Refer back to the 'key ingredients for explanation text' above and use these to focus feedback. Remember, though, that while the children should have included the ingredients, the key factor will be whether their explanation is clear and engaging. Does it work?

The writer now adapts aspects of their work in the light of their partner's comments, remembering that the final choice is the writer's. You may want to encourage them to write their own comment underneath their work focusing on what they think they have done well, how they have improved it and what may still need improving. The teacher then takes the work in for assessment and writes their comment so that it builds on the pupil's comment, creating a dialogue about the best way forward that can be continued in guided writing sessions.

When assessing the whole class' work, the teacher may find it useful to use a grid like the one below to help focus on what aspects of the writing particularly need improving if the children are to become skilled writers of explanations.

Grid to help assess what needs teaching next

Ingredients	Have these ingredients been successfully implemented? Which features now need to be focused on?
Plan it • Can they plan their explanation (box it up)? • Can they hook their reader by introducing what they are explaining in an interesting way? • Can they present explanation clearly and interestingly in logical order? • Can they round the explanation off with an engaging conclusion?	
Link it • Are they using topic sentences effectively to introduce paragraphs and guide the reader? • Can they link the text successfully with causal signposts?	
Express it • Can they add engaging detail appropriately to illustrate key points? • Can they use language that will interest the reader? • Have they used tentative language appropriately? • Are they using interesting and varied words and phrases appropriately? • Are they using a variety of sentence structures?	
Check it • Is there evidence that they are reading their work aloud to see if it sounds good? • Are they improving their work following the peer assessment? • Are they checking their spelling and punctuation?	

Your marking should lead directly into your next piece of teaching. Provide feedback on this work focusing on those areas that the children found most difficult and helping them understand how to edit their work effectively. A visualiser or iPad is a very useful piece of equipment that allows you to present exemplar work from the pupils immediately to the whole class to illustrate the improvements you are seeking.

Model for the children how to reflect on the effectiveness of writing. The more opportunities the children are given to talk about what works and what features make the writing engaging, the more they will be able to develop their own inner judge and craft and edit their own writing effectively. **Handout 5** is full of useful questions to help children reflect on what makes writing effective and discuss what works. If the teacher models this sort of reflection, the children will quickly pick up how to reflect on work. Focus on what makes the text engaging, not on the naming of parts.

Below is a list of some possible problems and the sort of work that may help rectify them.

The problem	Possible activity
Lack of cohesion	Sentence combination
Lacks depth	Provide more model text with additional features
Waffly expression	Improve
Can't judge what works	Compare

The grammar-based activity that research has shown to pay the greatest rewards is sentence combination. Turn whatever type of text you are focusing on into a series of unlinked machine gun sentences. For example:

- An asteroid collided with earth around 65 million years ago.

- Evidence supports the theory that this destroyed the dinosaurs.

- Dinosaur fossil records did not gradually die out over the years.

- Dinosaur fossil records abruptly disappeared.

- The massive collision with the asteroid caused dust to rise into the air.

- The sun was unable to shine through.

- The earth was plunged into a dim haze.

- There was a sudden dramatic change of climate.

- Dinosaurs could not cope with such a drop in temperature.

- Dinosaurs' main sources of food were wiped out.

- Dinosaurs quickly became extinct.

- It is estimated that 50% of all animal species died out.

Through shared writing, illustrate how to link the first few sentences coherently:

> Evidence would suggest **that** the dinosaurs were wiped out **by** an asteroid **that** collided with earth approximately 65 million years ago. **The key evidence supporting this theory** is **the fact that** dinosaur fossil records did not die out gradually over the centuries **but** abruptly disappeared.

Ask the class to complete the text, recasting the sentences in any way they think works best as long as the facts remain the same and then discuss what works.

One of the contributions that the Transforming Writing project made to the development of Talk for Writing was mini-lessons. This would be an excellent point within the unit to set up some mini-lessons so that pupils can focus on the areas that they need help with most (see pages 42–43).

Once they have polished their work you could display it in the classroom and around the school. Creating a book or magazine of the best of the explanations provides excellent exemplar material for future classes.

Stage 3: Independent application

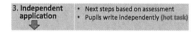

Figure 7.12

Task: Write independently a clear explanation of why an animal is in danger of becoming extinct (for example tigers, pandas) using all the skills you have learned.

Audience and purpose: Classroom display or school magazine.

Once the redrafting of the dinosaur explanations has been assessed, the teacher is now in a good position to move to the third stage where there is more choice. The assessment will direct what has to be focused on during shared and guided sessions.

For this topic, the children will need real information about why particular animals are in danger of extinction. The internet is an excellent source of such information:

- http://tiki.oneworld.org/biodiversity/home.html Tiki the penguin provides a useful guide to evolution and the threat to animal species for young children.

- http://www.planetozkids.com/oban/animals/endanger.htm provides a good overview of typical threats to animal species.

- http://www.kidsplanet.org/factsheets/map.html provides fact sheets on over 50 endangered species sorted by region. They are particularly useful for older children, providing key information about the animals as well as explanation about how and why they are threatened.

Again, model planning using a boxed-up planning grid before the shared writing. You could, perhaps, be working on a class version explaining the threat to koala bears and invite the children to plan and write explanations of the threat to gorillas, pandas or tigers.

The children, working independently, could then box up their plan. Once they have boxed up their plan, get them to turn it into icons and talk their text through. Then they will be able to compose their explanation text more easily as they will have rehearsed the phrases and structure that they want to use. The level of support provided for the independent writing will depend on the needs of the class. You may want to provide an exemplar text on the whiteboard and its related boxed-up planning on the writing wall to remind children of the process. This work could be written on yellow paper to indicate it is the hot task, or you could use a red sticker or tab so that the hot task can easily be identified.

Once the children have completed their work, ask them to read it through carefully and decide how to improve it. After your feedback and partner work, ask them to write their own comment on how well they have completed the task and what they have learned.

End of unit assessment

Final assessment   Compare cold/hot: assess progress

Figure 7.13

The teacher now assesses the final piece of writing (the **hot task**) and looks back at the cold task to see what progress has been made.

Adding your comment to the child's comment helps to promote the dialogue about what needs to be done to improve the child's work. Again, when the work is handed back, focus on one or two areas that everyone needs to improve. This could be indicated by highlighting the areas selected in a particular colour, for example *green for growth*. Provide some teaching relating to these areas and ask the children to immediately improve their work. Then ask them to reflect on their learning by looking back at the cold task and seeing what progress they have made.

The teacher is now in a position to decide which everyday language features will need focusing on in the next unit of work as well as to log any explanation features that will need strengthening when the class next revisits explanation writing across the curriculum.

Mastering the approach across the curriculum

Once children can cope with explanation writing independently, their skills can be applied and developed across the curriculum. This embedding of the skills in a range of contexts to provide depth and breadth is essential if the children are to achieve mastery of the skills that underpin effective explanation writing. Finding opportunities to embed skills across the curriculum is particularly valuable because it helps the children put their understanding of what they have learned into practice. For example, in technology they need to be able to explain how a particular thing works. The science curriculum is based on explanation. In

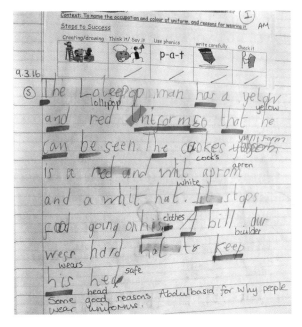

Figure 7.14   Reception child's explanation of why some people wear uniforms

history, it helps them explain a series of events logically and consider a range of perspectives; in geography they will need to explain a range of natural phenomena as well as how people have adapted the landscape in order to survive. Right across the curriculum so many things need explaining. Video clips 30–34 illustrate how the approach is being developed across the primary curriculum. If you choose a very simple explanation focus like *Why do some people wear different uniforms for their work*, then such embedding of skills can begin in reception as illustrated here, by a reception child from St Matthew's Primary, Nechells, Birmingham. This work was part of their People and Communities curriculum and built on the explanation skills they had learned in their English lessons.

However, explanation text is not always as easy to apply across the curriculum as the other non-fiction texts because the tune of explanation, in say science or maths, is often very different from that of explanation in more imaginative topics. Scientific and mathematical explanation has to be factual, accurate and precise. If the text you want the children to be able to write is significantly different from that which they have written in English, it may be advisable to take the children through the first two stages again. For example, science investigation is a mix of non-fiction text types including recount, information and discussion, but it is predominantly explanation. For such complex hybrid explanation text, it is useful to get the language of investigation into the children's heads using imitation and innovation techniques, after which they would be in a position to write up such

Figure 7.15   Year 1 child using a text map in science

investigations independently. The story of how the Talk for Writing approach has been developed to suit the needs of science investigations is an interesting one. With the help of secondary science teachers, the worked example below was developed. This approach proved to work so well that it has since been adapted to meet the needs of Key Stage 4 and Key Stage 5 science students as well as being adapted to introduce science investigations to Year 1, as pictured above at Selby Primary School, Yorkshire. Examples of these extensions are available after the worked example below.

Moving from imitation to innovation to independent application for science investigations

Non-fiction work in English will not have provided a similar enough model to the language required for science investigation to enable the children to write an investigation effectively. The children need to be guided through the imitation, innovation, independent application journey. It is not normally possible to do this within one unit as you will need a new topic to investigate in order to innovate on the investigation model. Therefore, it makes sense to see the first investigation as providing the model that can then be innovated on by subsequent investigations moving towards the pupil being able to independently write up any investigation.

So, this investigation into what happens to the heart when you exercise will provide the model to be imitated, and the next investigation will innovate on the model. The pupils will use each subsequent investigation to develop their innovation skills through internalising the pattern of language required until they can write up a science investigation independently in a range of ways.

- **Objective:** To write clear science investigations.

- **Task:** Write up your investigation into what happens to the heart when you exercise.

- **Context:** This would be taught at the end of a unit focusing on the effect on the heart of taking exercise. The children would have already carried out the investigation and therefore would have lots of knowledge about the topic but probably would lack the skills to express this knowledge effectively.

Establishing the baseline: At the beginning of a new investigation, it is not logical to set a cold task because prior to the unit the pupils would lack sufficient information to 'have a go'. But, to establish a baseline for expression, you could use features identified as needing attention from the last piece of written science work. To establish prior knowledge of content, KWL grids (What do I know? What do I want to know? What have I learned?) are useful.

The imitation stage

Devise an appropriate model text that contains the typical structure and language features of science investigation, suited to the level of the children. Then turn the text into a text map with images and symbols to help the pupils recall the text, and use this to help the children internalise the text orally. The text below covers the first four stages of a science investigation.

Figure 7.16   Text map for science investigation of the relationship between exercise and heart rate

Once the children have thoroughly internalised the text orally, show them the written version of the text.

Investigation: Does exercise affect heart rate?

I am investigating what happens to my heart when I take exercise.

My prediction, what I think will happen, is that exercise will make my heart beat faster because the heart has to pump blood faster to enable me to do the exercise.

To carry out an investigation, you must compare two variables: two things that change or vary. For this investigation, I will compare my heart rate when I am resting and when I am taking exercise.

However, it is important to make the test fair. To make this test fair, I must time my heart for exactly the same amount of time when I am resting as when I am exercising. It is essential that all the other conditions remain the same because, otherwise, I wouldn't know if it was the exercise or something else that was making the difference.

Boxed-up planning for a science investigation: 'Does exercise affect heart rate?'

Box up the basic pattern so that the underlying structure can clearly be seen. This will provide the basic structure for the children when they come to write another science investigation.

Boxing-up science investigations – establishing the structure	
• What is being investigated	
• Best guess (hypothesis)	
• The variables	
• Making it fair	

Figure 7.17

Lead the children through the annotation of the ingredients of each paragraph so that they identify the phrases that can be reused (see highlighted text below) as well as discuss the techniques that the writer uses. In this example, particularly stress the sentence signposts that help link the explanation together. The resulting science investigation toolkit should be displayed as this will drive the shared and independent writing, as well as informing self-peer evaluation and feedback from the teacher.

The children should draw their own text map to help them internalise the investigation. They could then write up the investigation for homework just using the text map to assist them. This would then have established the basic tune of science investigation.

The innovation stage

When the children do their next investigation, they could be shown how to innovate on the model text that they internalised. Display the text and highlight all the transferable generic investigation text that could be used for any science investigation, as illustrated below:

I am investigating what happens to my heart **when** I take exercise.

My prediction, what I think will happen, is that exercise will make my heart beat faster **because** the heart has to pump blood faster to enable me to do the exercise.

To carry out an investigation, you must compare two variables: two things that change or vary. For this investigation, I will compare my heart rate when I am resting **and** when I am taking exercise.

However, it is important to make the test fair. To make this test fair, I must time my heart for **exactly the same** amount of time **when** I am resting **as when** I am exercising. **It is essential that all the other conditions remain the same because, otherwise, I wouldn't know if it was the** exercise **or something else that was making the difference.**

How much support the class will need at the innovation stage will very much depend on the age of the class. Through shared discussion alone, older classes may now be in a position to co-construct orally how this text can be adapted to meet the needs of whatever they have just investigated. They could then create a text map for this innovation, talk the text in pairs and write it.

For younger classes not yet familiar with the pattern of science investigation, the class would need to be shown how to innovate on the original model through shared planning followed by shared writing. Illustrate how to plan writing up the investigation by continually referring back to the original plan, using it as a basis for creating a plan for the new version. In this way, you can use the highlighted sections of the original model to act as a talking frame and get the children to tell you what should be inserted to make the investigation fit the new investigation. This can then be summed up in your boxed-up planning. You can now, through shared writing, show them how to move from their plan to the actual writing. It helps to take this bit by bit, having the relevant paragraph from the original displayed on the interactive whiteboard, annotated and colour coded so that the language features stand out.

During the shared writing, once the children are more confident with the tune of science investigations, you can demonstrate how the standard phrases used to introduce each section can be varied, as well as alternative ways of best inserting the relevant information from the investigation. Display the plan you have just devised on the washing line where you and the class can see it, while you scribe the children's ideas on a flip chart.

Through shared writing, turn each section into fluent writing, involving the children in making decisions, suggesting words and developing alternative ways of expressing points.

The process is exactly the same as before:

- Gather facts for the new paragraph on the boxed-up plan.

- Refer back to the original.

- Turn the facts into similar sentences.

The children should then be in a position to innovate on this pattern and write an investigation independently themselves. This is why expanding pupils' writing across the curriculum is not just a case of technical vocabulary as the new curriculum would have us believe (see page 61).

Moving towards independence

Now that the children have the model in their heads, they will increasingly be able to adapt it to suit the requirements of any science investigation. Provide them with the original highlighted model text and the planning frame and remind them of the process. When you think the children are ready, challenge them to write up an investigation on their own, independently, without displaying the model or the boxed-up planning.

Figure 7.18   Text map for Year 1 science investigation

How this has been adapted to suit pupils from the age of 5 to 19?

At Selby Community Primary School in North Yorkshire, this approach is used to support children from EYFS to Year 6 with science investigations.

Look at the text map above and you can see that it is depicting the model text for a Year 1 investigation into what would happen if plants aren't watered, being innovated by asking what happens if plants don't get sunlight. When you look at the original model text for this below, you immediately recognise the generic high frequency phrases or 'science sentence signposts' that are being used. The children and staff at Selby CP have developed whole-school actions for the key generic vocabulary of science investigations and images of the children demonstrating the actions are displayed on the classroom wall. This has been turned into a handout – see **Handout 8** in Appendix 3 on **DVD 2**.

Figure 7.19   Fair test

What would happen if I didn't give a plant water?
I am investigating what happens to a plant if it has no water.

What I think will happen
I think that the plant will not grow because it has no water. The green plant will die as a result of lack of water. Plants need water to grow.

To carry out my investigation
I will compare two plants. One plant will have water and the other will not have water. I will put them both on the windowsill so that they have sunlight.

It is important to make our test fair. To make this test fair, I will put the same amount of seeds in the same size cup. It is essential that the conditions remain the same so that I know what a plant needs to grow.

My results
I left the cups on the windowsill for a week. The seeds in one cup grew. The seeds in the other cup didn't grow at all. This is because this cup didn't have any water. I have found out that plants need water to grow and stay alive.

The children internalised the model text so they could imitate it. The teacher then used Post-its to show them how to innovate this so that this time one of the plants was deprived of sunlight. The children then carried out their own investigation into this and wrote it up as illustrated.

Applying the approach to science is still relatively in its infancy but so far, due to the enjoyment of Talk for Writing across all years at Selby CP, it is having a positive effect. While we do not know what difference it would make if children were taught how to express and recall science like this throughout primary and on into secondary, the extra understanding of high frequency scientific vocabulary and the ability to form a coherent and well thought out experiment has shown promise so far.

The science department at Slough and Eton C of E Business College adapted this idea of using model text and boxing up answers for science investigations initially to suit the needs of Key Stage 4 pupils, in the hope of improving the pupils' attainment at GCSE. To the left is the boxed-up plan that the students applied to investigations. Pupils started to double their scores in tests, gaining 8–9/9, as opposed to 4–5/9. The science department found the approach so effective that they then started using it from Year 7 onwards and extended it into the sixth form where it helps the students answer synoptic essay questions.

Task

You are going to plan an investigation to find out how effective different washing powders are at removing stains. **Before** writing discuss how you will complete this investigation

You must include everything in the table below and complete the plan as a group A1 paper.

Aim	Rewrite the following changing the words in bold: Aim To investigate whether **light intensity** affects **the rate of photosynthesis**
Variables	For this investigation identify the : Independent variable Dependent variable Controlled variables (at least three) Use the pictures to help you remember the definitions for each
Method	Step by step instructions on how to complete th experiment. Write in bullet points Include specific measurements Make the experiment reliable

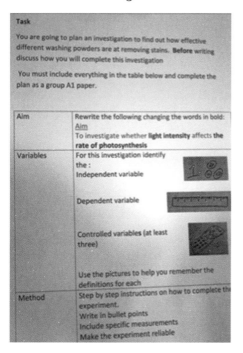

Figure 7.20 Generic boxed-up planning for science investigations

They also discovered the power of text mapping. Not only could text mapping be used to help pupils imitate investigations at the start of Key Stage 3 but it was also extremely powerful as a way of helping students internalise the content of the science curriculum at Key Stage 4. They found that if the teacher spoke a model piece of science text to the students, they quickly established the art of turning what they heard into symbols which helped them recall the facts as well as express them coherently. If you look at the images here of text maps in science, you will see that they are all very different. They are different students' ways of picturing the same text. The students like the approach because of its individuality and, of course, it makes them really concentrate as you cannot text map without

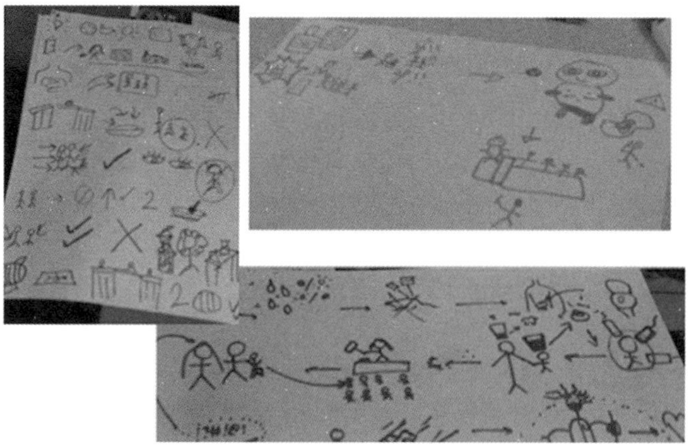

Figure 7.21 Text mapping allows pupils to personalise how they represent information

giving the process your full attention. The head of science summed up why they like the approach as follows:

- *The students feel pride in their own improvement and success.*

- *The staff really like it.*

- *It's slashed the time we have to spend on marking.*

- *There's a real sense of 'Let's see what we can do now'.*

- *There's much more conversation about teaching and learning now.*

Nasrin Ahmed, a teacher at Yew Tree Community Primary School in Birmingham, is developing a guide for progression in science enquiry year by year. The grid is divided into the following sections:

- Working scientifically – secure enquiry structure.

- Year group-specific enquiry types.

- Explanation-specific phrasing.

- Science vocabulary.

An extract from Year 1: Working scientifically is illustrated below. It is hoped that these will be available for teachers to purchase from www.talk4writing.com in the near future.

Year 1

Working scientifically – secure enquiry structure	Year group specific enquiry types	Explanation specific phrases	Science vocabulary (Not complete list)
Science Question Start to think about simple Science Questions by themselves (Are all material water resistant?) Prediction Make simple predictions Resources Identify simple equipment and resources	**Science Question** Children ask simple questions and recognise that they can be answered in different ways **Observation over Time** Pupils observe changes over time and use simple scientific language to describe this *(In Autumn the leaves fell and then in Spring the flowers started to blossom)* **Observation** **Observing closely, using simple equipment** *(hand lens, egg timers)*	Question Starters What is the best material for ... Who might ... How many layers of clothing might I ... When I observe ... I have sorted the animals that eat grass I predict that ...	deciduous evergreen, bulbs, stem amphibians, reptiles, fish, mammals, carnivores, herbivores, omnivores

Figure 7.22   Teaching guide for progression in scientific enquiry by N Ahmed, Yew Tree Community School, Birmingham

Persuasion

What is persuasion text?

Figure 8.1 Persuasion text map

Persuasion text is any text designed to persuade the reader to think or act in a particular way. From a very young age, most children have worked out that emotional blackmail can be a good way of persuading others to do what they want. This appeal to the emotions, hopefully in a less extreme form, is a key ingredient of persuasive text.

Like most non-fiction, persuasion writing begins with an introduction to inform the reader of what the writer is 'selling' – this is normally presented as a 'hook' to encourage the reader to want to learn more.

Ordering persuasive text is based on the logic of persuasion, with a series of points building one viewpoint. Paragraphs are ordered and linked to maximise their impact on the reader: emotive signposts draw the reader into the logic of the persuader. With short persuasive text, the opening statement is often the topic sentence for the whole piece: the following short punchy sentences back it up. With longer persuasive text, such as editorials, there will be a topic sentence for every paragraph as is usual for most non-fiction text. The style tends to be very personal, often directly addressing the reader as 'you', with exaggerated or deceptive language aimed at attracting the reader's interest.

To write an effective piece of persuasion, the author needs to have a very good eye for the audience being appealed to and to craft the text accordingly. They also need to have, or at least appear to have, a real enthusiasm for what they are promoting. This is why linking persuasion writing to real events like the school fete is so important because then children actually know something in detail about what they are trying to promote and will, hopefully, want to promote it.

We live in a world full of promotional text. Children, from an early age, need to understand the tricks of the persuasion trade in order to defend themselves against the more aggressive forms of advertising that may be subtly pitched at them. This is summed up disturbingly by this extract from *The Week*, in February 2010, from its column 'Spirit of the Age':

> *Children are being recruited by marketing agencies to promote fizzy drinks and computer games to their friends. The 'brand ambassadors', some as young as seven, can earn up to £25 a week in vouchers for 'chatting' about certain products – online or off – or hosting parties where the items are distributed. 'Don't start up a chat about the product,' advises marketing agency Dubit Insider. 'It's best to look for natural opportunities to drop it into the conversation.'*

Typical features of persuasion text

Audience	Someone you are trying to influence
Purpose	To promote a particular view or product in order to influence what people think or do
Typical structure	• Logical order • A series of points building one viewpoint • Paragraphs with topic sentence in introduction (and in all paragraphs for longer text) • Often includes images to attract attention
Typical language features	• Personal and direct, often informal (friendly) • Emotive sentence signposts • Opinions presented as facts • Use of the imperative • Use of language that sounds good, including slogans • Weasel words (emotive language designed to deceive/give best impression)
Examples	• Adverts • Newspaper editorials • Promotional leaflets • Pamphlets promoting a particular viewpoint

Choosing a persuasive writing topic

Research suggests that we are exposed to more than 3000 adverts a day and now, with the rise and rise of the internet, that advertising can be targeted precisely. Therefore, advertising is an obvious choice as a focus for persuasive writing. The trick is to come up with something that the children are interested in, like mobile phones, and devise work around that. Be prepared to be overwhelmed by their technical knowledge. Make certain that warm-up activities help the children to practise the language of advertising so that, by the time they come to design their adverts, they are alive with ideas about how to select just the right images, words and phrases to make their adverts effective. In addition, promoting school events can provide a real audience and purpose for the writing as well as easily accessible information on which to develop the promotional text.

Leaflets or letters promoting particular viewpoints can also be an excellent choice as long as they are linked to an issue that the children are genuinely interested in. I have seen children working enthusiastically on letters to the headteacher persuading her to tell the school to set more or less homework for children; linking this to Harry Potter and Hogwarts can be even more involving. School uniform, healthy eating, bullying, etc. provide real issues that the children care about. For this type of persuasive writing the children have to think carefully about their audience and decide on the best way to persuade them – will they need facts or can you just appeal to their good nature? They may need to try using counterarguments so that they tackle any queries the reader might have. It is also important to remind them not to overstate their case but rather to provide good reasons, helpful facts and explain why something might be important.

Whatever focus you choose, remember the golden rule: the topic must engage the children so they have something that they really want to express. Without this essential foundation, their persuasion cannot persuade.

Audience and purpose

Always provide some sort of audience and purpose for whatever focus is chosen. Clip 38 shows how making a film provides a great purpose. It can be useful to get the children to draw a picture of someone who is typical of the audience to help them remember who they are writing for and to pitch their persuasion accordingly.

Some key uses of persuasion writing skills across the curriculum

- Promoting school events and trips (cross curricular).

- Promoting particular viewpoints on school-related issues (English and PSHE).

- Promoting products or inventions (technology).

- Promoting localities, events or particular viewpoints (history, geography and RE).

- Promoting the perspective of characters from novels or mythical creatures (English).

- Promoting favourite reads (English).

Warming up the tune of the text

To help children write effective persuasion text, time must be spent helping them understand what language features give persuasion its particular flavour. They can then begin to recognise persuasive techniques when they hear or see them and begin to use them in their speaking and writing. What are the language patterns and sentence signposts, or the vocabulary, that are typical of persuasive writing?

Understanding the power of sentence signposts to link paragraphs, sentences and information within sentences is key to achieving cohesive text that flows logically. Appendix 3 (see **DVD 2**) covers linking text and includes useful handouts to support work in this area. The language of explanation can be used very persuasively. The picture here shows persuasive sentences crafted by Year 6 pupils from Burnley Brow Primary in Lancashire on Post-it notes.

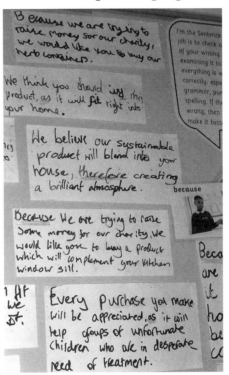

Figure 8.2   Displaying persuasive phrasing

For any work on persuasive writing, daily games like the one illustrated above need to be devised that will help the children familiarise themselves with the pattern of persuasive writing and the types of vocabulary that go with it, at an appropriate level for the class. Activities that co-construct understanding of what persuasive writing is like are an essential step in helping children master writing skills. Practising the tune of the text through talking will enable the children to manipulate what they have to say effectively, selecting just the right words, phrases and sentence patterns when they finally write it down. The examples below can all be adapted to suit a wide range of ages. Persuasive writing lends itself to:

Tuning into the language games

- **The persuasion game:** In pairs, swapping roles, take one minute to persuade in a monologue:

  - a snowman to come into the kitchen out of the cold;

  - a dragon to stop eating maidens.

- **The weasel words game:** Advertisements are often full of weasel words with positive associations that encourage the reader to want to buy the product being promoted. Devise an activity where the children have to sort the words and phrases like the ones in the boxes below into these categories:

  - negative (puts the reader off);

  - neutral (the reader has no associations with this word);

  - positive (the reader is attracted by this).

brown	natural	dull	exciting	usual	street
unique	dirty	day	deserted	brat	muddy brown
child	depressing	dusky brown	weather	hero	refreshing

- **The make-it-positive game:** Give the children a short negative passage, like the example below. Ask the children to rewrite it to make the impact positive without altering any of the nouns (underlined in the extract). This is a good game for reinforcing the function of nouns, adjectives, adverbs and verbs and the importance of selecting just the right word to create the effect that you want.

  > Ominous <u>alleyways</u> led to deserted <u>squares</u> where thin <u>cats</u> slinked in the <u>shadows</u> and the <u>street lamps</u> flickered. Strange <u>men</u> lurked in <u>doorways</u>, scowling fiercely as they played <u>cards</u>.

Help the children select words (mainly adjectives) that create a positive mood, like this:

> Charming <u>alleyways</u> led to secret <u>squares</u> where cosseted <u>cats</u> slept in the <u>shadows</u> and the <u>street lamps</u> welcomed. Old <u>men</u> chatted in <u>doorways</u>, quietly reminiscing as they played <u>cards</u>.

- **Magpieing persuasive language techniques from real text:** Provide copies of whatever type of promotional material you are focusing on and get the children to find examples of a range of persuasive language features. Encourage the children to magpie useful vocabulary from this activity. (See page 198 for a worked example.)

- **Cloze procedure targeting persuasive language:** Write a short persuasive passage related to the focus of your unit, then delete key emotive words. The children, in pairs, have to see if they can come up with appropriate words to fill the gaps. Encourage the children to magpie useful vocabulary from this activity. (See page 199 for a worked example.)

Tuning into persuasive sentence signposts games

- **Sorting the signposts:** Devise 16 or 20 sentence signposts printed on card signalling:

  - Ridicule

    o   anyone who thinks like this is an idiot (persuasion);

  - Neutrality

    o   different viewpoints need considering (discussion);

  - Complexity/uncertainty

    o   no easy definite view (discussion);

  - Agreement

    o   all sensible people think like this (persuasion).

For example:

- On the other hand . . .

- Now is the time to stand up . . .

- A counterargument is . . .

- Are we going to let . . .

- This is just the sort of namby pamby . . .

- We are all united . . .

- Is there anyone who . . .

- Perhaps the answer is . . .

- There can be no one who still thinks . . .

- One probable explanation is . . .

Ask the children in pairs to sort the cards into the four categories and to be prepared to read out the 'ridicule' and 'agreement' phrases in an appropriate tone of voice. Explain that some of the phrases could fit more than one category – it all depends on the context and the tone used. Pairs that finish first could come up with additional examples.

- **Spot the ridicule and agreement signposts:** Select some news articles that will interest the children and that are full of good examples of ridicule or agreement signposts (*The Sun* or *Donald Trump* can be relied on as a good source of these). Get the children, in pairs, to highlight them. Encourage them to magpie useful examples for future use.

Tuning into the text games

- **Role play:** Ask the children to enact aspects of the topic, for example telephone calls to a local secondary school enquiring about facilities, or from computer gaming companies or mobile phone promoters. This works best if the children sit back to back. Not being able to see the person you are talking to makes it easier to stay in role.

- **What = 'good' for this sort of writing:** Write four different introductions to whatever persuasive text you want the children to write, one of which is better than the rest. Include one example that is worthy but extremely dull and one that has lost the plot (i.e. it is not a piece of persuasive writing but is recount or instruction). There should be no surface errors in any of the text – you want the children to focus on the pattern of the language not surface error. Children select which is best, given the purpose, and suggest the ingredients that make it the best. This can be snowballed from pairs to fours to eights, and then the whole class can co-construct their key ingredients for an effective persuasive introduction.

- **Warming up the content when promoting a viewpoint:** The children brainstorm all the arguments they can in favour of and against the issue being focused on. Collate all the ideas then let each child choose which side of the argument they want to be on. They then practise in pairs presenting a persuasive argument in support of their view.

  This activity can then be strengthened by asking the children to decide in what order they want to present their points and getting them to draw a symbol to represent each point in order. Working in pairs, with just the symbols to support them, they present their argument to their partner, introducing and linking their points in a persuasive manner. Ask children to perform some of the more effective presentations to the whole class and encourage the children to magpie good phrases that they might want to use when they write their persuasive argument.

- **Sequencing the text:** Find a good short exemplar of whatever sort of persuasive text you are focusing on and rearrange the paragraphs – make sure that, when it is cut into paragraphs, the children cannot put it together again using the cut marks. In groups, the children have to sequence the text, then read the sequenced text aloud to check it is coherent, and finally be prepared to explain the order in which they have placed the text. Ask them to identify any sentence signposts that helped them decide on the order of the text and magpie these for future possible use.

Warming up understanding of design

- **Using book-talk techniques to warm up understanding:** Design usually plays a key role in persuasive text, so helping children understand design through warming-up activities is important. Set the children a design task that engages them, for example design a mobile phone advert pitched at the 9/10/11-year-old market.

- First, in pairs, ask them to discuss what ingredients they might want to include – what sort of images, colours, words and phrases they might use to persuade their audience to want to own this phone.

- Next, deepen their understanding by presenting them with an intriguing mobile phone advert and ask them to discuss with their partner very open-ended questions like 'Tell me what you can see'; 'Tell me what you think the purpose is'; 'Tell me who you think this advert is aimed at', etc. Don't be tempted to answer the questions yourself but slowly let the class, through their feedback, reflect on how the design and the text work together to help persuade the audience. Use the children's responses to build up an ingredients list for effective advert design. You may want to take this opportunity to model, through shared writing, how to annotate the advert to bring out the design features. The children, in groups, can then be challenged to make a rough draft of an advert design, and prepare to present the advert to a panel – *Apprentice* style – explaining why it would be effective. (Note, this is a hybrid text activity combining the language of persuasion and the language of explanation.) For a full explanation of Book Talk, see Aidan Chambers's *Tell Me* (Thimble Press).

How to plan a persuasive unit in Talk for Writing style

This image sums up the Talk for Writing process. If you have not already read Chapter 2, which explains this process in detail, you will find it useful to read that chapter before thinking about how the process can be applied to persuasive text. **Handout 1** is an expanded version of this process with more detail about the key essential features, as well as some optional suggestions that schools have found useful in helping children make progress – see Appendix 2, **DVD 2**.

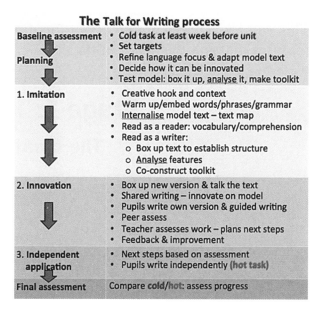

Figure 8.3   The Talk for Writing process

Worked example for persuasion text

Below is a worked example of the three stages of the Talk for Writing approach bookended by the initial and final assessments to ensure formative assessment is at the heart of the planning, teaching and learning process.

Objective: To be able to write persuasive text.

Topic for imitation, innovation and independent application: Promotional leaflets for local attractions.

Audience and purpose: Competition to produce the best promotional leaflet.

Baseline assessment and planning

Baseline assessment
- Cold task at least week before unit
- Set targets

Planning
- Refine language focus & adapt model text
- Decide how it can be innovated
- Test model: box it up, analyse it, plan toolkit

Figure 8.4

For any unit of work on persuasion you have to think first about what persuasive writing skills the class already possesses. As explained in Chapter 2, a good way of doing this is to set a **cold task**. This should be set at least a week before you begin to teach your unit so that you can alter your planning to suit the needs of the class. The pupils will need a familiar context (for example, write a leaflet promoting a forthcoming school event) so that they have something to write about that they know about and that interests them. Warm the topic up with a quick discussion but do not provide any teaching in how to write about this subject. This will help you pinpoint what specific skills to focus on in the unit to help the children progress. Assess this work and decide what language features to focus on within the unit as well as setting targets for children with different levels of attainment. This will also enable you to adapt the model text to ensure that it illustrates the features that suit the needs of the class.

Stage 1: Imitation

The creative hook

1. Imitation
- Creative hook and context
- Warm up/embed words/phrases/grammar
- Internalise model text – text map
- Read as a reader: vocabulary/comprehension
- Read as a writer:
  - Box up text to establish structure
  - Analyse features
  - Co-construct toolkit

Figure 8.5

Since the innovation focus later on in this unit is selling the school as a weekend attraction and the independent hot task will be on promoting the area as a tourist attraction, these entertaining topics lend themselves to becoming a competition which can be used as the hook for the start of the unit. You could ask the headteacher to come into the class and explain that both the school and the local council need more funds and so there is going to be a competition for who can come up with the best leaflets advertising the school as a weekend attraction and the area as a tourist attraction.

Warming up the tune of persuasion

Games and activities devised to familiarise the children with the typical language pattern of persuasive text and the context of the unit are key to success. As the games are played, flip-chart the vocabulary, sentence signposts and key sentence patterns that emerge and start to create a toolkit of useful ingredients for persuasion text to support the children's speaking and writing. Display these to make the learning visible and develop them throughout the unit. If the children have already been taught this text type in Talk for Writing style, build on their existing toolkit for persuasion.

Tune the children into the style of this sort of persuasive writing by reading leaflets to them and providing leaflets for them to read. This might be done in quiet reading or as part of guided reading.

Below are four warming-up-the-text activities to help the children become confident in the language of persuasive leaflets. The order of these activities is important. The first provides them with some of the key vocabulary that they will meet in the unit, the second introduces some of the key persuasive language techniques, the third scaffolds the use of this language and the fourth provides an opportunity for the children to start talking the language of persuasion.

To help children internalise new words for any non-fiction unit in English and across the curriculum, you might:

1. Begin with a Never-heard-the-word grid to flag up the key vocabulary of the unit

- List up to 20 words on a sheet.

- Give every pupil a copy of the sheet and present it as a challenge. If you think they haven't met the terms before, tell them not to worry if they get none of the words right at the beginning of the unit, but the aim is for everyone to get full marks when they revisit the sheet at the end of the unit and, of course, they should then be able to spell every word.

- Say each word clearly and then repeat it in a sentence which provides context but doesn't give away its meaning. It's important for pupils to understand that you know a word by the company that it keeps.

- Allow enough time after each word for the pupils to tick the *never heard the word* column, *heard it but not sure of its meaning* column, or to quickly jot down a meaning and/or example.

- Ask the pupils to put their score at the end of the activity. This activity will bring to the front of the pupils' minds vocabulary they may have heard before but had forgotten about, and it flags up all the key vocabulary coming their way soon. It also gives you a good idea of which words must be focused on most.

- Let them know that you are not going to go over any of the words now but will introduce each word in context as it's needed for the unit. Then, as soon as the words are introduced in context, provide alternative more familiar words for each word plus lots of opportunities for the children to practise using the words themselves in a range of contexts so that they start to internalise how the word can be used.

Below is the beginning of a Never-heard-the-word grid for this unit.

	Never heard before	*Heard – not sure of meaning*	*Know what it means: give a simple explanation plus an example*
1. attraction			
2. junction			
3. ample			
4. imperative			
5. alliteration			
6. rhetorical question			
7. . . .			

2. Magpieing persuasive language techniques from real text

Provide copies of genuine promotional leaflets for local attractions and give the children one example from these leaflets of each of a range of persuasive techniques as illustrated below:

- Informal language – see asterisked examples below

- Questions – *Are bored children driving you crazy?**

- Alliteration – *Dino Dig & the Wacky Workshop**

- Rhyme – *Dora the Explorer**

- Repetition – *Find us to find the fun**

- Imperatives (bossy sentences) – *Don't forget Lemurland!**

- Personal appeal – *You can get up close and personal**

- Boastful language – *The World's oldest tourist attraction*

- Patterns of three – *Visit. Shop it. Love it.**

- Short sentences – *Discover Wildwood*

- Language aimed at audience, e.g. *Txt**

- Play on words – *Make all your screams come true*

- Testimonials/quotes – '*Join us for a great day out*' – *David Bellamy**

Encourage the children to magpie useful vocabulary from this activity and turn the list into a poster of persuasive language tricks to support their later writing, as pictured here – note 'It's time you came and Saurus', a great pun from a dinosaur theme park. This will form a key part of the persuasion toolkit that will be co-constructed with the class throughout the unit.

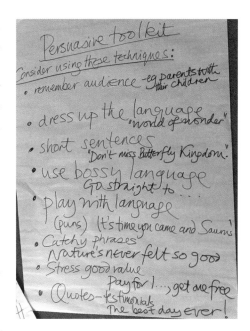

Figure 8.6   Persuasive toolkit – consider using these techniques

3. Cloze procedure targeting boastful language

The children, in pairs, have to see if they can come up with appropriate descriptive words to fill the gaps. It is also entertaining to play this game from the opposite perspective and get the children to select the negative language for the gaps. Encourage the children to magpie useful vocabulary from this activity.

For sale – a _____ opportunity to buy a _____, _____ school building, _____ for conversion. This _____ of a building would make a _____ setting for 6 flats, _____ placed for the shopping centre and railway, _____ grounds and _____ car parking is a _____ bonus. Complete with a _____ that money just cannot buy. The _____ school bell adds that _____ flavour.

4. Role play to tune the children into persuasive language

Now get the children to start talking in persuasive mode. Model a telephone conversation between a potential house buyer and a local estate agent. Displaying a picture of a wreck of a building is a useful visual aid here – and they are easy to find online. Then ask the children to hold their own mobile phone conversations.

Internalising the model text

Having warmed up the tune of persuasion, the children can now start to focus on imitating a persuasive text. Write a simple model persuasion text (in this instance a promotional leaflet for a mythical local attraction) that contains its typical structure and language features, appropriate to the level of the children but ensuring that there is an edge of challenge. Do not show the children the text at this stage. They are going to hear it and internalise it orally before they see it.

Now turn the text into a text map full of images and symbols to help the children recall the text. You may want to have one text map per paragraph and display them as a washing line. Talk the text for the children with actions, getting the children to join in. Move from whole-class retelling to groups and finally pairs so that ultimately everyone can retell the text on their own. You may want to refer to video clip 35 on **DVD 2** to remind you how to do this.

To help learn the text, children should draw their own text maps. These may be annotated with anything that causes problems.

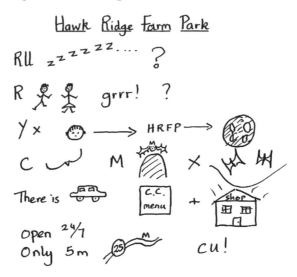

Figure 8.7 Text map for *Hawk Ridge Farm Park*

Retell the text in various different ways to help the children internalise the text:

- retell it silently;
- hold a race to see who can say it the quickest (see Clip 37);
- in pairs say it sentence by sentence;
- prepare to present to children in another class.

1a) Reading as a reader

Once the children have thoroughly internalised the text orally, present the text that they have internalised to the children and start by reading it as a reader.

Hawk Ridge Farm Park

Are you ever bored at the weekend? **Are the** kids driving you crazy? <u>**Why not** head straight to Hawk Ridge Farm Park and enter a world of wonder?</u>

- See eagles fly. Marvel at the bats' cave. Don't miss Butterfly Valley.

- There is ample parking, a cool café and a great shop.

- We're open all day every day from 10.00 am – 6.00 pm

- **Only** 5 minutes from junction 25 of the motorway!

See you there!

They should be able to read it because they have internalised the language, but that does not mean they have fully understood the meaning of the words. The more you have used actions and alternative words to help them understand the meaning, the more comprehension they will have of the meaning of the text.

Construct some comprehension questions for the children to initially discuss in pairs to open up discussion on the text and ensure the children have understood what they are reading:

- Why do you think the leaflet begins by asking if you are bored at weekends?

- Why do you think that eagles are the first attraction mentioned?

- Why do you think the leaflet mentions parking, the café and the shop?

- Why do you think the information about opening hours and how to get there is left to near the end, but isn't at the very end of the leaflet?

Read other examples and leaflets, gathering more persuasion techniques. These are readily available from most hotels, railway stations and information centres.

Help the children deepen their understanding of the text, becoming increasingly familiar with the structure and language patterns by using the following sorts of activities:

- Draw a map of Hawk Ridge Farm Park.

- Ring a friend, trying to persuade them to visit Hawk Ridge Farm Park with you.

- In role as the director of the park, explain why everyone should visit the park.

- Make a one-minute presentation, explaining what a good time you have had at the park.

1b) Reading as a writer

Once the children have fully understood the text, you can then start reading it as a writer, identifying the language features that can be reused as well as analysing the techniques that the writer has used to make the writing effective.

Boxing up the text

The first thing for the children to think about when trying to understand how a text has been written is its structure, so show the children how to box up this text. Normally that would mean counting the paragraphs and creating a boxed-up version with one box for each paragraph. But leaflets are often written in bullet points, like the example below, so here it is more a question of boxing up the clumps of information presented and deciding why it has been presented in this order.

Box up the basic pattern with the children, asking them to tell you what different clumps of information there are so that the underlying structure can clearly be seen. The more they see you create the structure in front of them, and are involved in analysing it, the more they will be able to understand it. See Clip 36.

Boxed-up planning for Hawk Ridge Farm Park leaflet

Heading for each section	*Key points*
Introduce venue with hook to engage reader	• Begin with personal problem in question form – Present attraction as a solution
Attractions	• Highlight three attractions – eagles; bats' cave; Butterfly Valley
Facilities	• parking • café • shop
Useful information	• When open • How to get there
Conclusion	• Slogan to seal deal

Display this boxed-up plan because it will provide the basic structure for the shared writing innovation and the children's work when they come to create their own versions.

Now help the children identify language features that can be reused as well as discussing the techniques that the writer uses. In this example, help the children identify the persuasive techniques and add them to the toolkit of persuasive techniques if they are not already there:

- speaking directly to the audience – imperatives and friendly informal language: *you . . .; kids . . .; Don't . . .*;

- use of rhetorical questions: *Are you . . .? Are the . . .?*;

- alliteration: *cool café; World of wonder*;

- patterns of three: *There is ample parking, a cool café and a great shop*;

- boastful (emotive) language: *wonder, marvel, cool*;

- short sentences: *Don't miss Butterfly Valley.*

It is worth taking specific sentence patterns and innovating on them to produce new sentences using the same underlying pattern, e.g.:

- *Are you ever bored at the weekend? Are the kids driving you crazy? Why not head straight to Hawk Ridge Farm Park and enter a world of wonder?*

- *Are you wanting life to be more exciting? Is daily life getting you down? Why not go straight to Fun Land and enter a world of wacky activities?*

- *Are you tired of dull hair? Are split ends driving you to distraction? Why not rush straight to Beautiful You and enter a world of glamour?*

Support understanding by flip-charting and displaying useful words and phrases built up throughout the persuasion unit. Where possible, this could be done by the teaching assistant (TA) or a pupil.

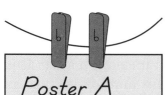

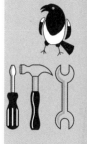

Poster A

Boastful language

- magnificent
- exciting
- wonderful
- marvellous
- superb
- unique
- enchanting
- thrilling
- unbeatable

Poster B

Use persuasive techniques

- Informal language — see all the examples below
- Questions — Are bored children driving you crazy?
- Alliteration — Dino Dig & the Wacky Workshop
- Rhyme — Dora the explorer
- Repetition — Find us to find the fun
- Imperatives (bossy sentences) — Don't forget Lemurland!
- Personal appeal — You can get up close and personal
- Boastful language — The World's oldest tourist attraction
- Patterns of three — Visit. Shop it. Love it.
- Short sentences — Discover Wildwood.
- Language aimed at audience, e.g. Txt
- Play on words — Make all your screams come true
- Testimonials/quotes — 'Join us for a great day out'

The image here is a flip chart of persuasive ideas to help a Year 6 class at Burnley Brow Primary in Oldham, Lancashire, compose an effective sales leaflet for a product. The key 'writing ingredients' for success, which we call a toolkit, can be established through these sorts of activities. It is essential that the children co-construct these ingredients, otherwise they will be meaningless to them. The toolkit of ingredients should be displayed as they will drive the shared, guided and independent writing, including self-peer evaluation and feedback from the teacher. A useful method is to flip-chart each ingredient as it is taught to help the children understand its significance. It is a good idea to keep the ingredients list as short as possible and back it up with a checklist that contains examples (see below). Support the short list with examples on the walls and in the children's journals from the activities they have taken part in.

By the end of the innovation stage, the ingredients toolkit may look something like this:

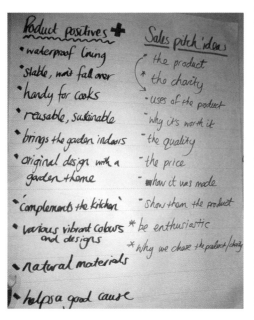

Figure 8.8   Flip chart demonstrating persuasive phrasing and ideas

Co-constructed persuasion writing toolkit

Plan it – order your ideas persuasively	<ul><li>Box up the content.</li><li>Begin with a hook to attract the reader: *Are you ever . . .?*</li><li>Follow this with enticing attractions: *eagles, bats, butterflies.*</li><li>Make the facilities appealing: *ample, cool, great.*</li><li>Include key information: *location, opening times, etc.*</li><li>Round off with a slogan to seal the deal: *See you there!*</li></ul>
Link it – join your ideas effectively	<ul><li>Link your ideas with sentence signposts: *Why not . . .?*</li></ul>
Expression – make your attraction inviting	<ul><li>Use persuasive language tricks to attract the reader (see poster B):</li></ul><ul><li>Rhetorical questions: *Are the . . .?*</li><li>Bossy verbs: *Don't miss . . .*</li><li>Use sentences of three: *There is ample parking, a cool café and a great shop.*</li><li>Use short sentences: *See eagles fly.*</li><li>Use boastful words : *World of wonder* (see poster A).</li></ul>
Check it	<ul><li>Read your writing aloud. Check it for flow and accuracy and improve it if it doesn't sound quite right.</li></ul>

Remind the class that you can include all the ingredients but still write a poor persuasive leaflet. They must remember to 'taste it' (read it aloud to test if it works) to help guarantee quality writing pitched at the right audience.

Of course, such checklists should be matched to the stage the children are working at, so they might be less complex or more demanding. These can be used as a guide for evaluation, marking and feedback. If the children have been taught previously in Talk for Writing style, then their existing toolkit for this type of writing should be built on to build in progress.

Stage 2: Innovation

2. Innovation
- Box up new version & talk the text
- Shared writing – innovate on model
- Pupils write own version & guided writing
- Peer assess
- Teacher assesses work – plans next steps
- Feedback & improvement

Figure 8.9

Task: Write a leaflet: 'Selling the school as a weekend attraction'.

Audience and purpose: Class magazine.

Now that the children have thoroughly internalised the pattern of persuasive text, they are in a position to innovate on this pattern by writing a promotional leaflet themselves, this time selling the school as a weekend tourist attraction. Provide a purpose for this, which could be for classroom display, for inclusion in a class magazine or for a competition. Support this process through shared planning and shared writing alongside appropriately devised role-play activities to further strengthen their familiarity with the structure and language patterns.

Use a similar boxed-up grid on a flip chart to act as a planner, to demonstrate to the children how to plan their leaflet.

Begin by getting the children to brainstorm some possible attractions the school could offer. Encourage them to be as imaginative as possible. Then, in pairs, get them to role-play a local resident ringing up the headteacher to find out what attractions are available. Using shared writing techniques, work on planning the leaflet, continually referring back to the original plan, using it as a basis for creating a plan for the new version.

Boxed-up planning for 'Selling the school as a weekend attraction'

Heading for each section	*Key points*
Introduce venue with hook to engage reader	• Bored by nothing to do? – visit Drax Primary School
Attractions	• Rare wall art • Magnificent sports facilities • State of the art IT suite
Facilities	• Car parking • Restaurant – gourmet
Useful information	• Where it is • When opens and closes
Conclusion	• Slogan to seal deal: Drax – max

Now, through shared writing, show the children how to move from their plan to the actual writing. It helps to take this bit by bit, having the relevant paragraph from the original displayed on the interactive whiteboard, annotated and colour coded so that the language features stand out. Alongside this, display the boxed-up plan you have just devised on the writing wall or washing line where you and the class can see it, while you scribe the children's ideas on a flip chart. The picture below shows a persuasion washing line at Front Lawn Primary, Havant. There are two useful handouts on shared writing in Appendix 2 (see **DVD 2**): **Handout 3** – *The art of shared writing* – lists the key ingredients that contribute towards successful shared writing; **Handout 4** lists useful phrases to use when doing shared writing.

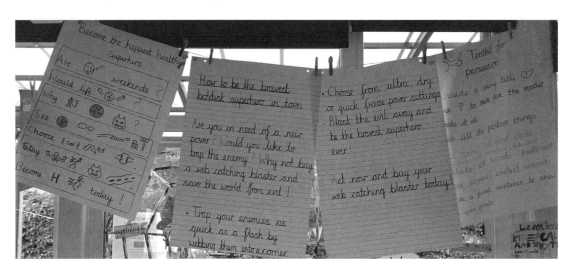

Figure 8.10   Using a washing line to display the model text, boxing up and word bank

Through shared writing, turn each section into fluent writing, involving the children in making decisions, suggesting words and developing sentences. As you do this, get the children to 'magpie' good ideas by jotting them down in their writing journals. Encourage them to never dodge a good word by putting a dotted line under words that are hard to spell (for example: graffiti), demonstrating how to focus on composition at this stage rather than spending time looking up the spelling. This can be done at the final draft stage.

Keep reading the shared writing through to get the children into the habit of reading their sentences aloud to see if they sound right. If you are teaching this after you have taught newspaper article writing, you may want to point out how the second paragraph hangs off the first paragraph without a topic sentence of its own, just as news articles often do. Given the shortness of these paragraphs, you probably won't want to build up this shared writing over a number of days but you may need to, depending on the children's confidence. The basic process is quite simple:

- Gather facts for the new paragraph and add to boxed-up planner.

- Refer back to the original.

- Turn the facts into similar sentences.

- Keep rereading to maintain flow.

- 'Test out' children's ideas to 'hear' whether they work.

- Ask children to develop sentences in pairs or on mini-whiteboards.

- Use the teaching assistant (or a pupil) to flip-chart key phrases and vocabulary to be turned into posters to support the writing.

Shared writing for 'Selling the school as a weekend attraction'

Are you driven to distraction by bored children at weekends? Relax – Drax Road School can solve your problems.

Gaze in wonder at the 21st-century graffiti, sample the stunning sports facilities **and** challenge the kids in the magnificent computer gaming suites.

Extensive car parking ensures trouble-free access.

And after all this fun, **why not** treat the family to the mouth-watering menu at our Michelin-starred restaurant? Chef's special – Fishy Chunks.

Conveniently placed opposite the sewage farm.

Open from 10.00 – 5.00 Saturdays and Sundays **throughout the year**.

Drax is max! – the local treat you just can't beat!

Once you have led the children through writing a class version of 'Selling the school as a weekend attraction', they are in a position to start planning and writing their own versions and should be bursting with ideas for what to say and how to say it. Help the children build up their own boxed-up plan of ideas and give them time to turn this into a text map and talk the text with a partner so that by the time they come to write, they know exactly what they want to say. Display the boxed-up planning, the text map, the shared writing, the toolkit and word and phrase banks to support them.

The children should write independently straight after the shared writing, gradually building their text. Use guided writing to teach and support groups in a focused manner. More confident writers might be asked to write a longer leaflet, adding extra information and moving away from the model (see pages 37–40 for an explanation of how to do this).

Once the children have completed their writing, they should be in the habit of sharing their writing with a partner to respond to each other's writing. This should be an opportunity to 'test out their writing', hearing how it sounds when read aloud. A discussion can follow about what works and what might be done to improve any places where the writing does not flow or engage the reader. Refer back to the 'toolkit' for persuasion text and use it to focus feedback. Remember, though, that while the children should have included the ingredients, the key factor will be whether the leaflet persuades the reader engagingly.

The writer now adapts aspects of their work in the light of their partner's comments, remembering that the final choice is the writer's. You may want to encourage them to write their own comment underneath their work focusing on what they think they have done well, how they have improved it and what may still need improving. The teacher can then take the work in for assessment and write their comment so that it builds on the pupil's comment, creating a dialogue about the best way forward that can be continued in guided writing sessions.

When assessing the work of the whole class, the teacher may find it useful to use a grid, like the one below, to help focus on what aspects of the writing particularly need improving if the children are to become skilled persuasive writers.

Grid to help assess what needs teaching next

Ingredients	*Have these ingredients been successfully implemented? Which features now need to be focused on?*
Plan it	• Did they think about their audience and what would appeal to them? • Did they begin with a punchy slogan to hook the reader's interest? • Did they include engaging attractions to interest their readers? • Did they mention key facilities that will appeal to their audience? • Did they provide key information? • Did they round off their leaflets with a slogan to seal the deal?
Link it	• Did they use a topic sentence to introduce to the reader what they were promoting? • Can they link the text successfully?
Express it	• Can they use a range of persuasive language tricks to help attract the reader? • Are they using interesting and varied words and phrases appropriately? • Are they using a variety of sentence structures?
Check it	• Is there evidence that they are reading their work aloud to see if it sounds good? • Are they checking their spelling and punctuation?

Your marking should lead directly into your next piece of teaching. Provide feedback on this work, focusing on those areas that the children found most difficult and helping them understand how to edit their work effectively. A visualiser or iPad is a very useful piece of equipment that allows you to present exemplar work from the pupils immediately to the whole class to illustrate the improvements you are seeking.

Model for the children how to reflect on the effectiveness of writing. The more opportunities the children are given to talk about what works and what features make the writing engaging, the more they will be able to develop their own inner judge and craft and edit their own writing effectively. **Handout 5** (see Appendix 2 on **DVD 2**) is full of useful questions to help children reflect on what makes writing effective and discuss what works. If the teacher models this sort of reflection, the children will quickly pick up how to reflect on their work. Focus on what makes the text engaging, not on the naming of parts.

Figure 8.11   Persuasive writing mini lesson on phrasing

On pages 177–178 is a list of possible problems and the sort of work that may help rectify them. One of the contributions that the Transforming Writing project made to the development of Talk for Writing was mini-lessons. This would be an excellent point in the unit to set up some mini-lessons so that pupils can focus on the areas that they need help with most (see pages 42–43).

The two pictures here, from a Year 6 class at Burnley Brow Primary in Oldham, Lancashire, show the teacher refining the class's ability to write persuasive sentences beginning with words such as *although* so that the writer counteracts doubts that the potential purchaser may have. He illustrated for the whole class 'on the carpet' how to do this, and those who felt confident returned to their seats to integrate the feature into their work. Those who felt they needed more help created a self-selected mini-group who stayed for further tuition. Examples of the class's ideas were displayed on Post-it notes to support the group crafting their ideas on mini-whiteboards.

The resulting persuasion text from such work can be turned into a book or magazine of the best of the leaflets to provide excellent exemplar material for future classes.

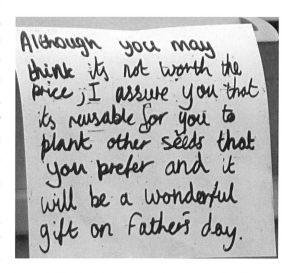

Figure 8.12   Post-it note displaying an example of how to counter potential negative points

Stage 3: Independent application

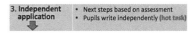

Figure 8.13

Task: Independently write a leaflet promoting your town or city as a tourist attraction using all the skills you have learned.

Audience and purpose: Make a presentation to a local council council representative who will judge its effectiveness in promoting the area as a tourist destination.

Once the redrafting of the leaflets has been assessed, the teacher is now in a good position to move to the third stage where there is more choice. The assessment will direct what has to be focused on during shared and guided sessions, including work on editing.

Again, model planning using a boxed-up planning grid as well as shared writing. You could, perhaps, be working on a class version of a pamphlet about a specific local attraction and invite the children to plan and write more general pamphlets encouraging tourists to visit the area. If possible, arrange for a member of the local council or the headteacher to judge the leaflets so the children have a real audience for their work.

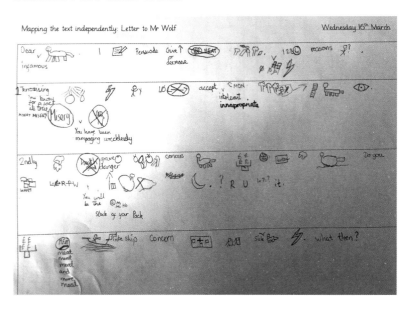

Figure 8.14 Year 6 child's text map for a letter to Mr Wolf

The children, working independently, could then box up their plan and turn it into a text map and talk their text through. (The illustration to the left is an independent text map by a Year 6 child at Penn Wood, Slough, for a persuasive letter to Mr Wolf.) With this level of support, the children will be able to compose their own persuasive text more easily as they will have rehearsed the phrases and structure that they want to use. The level of support provided for the independent writing will depend on the needs of the class. You may want to provide the model text on the whiteboard and its related boxed-up planning on the washing line to remind children of the process. Remember that the aim is to wean the children off using the model so, with older classes, the more alternative texts they encounter, the better. You may want to use the independence monitor illustrated on page 39 to help pupils to move away from the model text.

Once the children have completed their work, ask them to read it through carefully and decide how to improve it. When they have done this, ask them to write their own comment on how well they have completed the task. This will help them reflect on their learning and increase their sense of responsibility for their learning.

End of unit assessment

| Final assessment | Compare cold/hot: assess progress |

Figure 8.15

The teacher now assesses the final piece of writing (the **hot task**) and looks back at the **cold task** to see what progress has been made. Adding your comment to the child's comment helps to promote a dialogue about what needs to be done to improve the child's work. Again, when the work is handed back, focus on one or two areas that everyone needs to improve. This could be indicated by highlighting the areas selected in a particular colour, for example *green for growth*. Provide some teaching relating to these areas and ask the children to immediately improve their work. Then ask them to reflect on their learning by looking back at the cold task and seeing what progress they have made.

The teacher is now in a position to decide which everyday language features will need focusing on in the next unit of work as well as to log any persuasion features that will need strengthening when the class uses their persuasive writing skills across the curriculum.

Encouraging real independence, creativity and invention

Persuasive writing can be very entertaining and can be integrated into a wide variety of text, for example, creating a convincing character whose speech is full of weasel words and phrases. The end of a unit on persuasion is the perfect time to give the children the opportunity to practise their skills in the way that they choose. If children are to become effective creative writers who enjoy writing, they will need the motivation that comes from being able to choose your own topic and write about it as you choose. Such opportunities allow them to develop their skills in a whole range of exciting ways.

Mastering the approach across the curriculum

Applying their persuasive writing skills across the curriculum in a range of contexts will provide the depth and breadth that is essential if the children are to achieve mastery of the skills that underpin effective persuasive writing. Finding opportunities to embed skills across the curriculum is particularly valuable because it helps the children to apply what they have learned to a particular focus. For example, persuasive writing is important in technology since the children will need to be able to persuade people to be interested in buying a product they have made. In history, it can be applied to any period: persuading the Romans not to invade; persuading the Victorians not to employ children in mines, etc. Similarly, in geography, persuading consumers to want Fair Trade products, or persuading local populations to preserve the rainforest, etc. In PSHE, a wide range of issues lends itself to persuasive writing, for example persuading children not to encourage bullying. Given the fact that all school events need promoting, this provides a real audience to help the children hone their persuasive writing skills. And, of course, leaflets and adverts need design skills as well as copywriting skills, so this is the perfect opportunity to combine literacy and creative arts skills. As mentioned on pages 194–195, Book Talk techniques are invaluable here for helping children understand the thinking behind the design. Such an approach will enable the text type to be revisited and the language features embedded as part of the child's growing confidence as a young writer developing a flexible toolkit of writing skills that can be applied to any writing task.

A note on hybrid text

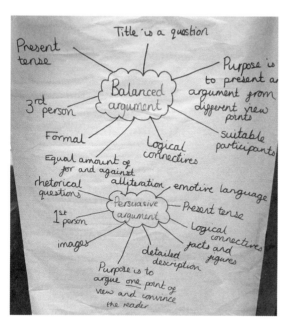

Figure 8.16 Toolkit display contrasting key persuasive and discursive writing techniques

Persuasion is probably the non-fiction text type that is most often encountered in a pure form, for example in adverts. But even adverts and promotional leaflets must contain information like how to contact the seller or how to get there. Meanwhile, many writers of discursive text use the techniques of persuasion to present their final conclusions. The flip chart pictured here from St Vincent de Paul Primary in Liverpool contrasts persuasive with discursive writing techniques.

The ultimate hybrid text is probably a guide book to a country or a place. Here you will have recount text about the history – but if this is accurate it will have to be discursive in parts where there are alternative interpretations. There will be information galore and explanation of particular cultural habits. Instructions will abound helping you find the places of interest. Running through every section will be the language of persuasion, encouraging you to visit various places and experience various things. A short guide book to an area provides an excellent topic for helping children exercise the full repertoire of their writing skills: it is the ultimate non-fiction hot task.

Discussion

What is a discussion text?

Discussion is extremely important because it helps us think and reflect. Whether it is discussing the merits of characters' behaviour in *Eastenders*, or debating the rights and wrongs of political shenanigans, human beings love to discuss. And, of course, it is central to the British values aspect of the Spiritual, Moral, Social and Cultural Development curriculum. The importance of discussion work in helping pupils express their ideas eloquently and learn from others is illustrated in video clips 39 to 41.

In education, discussion writing is highly prized because it involves considering all sides of an argument, weighing up evidence or ideas and trying to come to some sort of reasoned conclusion. Educationally, this form of thinking matters because it encourages children to empathise with different viewpoints, considering ideas and weighing up evidence before reaching a conclusion. Discussion lays the foundations for balanced discursive writing that will be used later on when writing history essays.

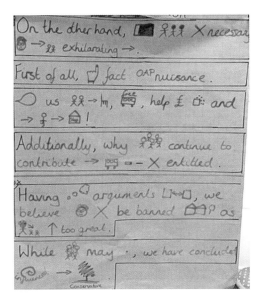

Figure 9.1 Discussion text map

In some ways, discussion is a close relative of persuasive writing – the important difference being that the author provides both sides of the argument and weighs up the evidence in a reasoned manner, drawing a conclusion.

Discussion writing at primary level is relatively simple to organise; compare and contrast essays are not so simple but these are not required of primary children . . . at least not yet! The writer begins by introducing the reader to the topic under discussion. As in all writing, the author is trying to hook the reader in, encouraging them to read further. This may well involve stating not just what is being discussed but also why this is a matter of interest, importance or particular relevance to the reader and current situation.

Currently, our class has been discussing whether or not football should be banned in the playground. This is a 'hot topic' because there is only limited space ...

In the main, at primary school, discussion writing follows a simple enough pattern. The writer opens by stating the topic under discussion, then provides the main reasons for a certain view, followed by reasons against, and ends with a reasoned conclusion. Ideally, ideas need to be backed with evidence or good reasoning. Following this in a formulaic manner runs the risk of leading to rather stilted writing, usually four paragraphs long. While this may be helpful for less confident writers, to develop the writing further, it is worth experimenting by using counterarguments and varying the way evidence is presented. For instance, this might involve using quotes from specialists, tables or graphs, photos or scientific information. It is worth teasing out the difference between opinions and actual evidence.

Obviously, discussion writing will be most powerful when the children have a strong connection to the topic in hand. Time needs to be spent building up information and different views so that the children are knowledgeable and have something to say. This can be led into by children developing presentations from both sides of a discussion, making notes and producing counterarguments.

Objective: To write engaging discussion text.

Typical features of discussion text

Audience	Someone interested or involved in the topic under discussion.
Purpose	To present a reasoned and balanced view of an issue.
Typical structure	Opening paragraph that introduces the reader to the issue. Followed by a series of paragraphs in logical order: – either beginning with all the arguments for, followed by all the arguments against; – or a series of contrasting points ending with a reasoned conclusion. Paragraphs usually begin with a topic sentence.
Typical language features	Sentence signposts to guide the reader through the argument that help to: • add on and order ideas and views, e.g. *The first reason, also, furthermore, moreover . . .* • introduce other viewpoints, e.g. *However, on the other hand, many people believe that, it might be thought that . . .* • conclude, e.g. *in conclusion, having considered all the arguments, looking at this from both sides . . .*
Examples	• Should healthy eating be compulsory? • Should children be allowed to choose where to sit? • Should mobile phones be banned in school? • How can we improve the playground?

Choosing a discussion writing topic

Almost everyone enjoys talking about their beliefs and ideas. As with all non-fiction writing, children need to be familiar with the topic in hand and have some sort of vested interest – otherwise any discussion may well fall flat (see video clips 39 and 41). There are many possibilities that work well:

a. Children's own concerns:

- Should school uniform be banned?
- Should a skateboard ramp be built in the playground?
- Should children have to stay at school at the end of the day to do an hour of homework?
- Should schools sell crisps at break time?

b. Fantasy:

- Should unicorns be held in captivity?
- Should dragons be kept as pets?
- Should the troll be sent to prison?
- Do giants exist?

c. Issues arising from stories:

- Should the Iron Man be captured?
- Should Goldilocks be in trouble?
- Should Danny help his father take the pheasants?
- Should Billy go into the forest at the start of the Minpins?

d. Real local issues:

- Should smoking be banned in all public places?
- Should the local park be closed at night?
- Should the village mobile library be cut?
- Should a new supermarket be built?

e. News:

- Should animals be used for testing?
- Should all children learn to swim?
- Should children be allowed to vote?
- Should the children of celebrities be photographed by journalists?

Audience and purpose

Holding classroom debates or 'trials' is a powerful way to help children gain a sense of audience. This might be enhanced further if a link can be made with a local secondary school with a 'debating team'. Ideally, the team visits, holds a model debate and then trains the children in debating techniques. The influence of older children is usually a very powerful motivator.

Some key areas for discussion writing skills across the curriculum

- PSHE:
  - Should bullies be punished?
  - Should boys and girls be taught separately?

- History:
  - Should children have been evacuated in World War II?
  - Was King Alfred a hero or a bully?

- Geography:
  - Should Fair Trade be encouraged?
  - Is recycling a good idea?

- Science:
  - Why should we have a balanced diet?
  - Should owl boxes be compulsory in all gardens?

Warming up the distinctive features of discussion text

When you overhear an argument in the playground, you are not likely to hear such phrases as *on the other hand, alternatively* and *from a different perspective*. While children will have heard adults discussing things at home, they may well be unfamiliar with the more formal language of written discussion. Quick-fire starters should help the children begin to become familiar with patterns such as *We are discussing whether or not* . . . . Children need to hear such patterns many times and attempt to use them orally before moving into the written form. In the long run, time spent on such starters pays off when children are writing whole texts as they are more familiar with the flow of language, having internalised it through playful, yet purposeful, repetition. Discussion writing obviously lends itself to any form of game that involves taking sides or giving viewpoints. When devising tuning-in games like the ones below, it is often best to select fictional topics. This enables the children to focus on the language patterns and not worry about accuracy of information.

Tuning into the subject: vocabulary games

- Focus on the topic to be discussed – provide the children with a list of the key technical terms to be used plus their related definitions. In pairs the children have to match the terms to the definitions. This works best if the words and their definitions are printed on separate cards so they can be physically matched.

- Produce a list of evidence and opinions for children to sort into two categories – proper evidence versus someone's view.

- Draw up charts or lists of views, reasons and evidence.

Tuning into sentence signposts and generalisers games

Understanding the power of sentence signposts to link paragraphs, sentences and information within sentences is key to achieving cohesive discussion text that flows logically. Appendix 3 (**DVD 2**) provides more information and useful handouts on linking text.

- Rapidly read a paragraph and underline the signposts that might be used in other discussion pieces.

- Rehearse using more challenging signposts to create fantasy sentences, for example:

We are discussing whether or not dragons exist.
We are discussing whether or not unicorns can fly.
We are discussing whether or not gerbils can sing.

Tuning into the sentence games

- Play sentence signpost tennis, where the first half of a key pattern is spoken by one child and the second half by the other. In this way, sentences can be bounced back and forth, for example:

Child A – *The main reason for suggesting that unicorns make good pets . . .*
Child B – *. . . is that they tend to bite.*

- Provide the children with a viewpoint: for example, aliens exist. They then have to rapidly create sentences that provide reasons for believing this:

I believe that aliens exist because I saw an alien last night in the back yard.
I believe aliens exist because my Nan says it is true.
I believe aliens exist because I found a space suit.
I believe aliens exist because my friend Charlie comes from Pluto.

- Play sentence tennis.

  a. Player A says – *We believe that cyborgs are good . . .*
  b. Player B completes the sentence using 'because' – *because they help with the washing up.*
  c. Keep playing the sentences back and forth until someone makes a mistake.

- Choose a sentence signpost that helps you to add on another point of view, such as *also, moreover, additionally* or *furthermore*. See who can keep adding on an extra point. Provide a topic for discussion – for example, *Should giants be allowed into the neighbourhood?* Start by saying, *We believe giants should be allowed to live locally because they can help move fallen trees . . .* Then the game begins with the children adding more ideas in support.

- Try playing a game where one child makes a statement and the other player has to give the counterargument, for example:

  Player A – *I believe that dragons exist because their bones have been found.*
  Player B – *On the other hand, many people believe that dragons do not exist because none have ever been seen.*

- In pairs, discuss whether unicorns exist, providing three good ideas for your side of the argument. A good way of extending this activity is to first get the children to present their arguments as if no other viewpoint were possible. Then ask them to present their argument tentatively, showing that they have listened to the other side and recognised that it is a complex issue. This works best if you model it for the children first.

Tuning into the text games

Compare different opening paragraphs and decide which is the best written and why. Use this to draw up a simple chart based on the children's ideas: *In order to write a good opening to a discussion, you need to remember to . . .* For example:

Text A: *Currently, there is a heated debate in our class because one of us can be nominated by the intergalactic council for hero status. Would becoming a superhero be a good idea or not?*

Text B: *Would you make a good superhero? Do you believe that a life rescuing those in disasters and becoming a freedom fighter against the tyranny of street crime would be for you? Here's some things you might want to think about before committing yourself to taking up the cape!*

Text C: *In our class, we have been debating whether or not it would be advisable to become a superhero.*

Improve – Provide a poorly written example for the children to improve. This is especially useful if the teacher builds in the sort of weaknesses or errors that children commonly make, for example:

> *In our group, we have been discussing whether or not computers are good for you.*
>
> *Some people argue that you can learn from using the computer and they have programs to help them read and improve their maths and that they use the computer to find out information and that the computer is going to be used in the future in many jobs and we should get used to using them.*

Role play

- Role-play a discussion between two people sitting on a bus who have different views on a subject.

- Role-play a TV discussion.

- Role-play being visiting professors with opposing views on the topic.

- Hold a full-blown trial, perhaps based on a well-known tale, picture book or class novel. I saw a great trial held by Year 4 children where they had the troll in the dock for threatening behaviour. He managed to persuade the jury that the goats had dangerous horns, were threatening and he was only protecting the rare flowers from their destructive ways!

Warming up the specific content

- Use a simple grid to list reasons for and against a topic.

- Put the reasons into an order – discuss whether you should start with the best reason or end on that.

- Provide evidence for each reason.

Sequencing the text

Provide the class with a discussion piece that has been jumbled up. This could be a whole text or a paragraph. The activity focuses on being able to re-sequence and then explain decisions, identifying the clues and links. For instance:

> *On the other hand, some people argue that Jack was on the edge of starvation and was forced to steal in order to save his dying mother. Furthermore, it could be argued that the giant was a danger to the local area and had been responsible for stealing sheep and cattle to feed himself and his wife. Indeed, some people believe that Jack should be further rewarded for ridding the locality of this terrible creature.*
>
> *Having considered all the arguments, I believe that while stealing should normally be punished, on this occasion Jack acted in the best interests of his family and the local area.*

Many people think that Jack should be sent to jail because he stole the giant's magical hen that lays golden eggs. Additionally, he returned to the giant's castle and took a never-ending purse plus the giant's talking harp. Furthermore, he was responsible for killing the giant.

We have been discussing whether or not Jack should be imprisoned for theft.

How to plan a discussion unit in Talk for Writing style

The Talk for Writing process

Baseline assessment	• Cold task at least week before unit • Set targets
Planning	• Refine language focus & adapt model text • Decide how it can be innovated • Test model: box it up, analyse it, make toolkit

1. Imitation	• Creative hook and context
	• Warm up/embed words/phrases/grammar
	• <u>Internalise</u> model text – text map
	• Read as a reader: vocabulary/comprehension
	• Read as a writer:
	   o Box up text to establish structure
	   o <u>Analyse</u> features
	   o Co-construct toolkit

2. Innovation	• Box up new version & talk the text • Shared writing – innovate on model • Pupils write own version & guided writing • Peer assess • Teacher assesses work – plans next steps • Feedback & improvement
3. Independent application	• Next steps based on assessment • Pupils write independently (hot task)
Final assessment	Compare cold/hot: assess progress

This image sums up the Talk for Writing process. If you have not already read Chapter 2, which explains this process in detail, you will find it useful to read that chapter before thinking about how the process can be applied to discussion text. **Handout 1** is an expanded version of the process with more detail about the key essential features, as well as some optional suggestions that schools have found useful in helping children make progress – see Appendix 2, **DVD 2**.

Figure 9.2   The Talk for Writing process

Worked example for discussion text

Below is a worked example of the three stages of the Talk for Writing approach bookended by the initial and final assessments to ensure formative assessment is at the heart of the planning, teaching and learning process.

Objective: To write a discussion piece that would interest the reader, providing all sides of the argument.

Topic: *Doctor Who*: **Imitation** – Should Daleks be allowed to live on earth? **Innovation** – Should Doctor Who give up being a Time Lord? **Invention** – Children put on trial The Master for crimes against the universe.

Audience and purpose: Class hold mock trial to entertain other classes and write up the trial for a simple broadcast.

Initial assessment

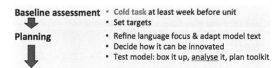

Figure 9.3

For any unit of work on discussion you have to think first about what discursive writing skills the class already possesses. As explained in Chapter 2, a good way of doing this is to set a **cold task**. This should be set at least a week before you begin to teach your unit so that you can alter your planning to suit the needs of the class. The pupils will need a familiar context (for example, ask the children to write a piece entitled *Should school uniform be optional?* giving all sides of the argument) so that they have something to write about that they know about and that interests them. Warm the topic up with a quick discussion – but do not provide any teaching in how to write about this subject. The discussion cold write pictured here, from Knowle Park Primary School, Bristol, focuses on whether aliens exist. The teacher has listed the pupil's targets clearly underneath.

This cold write will help you pinpoint what specific skills to focus on in the unit to help the children progress. Assess this work and decide what language features to focus on in the unit as well as setting targets for children with different levels of attainment. This will also enable you to adapt the model text to ensure that it illustrates the features that suit the needs of the class.

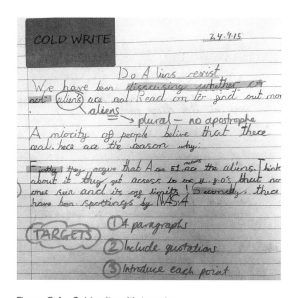

Figure 9.4 Cold write with targets

Stage 1: Imitation

The creative hook

Figure 9.5

The discussion focus for this unit is all related to *Doctor Who*, which is always guaranteed to engage children and lends itself to great displays and sound effects. To catch the children's interest try any of the following:

- Show them 'clues' to see if they can guess which story they are going to work on, e.g. a miniature police box, a stethoscope . . . Play the theme tune.

- Mock up a headline for the local newspaper, e.g. *Daleks move into Swindon.*

- Create a pretend news bulletin to play the children, e.g. an interview with a family of Daleks that have moved in locally.

- Take the children on a 'walk' through the BBC's *Doctor Who* website (http://www.bbc.co.uk/doctorwho/dw) or Wikipedia.

Warming up the tune of discussion text

Games and activities devised to familiarise the children with the typical language pattern of discursive text and the context of the unit are key to success. As the games are played, flip-chart the vocabulary, sentence signposts and key sentence patterns that emerge, and start to create a toolkit of useful ingredients for discursive text to support the children's speaking and writing. Display these to make the learning visible and develop them throughout the unit. If the children have already been taught this text type in Talk for Writing style, build on their existing toolkit for discussion text.

- **Begin with a Never-heard-the-word grid** to flag up the key vocabulary of the unit – see pages 197–198 for the instructions on how to do this.

Below is the beginning of a Never-heard-the-word grid for this unit

	Never heard before	*Heard – not sure of meaning*	*Know what it means: give a simple explanation plus an example*
1. controversy			
2. beneficial			
3. intergalactic			
4. considerably			
5. exterminate			
6. compassion			
7. occasion			
8. influenced			
9. . . .			

- Play tuning into sentence signpost games, amending the examples to suit the context chosen for your unit (see pages 217–218).

- **Create a simple discussion text, omitting all sentence signposts to produce a cloze procedure**, for example:

  _____ there is a hardcore section of the community who think that the idea of aliens visiting Warminster is ridiculous. _____, these people believe that it is hard enough to encourage visitors from local towns to visit and shop, let alone anyone from a million light years away! _____ they believe that the crop circles are manmade _____, they suggest that sightings of spaceships are caused by atmospheric pressure changes _____ they dismiss reports of alien abduction as being impossible.

- **What = 'good' for this sort of writing?** Write three different discussion paragraphs about the same subject so the children can consider which works best. Discuss what makes it effective. Which is the weakest? Why? What advice would you give to the weaker writer? Use this activity to draw up a wall chart titled, 'What you need to do to make discussion writing interesting'. Try comparing these three paragraphs as a start:

  Text A: *The most compelling argument against only providing healthy food at lunchtime is that many of us just don't want to eat it. When you are picturing a luscious hamburger encircled by crisp golden chips, it's really depressing to know that all you have to choose from is limp lettuce leaves surrounding assorted cold crunchy so-called healthy options. It's enough to make you want to give up eating.*

  Text B: *Well, most of us are fed up with having to eat salad and vegetables and healthy stuff like that all the time because it's like boring and then you don't want to be bothered with eating it and then you think why can't I have crisps and chocolate.*

  Text C: *A key problem with only providing healthy food at lunchtime is that many of us do not like it. We would much prefer to have some of our favourite foods like hamburgers, pizza, chips and chocolate, rather than having to eat salad and fruit all the time.*

Internalising the model text

Figure 9.6 Discussion text map from Knowle Park – each paragraph is on a separate flip chart

Use an interesting version of a discussion piece that contains the expected structure and features appropriate to the level of the children so that there is an edge of challenge. Do not show the children the text at this stage. They are going to hear it and internalise it orally before they see it.

Turn this into a large class text map. Since this text will have several paragraphs, it lends itself to being displayed on a washing line with one sheet of flip-chart paper per paragraph. Learn the text together as a class with actions or divide it up so that groups can learn a section and then teach each other. Move from whole-class retelling to groups and finally pairs so that ultimately everyone can retell the text. Learn the text with a view to performing it at an assembly. This example is pitched for a strong Year 6 class.

To help learn the text orally, children should draw their own mini washing lines or text maps. These may be annotated with anything that causes problems.

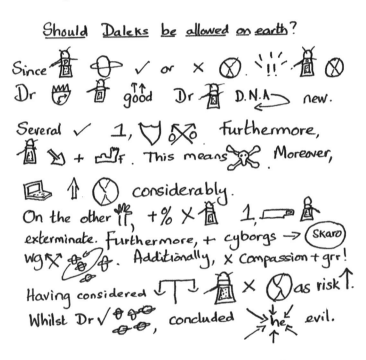

Figure 9.7   Text map for *Should daleks be allowed on earth?*

Retell the text in various different ways to help the children internalise the text.

Apart from the standard ways of helping the class internalise the text (see list on pages 21–22) you might also want to try:

- retell the text in role as a Dalek;
- retell it in role as a Time Lord;
- prepare to present to children in another class.

1a) Reading as a reader

Once the children have thoroughly internalised the text orally, present the text that they have internalised to the children and start by reading it as a reader.

Should Daleks be allowed to live on Earth?

Since the arrival of the Daleks on this planet, there has been much discussion about whether or not they should be allowed to live on Earth. This raging controversy is of vital importance because the Daleks have asked the world's parliament if they can stay.

The Doctor, the famous Time Lord, has argued that the Daleks might be allowed to stay because they could be used as a force for good. The Doctor has suggested that by changing the Dalek's basic DNA, a new breed could be created. There are several reasons why this might be beneficial. First, they would act as ideal defenders in any intergalactic battle. Furthermore, the Daleks are tireless workers and totally fearless. This means that they might be prepared to work in areas that are dangerous. Moreover, The Doctor argues that their skill in technology would help the earth considerably.

On the other hand, the large majority of people on planet Earth do not believe that the Daleks should be allowed to stay. First of all, they point to the fact that when the Daleks have previously visited, they have attempted to exterminate all other life forms. Furthermore, they add that these cyborgs from the planet Skaro have been waging war around the galaxy. Additionally, the Daleks are known to have no compassion and only feel hate.

Having considered the arguments from both sides, we believe that the Daleks should not be allowed to stay on Earth as the risk is too great. While The Doctor is usually right and has saved the galaxy on many occasions, we have concluded that perhaps he has been influenced in some way by these evil creatures!

The children should be able to read the model text because they have internalised the language, but that does not mean they have fully understood the meaning of the words. The more you have used actions and alternative words to help them understand the meaning, the greater comprehension they will have of the meaning of the text.

Help the children deepen their understanding of the text, becoming increasingly familiar with the structure and language patterns, by using the following sorts of activities.

- **Play the alternative words game:** List some of the tricky words from the text and ask the children in pairs if they can come up with alternative words or phrases that mean the same thing. For example:

controversy	exterminate
beneficial	compassion
intergalactic	occasions
considerably	influenced

- **Construct some comprehension questions** for the children to discuss initially in pairs, to open up discussion on the text and ensure the children have understood what they are reading:

  - Explain, in your own words as far as possible, the arguments in favour of the Daleks being allowed to stay.

  - Explain, in your own words as far as possible, the arguments against the Daleks being allowed to stay.

  - Explain which of these arguments (for or against) you think is the most convincing and why you have chosen it.

  - Explain why you think the writer has concluded that the Daleks should not be allowed to stay and if you agree with this conclusion.

- Interview The Doctor for *Space News*, asking his opinions over this controversial possibility.

- Interview or hot-seat a Dalek.

- Hold a town meeting to gather views for and against.

1b) Reading as a writer

Once the children have fully understood the text, you can then start reading it as a writer, identifying the language features that can be reused as well as analysing the techniques that the writer has used to make the writing effective.

Boxing up the text

The first thing for the children to think about when trying to understand how a text has been written is its structure, so show the children how to box up this text. If the class is already familiar with boxing up, ask them to box it up in pairs and discuss as a class. Count the paragraphs and create a boxed-up version with one box for each paragraph.

Box up the basic pattern with the children, asking them to tell you what the focus of each paragraph is so that the underlying structure can clearly be seen. The more they see you create the structure in front of them, and are involved in analysing it, the more they will be able to understand it.

Boxed-up planning for 'Should Daleks be allowed to live on earth?'

Heading for each section	*Key points*
Introduce what is being discussed and why this matters	– much discussion about whether or not they should be allowed to live on earth – have asked to stay
Key arguments for	The Doctor arguing for Daleks – a potential force for good if they change DNA: – powerful defenders – tireless workers – technologically advanced
Key arguments against	Majority of people arguing against When visited earth before: – attempted to exterminate all other life forms – wage war around the galaxy – known to have no compassion and only feel hate
End round the story off	Daleks should not be allowed to stay on earth – too risky – The Doctor is usually right but perhaps influenced by these evil creatures!

Display your boxing up, so the children know how to plan their discussion writing. This will provide the basic structure for the children when they come to create their own versions.

Help the children to become increasingly familiar with the structure and language patterns of the text by devising activities that help them analyse the patterns of language in the paragraphs, for example:

- **Identifying discursive sentence signposts**: Ask the children to highlight all the sentence signposts they can spot in the text and then categorise them into those that signal:

  - introducing a point;

  - adding on more information;

  - introducing a different viewpoint;

  - the conclusion.

Create a poster of useful discursive signposts so they are there to support the children when they come to write (see below).

- **Imitating the sentence pattern:** It is worth taking specific sentence patterns and innovating on them to produce new sentences using the same underlying pattern, for example:

  - *Since the arrival of the Daleks on this planet, there has been much discussion about whether or not they should be allowed to live on earth.*

  - *Since the arrival of the new players to the team, there has been much discussion about whether or not the transfer fee was money well spent.*

  - *Since the introduction of healthy eating to the school, there has been much discussion about whether or not it is a good idea.*

  - *Doctor Who, the famous Time Lord, has argued that the Daleks might be allowed to stay because they could be used as a force for good.*

  - *Fred Smith, the well-known footballer, has argued that he hasn't done anything wrong because everyone tries to avoid paying tax.*

  - *Rex, the school dog, has suggested that he should be allowed to sleep all day because he is a tired dog.*

Support understanding by flip-charting and displaying useful words and phrases built up throughout the information text activities.

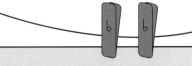

Poster A

Sentence signposts adding on more information:

- *In addition,*
- *Furthermore,*
- *Moreover,*
- *Also,*
- *Additionally,*

Poster B

Sentence signposts signalling a different viewpoint:

- *On the other hand,*
- *Alternatively,*
- *However,*
- *It could be argued that . . .*
- *Many people disagree, arguing that . . .*

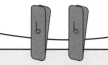

Poster C

Sentence signposts signalling the introduction of a point:

- Since x, there has been much discussion about . . .
- There are several reasons why . . .
- First of all . . .
- This means that . . .

Poster D

Useful words for introducing opinions:

- believe
- think that
- suggest
- claim
- state

Poster E

Generalisers for referring to groups of people:

- All
- Everyone
- Most
- Some
- Many
- A few
- Lots of people
- The vast majority
- A significant minority

Poster F

Useful phrases for your conclusion:

- In conclusion,
- Having considered all the arguments,
- Looking at this from both sides,
- There is much to be said for both viewpoints.

The key 'writing ingredients' for success, which we call a toolkit, can be established through these sorts of activities. It is essential that the children co-construct these ingredients, otherwise they will be meaningless to them. The toolkit of ingredients should be displayed (see below), as they will drive the shared, guided and independent writing, including self-peer evaluation and feedback from the teacher. A useful method is to flip-chart each ingredient up on the toolkit as it is taught, to help the children understand each one's significance. It is a good idea to keep the ingredients list as short as possible and back it up with a checklist that contains examples and is related to the posters displayed next to it on the writing wall.

Co-constructed discussion writing toolkit

Plan it – order the information logically	• Box up the argument into chunks – reasons for and reasons against in logical order. • Begin by introducing the reader to the topic, including a hook that encourages the reader to read on. • End with your conclusion, explaining your decision.

Link it – make your points fit together well	• Link your argument together using sentence signposts that:
	  – help to add on more points of view (see poster A);
	  – signal the alternative arguments clearly (see poster B);
	  – signal the introduction of a point (see poster C).

Express it – make your points of view sound interesting	• Use interesting, varied language to keep your reader wanting to read on (see poster D). • Use generalising language that sums up information (see poster E). • Vary sentence lengths, using short ones to make key points, e.g. *There are several reasons why this might be beneficial.* • Make a point and then explain it further using words such as *because*. • Try to relate what you are saying to the reader, e.g. *Young people believe that . . .; you might be one of the many people who think . . .*
Check it	• Read your writing aloud, check it for flow and accuracy and improve it wherever it does not sound quite right.

Remind the class that you can include all the ingredients but still write a poor discussion. They must remember to taste it (read it aloud to test if it works) to help guarantee quality writing.

Of course, such checklists should be matched to the stage the children are working at, so they might be less complex or more demanding. These can be used as a guide for evaluation, marking and feedback. If the children have been taught previously in Talk for Writing style, then their existing toolkit for this type of writing should be built on to build in progress.

By this point, the children should be very clear about the discussion surrounding the imminent arrival of the Daleks who may well be taking up residency in a street nearby!!

They will also be very familiar with the overall pattern of the text and the various language features – they will have heard, spoken, read, discussed and played with the sentence types until they have begun to become part of their linguistic repertoire. It would be ideal to end this stage with some sort of enthusiastic performance to other classes. Envoys might visit classes to discover what they believe, having heard the different sides speak.

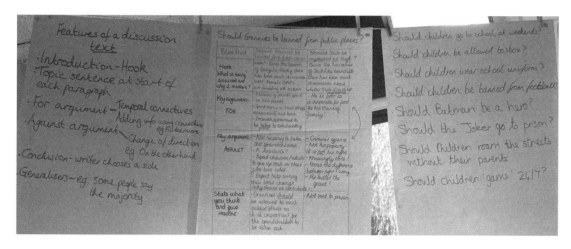

Figure 9.8   Washing line supporting a discussion unit

By the end of the imitation stage you should have a fine display on your washing line or working wall of the model text, the boxed-up plan, the toolkit and some useful words and phrases to support the innovation stage. The discussion washing line displayed here is from Front Lawn Primary, Havant.

Stage 2: Innovation

2. Innovation
- Box up new version & talk the text
- Shared writing – innovate on model
- Pupils write own version & guided writing
- Peer assess
- Teacher assesses work – plans next steps
- Feedback & improvement

Figure 9.9

Staying with the *Doctor Who* theme, you might then move into the second phase by raising the following topic for discussion: 'Should The Doctor give up being a Time Lord?' Perhaps a letter or email arrives for the class, or a message is left on the Class Blog from The Doctor, giving his reasons for wanting to pack in his endless years rescuing life in the known universe.

- Hot-seat The Doctor or interview him for a mock news bulletin.

- Have a panel of children in role as politicians and other Time Lords discussing what The Doctor should do.

Use the boxed-up grid showing the structure of the model text and use the same structure to plan your innovation. Gather points of view and organise them on the boxed-up planner so the children see how to plan their work. This might be done by children taking on different roles, such as The Doctor, another Time Lord, a Dalek, a Cyberman, a Prime Minister.

It helps if you keep the original model clearly displayed so that you can keep referring to it. You are about to lead the children through writing a class version of 'Should The Doctor give up being a Time Lord?' This will then be followed by the children writing their own versions.

Boxed-up planning for 'Should The Doctor give up being a Time Lord?'

Heading for each section	*Key points*
Opening hook – what is being discussed and why this matters	• must be discussed • The Doctor has a vital role in defending universe
Key arguments for	• has saved many planets, etc. from destruction • only person who can work TARDIS • unlike humans, The Doctor can regenerate
Key arguments against	• tired of battles against enemies • perhaps someone else might beat them for good • danger of The Doctor becoming like the Master • nearing the end of regeneration
End – state what you think is right and give reasons	• encourage Doctor to continue, BUT • find a replacement

Use shared writing to turn each section into fluent writing, involving the children in making decisions, suggesting words and developing sentences. This can be done paragraph by paragraph over a number of days, depending on the children's confidence. The process is quite simple:

- Gather points of view and evidence/arguments for the new paragraph.

- Refer back to the original.

- Turn the ideas into sentences; keep rereading to maintain flow.

- Test out children's ideas to 'hear' whether they work.

- Underline or highlight key features, like sentence signposts.

- Ask children to develop sentences in pairs or on mini-whiteboards.

- Pace the writing over two or three days to ensure quality.

- Ask the teaching assistant (or a pupil) to flip-chart key phrases and vocabulary to be turned into posters to support the writing.

There are two useful handouts on shared writing in Appendix 3 (see **DVD 2**): **Handout 5** – *The art of shared writing*, lists the key ingredients that contribute towards successful shared writing; **Handout 6** lists useful phrases to use when doing shared writing.

An example of shared writing developed from the plan

We have been debating whether or not The Doctor should give up being a Time Lord and settle down. It is vital to think about this because of his key role in defending the universe.

The large majority of people that we have interviewed believe that The Doctor should continue in his role as a Time Lord and they have a number of good reasons for suggesting this. First of all, they make the point that The Doctor has saved many planets, galaxies and civilizations from a range of intergalactic enemies. Furthermore, they add that The Doctor is the only person who is capable of controlling the Tardis (Time and Relative Dimensions In Space) and so no one else could make good use of the time travelling machine. Additionally, they point out that no one else has the capability to regenerate their body after death so The Doctor is irreplaceable.

On the other hand, The Doctor has become increasingly tired of what seems to be endless battles against his old enemies the Daleks, Cybermen and Autons. First, he has argued that perhaps someone else might be able to vanquish these tyrants for good. Furthermore, The Doctor's friends have suggested that they are concerned in case The Doctor transmogrifies in the same way that the Master did to become a renegade Time Lord. This could mean that The Doctor turned into a force for destruction and is, therefore, not a risk that should be taken! Finally, The Doctor argues that it is time to hang up his cloak as Time Lords can only regenerate 12 times so his career as a space and time saviour is almost over.

Having considered the arguments from both sides, I personally believe that The Doctor should be encouraged to continue in his role as a Time Lord as there is no one else who could fill his shoes! However, the Interplanetary Parliament must seek a

> **new Time Lord as The Doctor has regenerated on eleven occasions and, therefore, his time is running out!**

You will notice in the example above that the class has hugged fairly closely to the original. However, they have also drawn from other samples of writing. It is worth building up a bank of each text type.

The children should write independently straight after the shared writing, gradually building their text over a number of days. Use guided writing to teach and support groups in a focused manner. More confident writers might be asked to write more paragraphs, perhaps adding in counterarguments, for example:

> **While some Time Lords have argued that The Doctor has never really succeeded in his intergalactic battles, others claim that he should be further supported. They suggest that a junior Time Lord should be assigned to The Doctor for future training and development.**

Children should also be using ICT to add in images that make a point, as well as using graphs, tables and charts to back up points of view with evidence.

Once the children have completed their writing, they should be in the habit of working with their partner to respond to each other's writing. This should be an opportunity to 'test out' their writing, hearing how it sounds when read aloud. A discussion can follow about what works and what might be done to improve any places where the writing does not flow or engage the reader.

The writer now adapts aspects of their work in the light of their partner's comments, remembering that the final choice is the writer's. You may want to encourage them to write their own comment underneath their work focusing on what they think they have done well, how they have improved it and what may still need improving. The teacher can then take the work in for assessment and write their comment so that it builds on the pupil's comment, creating a dialogue about the best way forward that can be continued in guided writing sessions.

Your marking should lead directly into your next piece of teaching. Provide feedback on this work, focusing on those areas that the children found most difficult and helping them understand how to edit their work effectively. A visualiser or iPad is a very useful piece of equipment that allows you to present exemplar work from the pupils immediately to the whole class, to illustrate the improvements you are seeking.

Figure 9.10 Playing sentence doctor

The picture here from Montgomery Primary School, Birmingham, shows a class involved in sentence doctor activities to help them check their discussion writing carefully.

Model for the children how to reflect on the effectiveness of writing. The more opportunities the children are given to talk about what works and what features and ideas make the writing engaging, the more they will be able to develop their own inner judge and craft and edit their own writing effectively. **Handout 5**, on **DVD 2,** is full of useful questions to help children reflect on what makes writing effective and discuss what works. If the teacher models this sort of reflection, the children will quickly pick up how to reflect on work. Focus on what makes the text engaging, not on the naming of parts.

On pages 177–178 is a list of possible problems and the sort of work that may help rectify them. One of the contributions that the Transforming Writing project made to the development of Talk for Writing was mini-lessons. This would be an excellent point within the unit to set up some mini-lessons so that pupils can focus on the areas that they need help with most (see pages 42–43).

Stage 3: Independent application

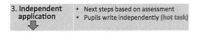

Figure 9.11

It is tempting to stop at the end of the second phase – everyone has written their own discussion piece and there may be a sense that you have to move on to cover other aspects. However, you do have the advantage of being able to assess their writing and provide feedback to the class and individuals. This can then drive what happens in the third session. You may want to focus on particular aspects of the writing by providing a mini model of a paragraph, for example, concentrating on how to engage the reader in the opening.

Of course, you will also want to see what the children can do when writing about a topic of their own choice. You might wish to provide a list of possible subjects for writing in the form of a 'discussion menu'. The children then choose a topic that interests them – for example, should spiders be allowed to climb down plugholes. Alternatively, you might wish to stay with the same theme and generate ideas for further *Doctor Who* discussions – e.g. Do robots make good pets? Would a Cyberman be a good teacher? Should the Master be trusted? The picture here captures a discussion at Knowle Park Primary, Bristol, about whether Little Red Riding Hood should have been allowed to set off for her grandmother's house alone.

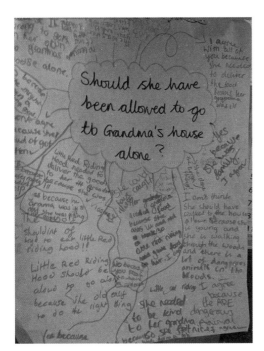

Figure 9.12   Discussion brainstorm

You will still need to use shared and guided writing, but it has the advantage of working off the back of the children's writing and will therefore become much more focused on what needs to be developed. Select a topic for the class discussion piece. Ideas might be gathered, a simple text map drawn and children orally rehearsed. Move from this into a simple writing grid that shows the main points of view, carefully boxed up. Move from this plan into the writing. This drives the children's own planning, oral rehearsal and writing where they craft their ideas.

The children, working independently, could then box up their plan. Once they have boxed up their plan, get them to turn it into icons and talk their text through.

Figure 9.13   Boxed-up planning supporting writing

Then they will be able to compose their discussion more easily as they will have rehearsed the phrases and structure that they want to use. The picture here shows a girl at Warren Farm Academy, Birmingham, writing about whether people should be sent to Mars. You can see that on the left-hand page she has boxed up her plan, thought about the key phrases that she wants to use and is now using her planning to support her writing.

Try building in mini-pauses so that children can read their paragraph aloud to their partner as they write, allowing them to get used to carefully refining their writing rather than the 'hundred yard dash' method of writing!

An interesting idea for discussion writing is for children to work in pairs – jointly crafting an opening and then each taking different sides – and finally drawing a conclusion.

The level of support provided for the independent writing will depend on the needs of the class. You may want to provide an exemplar text on the whiteboard and its related boxed-up planning on the washing line to remind children of the process. This work could be written on yellow paper to indicate it is the hot task or a red sticker or tab be used so that the hot task can easily be identified.

Once the children have completed their work, ask them to read it through carefully and decide how to improve it. Once they have done this, ask them to write their own comment on how well they have completed the task. This will help them reflect on their learning and increase their sense of responsibility for their learning. The hot write overleaf from Knowle Park can be compared with the same child's cold write for a discussion unit of work – see page 221 near the beginning of this chapter.

An exciting way to end this unit of work would be to put the Master on trial and hold a courtroom scene with children playing different roles. In order to carry out the debate, gather key signposts onto cards to help children express their ideas:

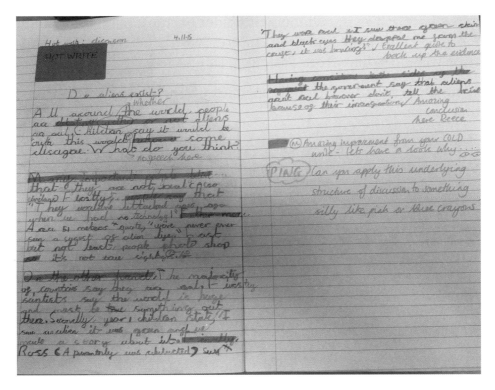

Figure 9.14   Discussion hot write

The team that agrees

We believe . . .	Our first reason is . . .	Another reason for saying this . . .	Furthermore . . .	Also . . .
It is true that . . .	We think . . .	. . . because . . .	The main reason to . . .	Finally . . .

The team that disagrees

On the other hand . . .	Other people suggest that . . .	Alternatively . . .	However . . .	A different view is to suggest that . . .
If . . .	It is not right to say . . .	. . . because . . .	It is incorrect to suggest . . .	Finally, the most important reason . . .

Conclusion

It is clear that . . .	Having listened to . . .	I believe that . . .	In conclusion . . .	I think . . .
Because	As a result of	I feel that	The evidence suggests that	Finally . . .

As a theme, *Doctor Who* is a winner with older primary pupils. You might want to make more of it by challenging the children with other tasks that hone all their non-fiction writing skills – from designing Daleks to writing in role. For example:

- Write reports about different enemies of The Doctor and different planets that he has visited.

- How to operate the Tardis – the lost instructions!

- Vital instructions – how to defeat a Cyberman.

- Explain how a Dalek works.

- Create newspaper articles entitled 'Dalek Invasion'.

- Write an advert to try and tempt another Time Lord to join The Doctor.

End of unit assessment

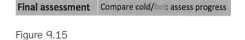

Figure 9.15

The teacher now assesses the final piece of writing (the **hot task**) and looks back at the **cold task** to see what progress has been made. Adding your comment to the child's comment helps to promote a dialogue about what needs to be done to improve the child's work. When the work is handed back, focus on one or two areas that everyone needs to improve. This could be indicated by highlighting the areas selected in a particular colour, for example *green for growth*. Provide some teaching relating to these areas and ask the children to immediately improve their work. Then ask them to reflect on their learning by looking back at the cold task and seeing what progress they have made.

The teacher is now in a position to decide which everyday language features will need focusing on in the next unit of work as well as logging any discursive features that will need strengthening when the class next revisits discussion writing.

Mastering the approach across the curriculum

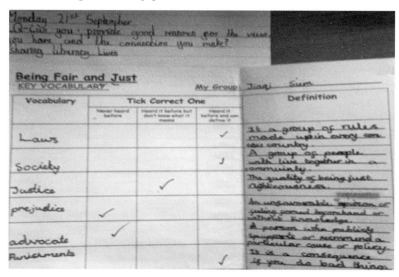

Figure 9.16   Never-heard-the-word grid for RE

Once pupils can write discussion text independently, their skills can be applied and developed across the curriculum. Discussion writing and talk can be used on a regular basis within all subjects and topics and for all years. It is especially useful in history, geography, science, RE (religious education) and PSHE (personal, social and health education). For example, discussion lies at the heart of PSHE. With Year 1 children, discussion might revolve around how we treat each other, but by Year 3 they may be focusing on how to improve break time, moving on to more sophisticated topics like 'Is it right to fight for what you believe in?' as they get older. Equally, discussion is central to history since all study of the past is subject to interpretation. While Year 2s may be focusing on whether Queen Elizabeth I was a good queen, by Year 6 they may be discussing whether workhouses should be reintroduced. Geography, too, is fundamentally a discursive subject with vital environmental topics to discuss like global warming and the decline of the rainforests. The picture above shows a Year 6 child's RE work from St Matthew's in Birmingham. To warm up the vocabulary for a unit on fairness and justice, the children have used a Never-heard-the-word grid (see pages 197–198).

Though science in primary will focus more on information and explanation, discussion comes in here too, for example around healthy eating. Discussion is the text type that most encourages pupils to think and express their views while, most importantly, also encouraging them to listen and adapt their views in the light of the ideas of others, and to recognise that most issues are complex. As they move up the school, they should be being encouraged to see that there are usually more than two sides to any argument and that where there is a lack of proof they should present their ideas tentatively rather than absolutely. It is useful to model for the children how to introduce a contradictory point tentatively as people are more willing to accept an alternative proposal in this manner, as illustrated here by the sentence display from St Joseph's, Derby.

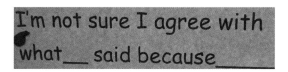

Figure 9.17   Displaying key discursive sentence patterns

A note on hybrid text

Pure discussion text in real life is fairly rare. Very often the text will contain sections of information and explanation. For example, if you are discussing the destruction of the rainforest, you need to provide information about the topic and explanation of some of the features of rainforests.

Moreover, many topics lend themselves to writing in a wide range of genres. Warren Farm Academy in Birmingham in Year 6 have a ghostbusters unit linked to a nearby stately home (Aston Hall) that looks as if it could be haunted. This provides scope for a wide range of imaginative non-fiction writing, as illustrated by the extracts below.

I trust that, in the light of my considerable experience you will take me as a suitable candidate for a position as a paranormal investigator. How could you do without my unique qualities? Should you require references, I would be happy to provide them; there are many teachers who could verify my suitability for this position. I can not wait to be the paranormal investigators.

Yours Sincerely
J. Adoghe   I will gladly provide references!

Figure 9.18   Pupil writing an application to be a ghostbuster (persuasive writing with dashes of information)

Figure 9.19   Pupil, in role as a ghostbuster, describes their experiences at the hall (recount)

the ghosts to We climbed up the stairs to see the great dining room. We moved on to the green drawing room. However there were no paranormal activity, occuring. As we entered the King Charles room, the presence of the paranormal became apparent. We heard infinite swords clashing and lightening flashing. Furthermore, in the long gallery, we were all running to the never-ending footsteps; mysteriously a classmate fell, her shoe came off and her pencil snapped in

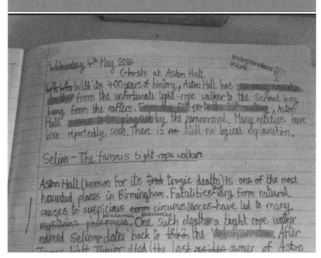

Report- Ghosts of Aston Hall

Wednesday 4th May 2016   Independent Work
Ghosts at Aston Hall.
With its 400 years of history, Aston Hall has from the unfortunate tight-rope walker to the Servant boy hung from the rafters. Aston Hall by the paranormal. Many entities have been reportedly seen. There is still no logical explanation.

Selina - The famous tight-rope walker

Aston Hall (known for its tragic deaths) is one of the most haunted places in Birmingham. Fatalities vary from natural causes to suspicious circumstances have led to many mysterious phenomena. One such death a tight rope walker named Selina dates back to 1862, the After

Figure 9.20   Pupil provides information about the ghostly history of Aston Hall

Figure 9.21   Pupil discusses the rights and wrongs of using ghosts as a source of entertainment

The vast majority of the public are talking about the new trend of forcing ghosts to entertain. This issue has provoked strong opinions from many of the alerted public. However, most people think necessary on many occasions. Firstly, certain people haven't yet seen, or entering face to face; this might help them to overcome their fear of them. Also, this could boost up their courage. For my point, at party attenders might want to feel the thrill of experiencing a haunt phenomenon. Moreover, mischievous at halloween, who have run out of tricks, they could rent a ghost for an ultimate scare. They may even get ideas from the apparition and possibly make friends with it. Thirdly, there is a finincial benefit to this as well if this B.O.O business is successful Some of the money could go to the government who could split it to the council and charities, therefore, roads, street lights, police stations and fire services could be upgraded.
On the other hand, some argue
On the other hand, some argue that we are treating them differently and it is similiar to slavery. They also believe we shall let them feel alive or they could turn

CHAPTER 10

Spreading Talk for Writing across a school

Children make good progress when they are taught in a systematic and cumulative manner. Effective schools have established and refined systems that are proven to be effective. New teachers are inducted into the schools' approaches and not left to their own devices.

Some of these schools have developed their teaching of reading and writing by using the principles of Talk for Writing across the whole school. This can have a dramatic effect on children's progress in writing.

> We attended the original East Midlands pilot (PNS 2008). Talk for Writing strategies have been continually embedded across the school with great results. Despite pupil premium on a white working class estate at 70%, so a difficult group to move traditionally, Talk for Writing has had a huge impact on writing progress, passion and enjoyment of both children AND teachers.
>
> *Birmingham conference delegate, 2013*

> We started Talk for Writing 'by accident', after stumbling across *Talk for Writing Across the Curriculum* on Amazon. The impact on children's work is quite remarkable. Previously poor writers no longer sit and twiddle thumbs, staring into space, but are motivated and engaged and are achieving success. The good writers are flying and producing work of a high standard. Children look forward to writing and want to start another piece of writing, once one piece is completed! Our Headteacher is very impressed with the standard of writing we are producing and is keen to roll it [out] across the school. Great to see how grammar fits into writing in an innovative, meaningful and creative way. Thank you so much. Hope to see you in Scotland one day.
>
> *Conference delegate from Scotland*

> 'We have only been following the Talk for Writing approach for a few months but we are already seeing AMAZING progress. The children love the approach – actions, drama, text maps and boxing up. Our children have very poor vocabulary, but are beginning to internalise things and it's all because of Talk for Writing. I feel even more confident after today and cannot wait to share all I've learned! Thank you for sharing your great ideas!'
>
> *Newcastle conference delegate*

> 'Talk for Writing provides a framework to be consistent from nursery to Year 6. Staff confidently deliver fun and engaging lessons where the children are confident to write at whatever stage they are starting. There is a real buzz in the corridors! As a school, we now use text mapping across all areas of the curriculum.'
>
> *Sarah Gordon-Weeks, Senior Leader,*
> *Dashwood Academy, Banbury*

Research by Robert Coe (Professor in the School of Education and Director of the Centre for Evaluation and Monitoring, Durham University) tells us that if you want to transform practice you need at least 15 hours' intense input/trialling – preferably 50 hours:

- spread over at least two terms;
- focused on the teacher's knowledge and how children learn;
- with time to try ideas out and discuss;
- with support networks to help sustain and improve;
- that leads to feedback and evaluation;
- focused on evidence-based strategies.

Our experience of working with schools would support this. The real potential of Talk for Writing is only seen after three or four years. The power of any approach comes with time, where learning becomes cumulative and progressive. Where schools have been determined to establish the principles and refine the approach, customising it to meet the needs of their children, dramatic results follow as illustrated on pages 2–4.

A whole-school approach can be launched with a development day but our experience is that schools find that one day is insufficient. It takes time for all staff to become skilled at the various aspects of teaching. For example, one teacher in Sheffield, while attending termly training over a year on Talk for Writing, set about introducing and then embedding the approach in the following manner. For six months she trialled the idea in her own classroom, building her own confidence in the approach and establishing evidence of its impact. She then used this evidence to convince the headteacher that this was the way forward for the school. Consequently, all staff training days and twilight sessions were then devoted to developing the approach. As a result, the whole school enthusiastically supported and developed the approach and the children's attainment improved. The Year 6 teacher, with seven years' experience of teaching this age group, explained that over the years they had tried several different methods to raise writing standards. Nothing had worked until they tried Talk for Writing. Now they put all non-fiction genre into a topic that the children really enjoy so that they can build on children's existing knowledge and imagination. 'This approach has made literacy really exciting for me and the children. They look forward to the lessons. Now that the approach is embedded in reception, we can really make a difference.'

The literacy coordinator summed up why it has worked:

- 'everyone is on board because it makes sense;

- the approach is very accessible – which makes it so perfect;

- it has become part of everyday practice – integrated in all that we do'.

If genuine progress is to be made, time and focus will be essential. Indeed, in some schools teaching reading and writing will always have to be a focus for development because of the nature of their catchment area.

There are many different ways to bring about change. Here are a few key points that we have learned from working with teachers and schools about what works well:

How to begin

- Establish the Talk for Writing approach in your own classroom.

- Track progress carefully so that you have evidence to show the rest of the staff, demonstrating that the approach makes a difference in your school, with your children.

How to build support

- Begin to spread the approach by working with a few like-minded colleagues, including a member of senior management, as commitment from the senior management team will be crucial to establishing a whole-school approach.

- Observe each other or team teach so that you can learn together.

- Use each other's classes as an audience.

- Support each other in producing model texts.

How to engage the whole staff

- Use staff meetings and development days to involve all staff and establish and refine approaches.

- All take a text and learn it across the whole school, or key stage, so everyone is working together and approaches can be shared.

- Send staff on as much quality training as possible.

- Set up systems that help teachers internalise the process, for example:

  - Have consistent actions for the key connectives illustrated by children on the writing walls (see **Handout 7**, Appendix 3, **DVD 2** for suggested actions).

  - Ensure that the exemplar texts build in progress from year to year.

  - Guard against teachers becoming stuck in imitation mode by having washing lines in every room showing the progress from imitation, innovation to independent application.

The Head, the 'resident coach' and the team

The two key ingredients needed to start an initiative across a school are the Head, who will lead and manage the approach, and the expert enthusiast 'resident coach', whose role it may be to help teachers increase their subject knowledge and develop classroom skills. We know that a strong teaching model helps teachers imitate practice until they are able to adopt the style as their own. There is also the skill of gradually staging a teacher's learning in bite-sized chunks so that they gain success and increase their repertoire over time.

However, working on their own, the Head and coach may struggle unless the school team is involved. Good ideas stem from talented people working collaboratively, often using a simple form of teacher research where ideas are tried out, refined and developed over time with an eye constantly kept on the question, '*Is this improving children's learning?*'

And, of course, the coach may leave and everything will fall apart if there is no team that can take over. Including a leading teaching assistant (TA) in the team has worked well in many schools because it helps to ensure that all the TAs are on board, as illustrated by video clip 42 on **DVD 2** from Montgomery Academy in Birmingham and reinforced by the TA below:

> ❝It helps me feel more involved in the lessons and has raised expectations of both the pupils and myself.❞
>
> *Louisa, TA at Dashwood Academy, Banbury*

All of this has to be led by someone who is prepared to keep their eye on the ball. The headteacher has to be involved in ensuring that the overall management strategies are in place, for example:

- Analysis of data, inspection evidence and SATs to focus on aspects that need development.

- Setting sensible targets to ensure progress.

- Termly or half-termly monitoring of progress in writing.

- Weekly 'learning walks' round the school to focus on an aspect.

- Regular 'drop-ins' to keep in touch with what is happening.

- Observation of teaching and discussion with children.

- Work scrutiny.

- Feedback from monitoring.

- Peer observation systems and coaching.

- Allocated staff meetings each term and development days each year.

- Training opportunities for staff.

- Phasing in different aspects of the approach (see **Handout 1** for a list of the teaching processes involved in the Talk for Writing approach).

To establish such routines, schools will find *Standard for teachers' professional development*, published by the DfE in July 2016, very useful. It has much in common with its excellent predecessor, the ISP programme. The 2016 document can be accessed from: https://www.gov.uk/government/uploads/system/uploads/attachment_data/file/537031/160712_-_PD_Expert_Group_Guidance.pdf

However, many schools struggle to establish common policies that work. They may well have development days, but do not seem to be able to then use what has been introduced. Schools that are most successful have very clear expectations of what has to be done, based on the evidence of what helps their children make good progress. These routines, understandings and approaches are co-constructed, constantly developed and refined over time – and, once established, are **non-negotiable**: a systematic approach is key to children developing their learning year on year.

Fitting the approach into the curriculum

Each curriculum unit needs to be built around an intriguing, exciting experience or idea – which may well relate to a book being studied or another focus of study. It is crucial that the writing is based on an experience that really captures the children's imaginations and interest. If a school decides to cover each of the key text types every year, then this means that at least six central experiences or themes will need to be resourced.

A school would need to make sure that everyone had checked across the curriculum and identified places where text types would be revisited. An overall plan should be drawn up, showing where in each year group all the text types will be taught in English and where they will be applied across the curriculum. And time needs to be found at the end of units to foster real independence, creativity and invention by giving children the opportunity to choose both their own topic and how to write about it.

Over time, a school would need to build up a bank of texts that have been specifically written and work well as a basis for oral learning as well as containing the key features. These would have to be matched by a clear idea of what constitutes progress in writing. In some schools, the deputy head or literacy coordinator double-checks the models to ensure progress from year to year. This will take time and involve redrafting models. The truth is that it is only through 'trying' a model out with a class that a teacher can really tell whether it works:

- Is it sufficiently memorable and rhythmic to making oral learning easy?

- Is it sufficiently interesting to hold attention and fascinate?

- Does it act as an effective model, having both the overall structure as well as key language patterns?

How the teaching of reading fits in

Furthermore, a school would also need to consider how the teaching of reading fits into this approach. Obviously, the early stages of a unit focus on reading and interpreting the text type. Moreover, during the stages of writing, the class will also be discussing what makes effective writing, drawing on their reading. However, this would need to be supplemented with a strong phonic programme for younger and less confident readers, shared as well as guided reading and independent practice. For instance, some schools devote 45 minutes a day to teaching reading and a similar length of time to teaching writing.

We know that the most proficient writers in schools are those who read. The implication of this is that to raise standards in writing, schools need to find strategies to increase children's enthusiasm for reading non-fiction. They might:

- read quality non-fiction texts to the class;

- provide garage boxes of different text types for independent reading;

- link the texts selected for guided reading to the writing;

- display and promote interesting non-fiction books;

- give non-fiction a similar status to fiction;

- discuss why non-fiction is central to living;

- provide visual images and male role models.

The school's professional development culture

All schools and teachers differ in the levels of support and challenge that will be needed. Having said that, there are underlying principles that are common to curriculum development and improving teaching across a school.

Whole-school movement occurs most powerfully when there is a general recognition that something needs to be done and everyone is motivated to ensure that improvement happens. This may be because teachers become excited by an idea or because they are disturbed by a sense that things could be improved. Ideally, this leads to a communal and collaborative approach to improving teaching and learning. No one should be allowed to opt out.

The analysis of SATs, as well as ongoing monitoring of pupil progress, has enabled schools to establish sophisticated strategies for pinpointing strengths and weaknesses both in teaching and learning, therefore targeting time and effort to ensure improvement. However, while this may identify where schools need to focus staff development, the key challenge of improving teaching remains. Some teachers find they can attend a course and seem able to return and instantly apply what has been learned. Others return from courses and find that what was introduced is too demanding to apply or that the school system will not allow different approaches to be trialled.

Establishing procedures to gain consistency and improve teaching involves utilising a range of approaches, adapted to meet the needs of teachers. The following principles are characteristic of success.

Time and focus

Genuine change is a process that takes time. New procedures and routines are simple enough to establish but changing understanding and belief about learning and teaching takes longer. Teachers need time to experiment, gradually refining their skills and deepening their understanding.

A genuine focus for improvement has to be built into the school's development plan as well as teachers' own learning plans. This can focus time, support and resources. Any programme of development needs to be coupled with effective short-term monitoring to pick up on and spread successes as well as supporting the less confident. Such programmes need well-defined aims related to carefully identified need analysis, alongside a range of relevant staff development activities, monitoring and feedback procedures to track impact. Schools may need to consider deploying regular staff meetings and development days, accepting that more demanding issues need time as these often require a multi-stage process focused on system-wide improvement.

Where schools have too many initiatives, genuine progress will struggle because there is too much going on. Improving writing may need a school to work hard for two or three years in order to improve everyone's teaching and secure real improvement. However, this sort of attention is worthwhile because improving writing helps to improve learning across the curriculum, as the impact of Talk for Writing has shown.

Showing a genuine interest

One key role of senior managers is to show a real interest in what teachers are attempting to establish. This encourages and actively promotes professional discussion about teaching and learning within a 'safe' context. Praise is vital. Healthy schools, where teachers are excited about improving teaching and learning, are often underpinned by mutual respect and the ability to work together.

Trying it out

Teachers may need time to try different approaches, developing their skills. However, many teachers need more than this, as 'self-improvement' can only get you so far. While most teachers are reflective and can identify what worked and what did not, most of us benefit from a more collaborative, collective and cooperative venture where teachers learn in pairs or small groups, using each other's strengths.

Tried and tested staff development activities

Improvement has to be energetically and enthusiastically driven, celebrating successes and accepting issues as part of the process of learning about teaching and learning. It works best where schools recognise collectively that there is an issue and wish to do something about it. The most powerful approach involves teachers working collaboratively and collectively, using a range of strategies appropriate to their differing needs, until all staff have improved the effectiveness of their teaching, thus accelerating the rate of progress across a school. Any reform will stem from the Head's vision of what it might look like but also involves reflective teachers as essential contributors. Many teachers will be aware of what sort of activities might help them learn. The following ideas have all been shown to work.

Establish a clear direction

- Agree and establish, through the Head working with staff, a few simple, clear routines and practices that are 'non-negotiable' as they are known to work – for example, story maps and text maps on walls, a bank of stories to be learned, daily spelling games, etc.

Build in opportunities to learn, trial and reflect

- View staff meetings as a chance for learning rather than just the dissemination of information.

- Hold a staff meeting in which the 'coach' teaches everyone something – followed by all trying this out and then reviewing it at the next meeting.

- Use coaching of teachers – staging learning in bite-sized chunks so everyone can 'observe' simple and effective teaching that they can imitate; and discuss their teaching in a 'non-threatening' environment.

- Use a staff meeting for the coach to teach a class with others watching – then the observers go off and try the same lesson/approach.

- Pair teachers – so they can plan and teach together. Pairs can work together with one observing learning (non-threatening observation) followed by discussion.

- Use informal 'drop in' visits to engage with classroom activities so that professional discussions are well informed.

- Use weekly 'learning walks', focused on an aspect of learning – with staff meeting feedback.

Help teachers learn from experience

- Ensure that teachers develop confidence through experiencing being taught writing themselves.

Learn from other schools and experts
(also see the following two sections)

- Establish local networks that are focused on a single issue – mutual observation, paired teaching, class swaps.

- Set up visits to other schools.

- Hold a cluster development day that is followed up by putting teachers from different year groups together to share ideas, approaches and plans, and look at work from each other's classrooms.

- Establish reading of relevant professional material as well as viewing of video clips of teaching – both from other schools and 'in-house'.

- Utilise local and national courses and expect teachers to make good use of what has been learned.

Involve the children in the process

- Involve the children in teacher-research so that their views are part of the school's information about what works and what hinders progress.

- Hold discussions with children about aspects of learning.

Provide a focus to achieve momentum

- Build in a 'whole-school' initiative to kick-start a process, for example a storytelling week.

- Have one unit a year where everyone works on the same text – the shared writing can differentiate the outcomes, illustrating how a simple tale like *The Little Red Hen* can be transformed into a subtle text in flashback or change-of-perspective mode.

Review and celebrate progress

- Use regular 'book/work' reviews as a strategy for discussing progress and teaching.

- As a staff, review a child's work and discuss what guided work might be appropriate.

- Review one child's progress, looking at the progress between the cold and hot tasks, discussing relevant teaching.

- Review a range of children's writing, discussing 'national assessments'.

- Review children's progress across the school in a staff meeting.

- Establish a strong reward system, such as certificates for children and classes making progress.

Provide the appropriate resources

- Ensure the provision of materials that are needed, such as cards with sentence signposts and a visualiser (or some other electronic means of projecting children's work on screen) for each classroom.

The key to running successful Inset – experience not telling

When running staff Inset, it is important to ensure that teachers 'experience' what is being focused upon. Sticking teachers in a room and telling them what to do can only really work at the lowest level of sorting out simple routines. To help teachers learn in a more effective manner, they need to experience what it means to be in the shoes of the learner, reflect on this and consider the implications for class teaching. In other words, they will need to be directly taught in writing workshops so that they experience writing for themselves.

Making the most of external Inset

We have all had the experience of returning from a course, excited by the possibilities, only to be given a 15-minute slot at the staff meeting three weeks down the trail to pass over what had taken a whole day! A 'course' can only hope to introduce an idea or strategy. The teacher then has to try it out, gradually refine their practice and gain confidence. This phase of 'experimentation' may need support or, at the least, the chance to step out of the usual routine.

Some teachers may be confident enough to move straight into running a staff meeting but it is always best to teach from practice. Encourage staff to try out what they have learned so that they can talk from experience and be certain that it has helped the children make better-than-expected progress. The next challenge is to spread what has been learned right across the school until it becomes part of established practice.

All of this needs leading and managing. We have had the experience of working over a number of years in different parts of the country, training many teachers but, in the end, if the headteacher does not lead a coherent and coordinated plan for improvement over time, then nothing much will happen. I recall one teacher who had been thoroughly inspired by a day's training but was certain that she would not be able to implement the approach back in school since all planning and approaches were fixed in stone. Where headteachers do not allow their staff to learn, develop and try out ideas, money spent on training is wasted.

Visit www.talk4writing.com for conference information and accredited training schools and trainers.

School clusters collaborating

Many schools work in small clusters that share similar needs but also where the Heads share similar values and enthusiasms. This can be extremely productive as a way forward for genuine professional development.

Moreover, a number of outstanding schools across the country have begun to open their doors to work with other schools. It is possible to visit schools where writing is taught effectively. Such sessions often involve observation of teaching. In this way, schools are beginning to increasingly make use of the talent that lies within. Across the country, there is sufficient excellence in teaching that can be used to influence others. If you are interested in visiting a Talk for Writing Training School to see the approach in action, see www.talk4writing.co.uk/training-centres. All the training schools provide dates when their schools can be visited, and they and the Talk for Writing consultants can also be contacted to provide in-school training including extended projects.

Any training has to be managed and developed. Our experience is that 'return visits' are most useful as well as reciprocal visits. Imitation and repetition are crucial to developing teaching. Indeed, teachers learn well by observing a confident teaching model. As they try out similar approaches in their own classrooms, they gradually begin to innovate and refine their skills and understanding. In the end, this leads to teachers becoming more confident to develop new insights and approaches. If teachers are not free to experiment, we will never move forward.

Common sense, as well as international research, suggests that where teachers collaborate and support each other's development, then standards are more likely to rise. Interestingly, in countries where competition is used as a lever to raise standards, national progress is slower. It seems that working together has more effect than working in isolation or against each other. Obvious really.

Progress across the curriculum

In conclusion, one thing that we have noticed is that where a school makes a concerted effort to improve the teaching of non-fiction writing this has had great benefits in other areas of the curriculum. Teaching non-fiction writing effectively not only helps children learn across the curriculum but it also provides them with a key tool for future learning, which in turn helps them cope with life beyond school. The Talk for Writing approach, well taught, raises standards significantly while providing children with a flexible toolkit that will enable them to become life-long confident writers and communicators.

The final word: what teachers say about the difference it makes

> The perfect way to engage and inspire all children from all backgrounds and all abilities.

> Talk for Writing has been instrumental in making my school the inspirational and outstanding educational establishment it is today and even better one it will be in the future! Thank you.

> Talk for Writing REVOLUTIONISED OUR SCHOOL!

> This *will* change the education for children – it's inspiring, challenging and will transform my teaching!

> Massively improved enthusiasm for literacy amongst staff and children since rigorous Talk for Writing implemented.

> I thank you and all of my children thank you. Talk for Writing has transformed the quality of my teaching and their learning.

> 'I've had such a great time in the last year doing Talk for Writing with my class that I really want to share this. The effects were extraordinary. I could see the effect in all the subjects and the evidence in the books is amazing. When you watch the children write now, you can see them thinking about how to compose.'
>
> *Shona Thomson, teacher showcasing impact of the approach at the non-fiction Lewisham conference*

Involving parents to enhance learning and build the school community

The more the parents of children at your school understand the Talk for Writing process, the greater the children's progress can be: parental involvement enhances the children's language acquisition and, of course, it builds the parents' confidence and enthusiasm for learning as well as their children's. For guidance on how to involve the parents of Early Years children, see *Talk for Writing in the Early Years*, chapter 10.

If you watch the family involvement extracts on the Early Years DVD, you can see parents from Lowedges Primary in Sheffield movingly explain how getting involved in the school's storytelling approach has started to influence home culture. As one mother called Kelly states, the power of the approach is the fact that it is fun for the children and this fun can be continued at home: 'I don't think the kids see this as learning. I think they see it as they're having fun. They don't feel like they're learning something so I think they do it a lot more than what they'd do if they saw it as learning – if they didn't see it as a chore, and that's what they're not seeing it as – a chore – it's a game. It's fun – fun for all the family.' Mark, the father of a child called Ollie, agrees: 'That's why Ollie's inviting everyone because she thinks it could be fun for all the family.'

The difference that this could make over time is explained by another parent, Sarah, whose son was involved and then, two years later, her daughter Page was in reception: 'I'm a lot more confident in myself doing it but I've also seen the change in Page. When she first started school, she used to basically play on her own all the time and now she's coming home and saying, "I've been doing this at school." She used to be really shy but now she's a right chatterbox telling me what she's done, 'specially with *The Little Red Hen*. My son, he'll help. He'll show me and we'll actually perform it together.'

Once the parents are familiar with the storytelling approach, you can start a new story in school and then get the children to go home and teach their families the new story – the child takes home a text map and gets the whole family joining in. As the approach moves up the school, the children are the key ambassadors.

Schools in Sheffield that were already using the Talk for Writing approach and which then successfully involved the parents of reception children in the storytelling process found that this doubled the rate of progress the children made. Moreover, it also had a big impact on parents' involvement with the school, as reception teacher Katie Hanson from Porter Croft School explains:

> *Family storytelling has not only brought parents into the school but has changed their attitude towards the school. It's opened up the conversation about children and learning. Parents have stopped demanding to see the writing and understand the key role talk plays in children's development. Parents are now much more confident about how to support their children's learning at home . . .*

This is endorsed by the school's headteacher, Jim Dugmore: 'Books and reading are now high profile. Because the storytelling has involved the parents, it has become easy to get parents to volunteer to support reading. The more your school uses the Talk for Writing approach to engage the parents as well as the children, the more progress the children will make.'

At Selby CP School in North Yorkshire, the reception teacher sends non-fiction text maps related to science for the children to practise at home, as well as story maps from fiction units. The accompanying letter asked parents to report back on what happened. Parents were delighted by the progress their children made and by how much they enjoyed talking about Space and the Universe, as demonstrated by these pictures sent in from one parent and the short video clip on **DVD 1**.

Figure 11.1   Reception-age boy using a text map at home to help him present information about the Universe

This reception-age boy had six text maps in front of him. Below is one of these text maps plus the text about the universe that the maps depicted. When you look at the map, you can see that it refers to the last two paragraphs.

Figure 11.2   Text map about the Universe

The model information text: Space

Planet Earth: We live on Earth. Earth is a planet. It is surrounded by space.

The Sun: The Sun is a big bright star. It gives Earth light and heat.

Day and Night: We have day and night because the Earth slowly spins around. When our part of the Earth faces the Sun, we have daylight.

The Moon: At night we see the Moon in the sky. The Moon does not give light. It is lit by the sun.

Moving Moon: The Moon goes around the Earth. It takes 27 days for the Moon to go around the Earth.

The Stars: At night we see the stars. Stars make pictures called constellations.

The Solar System: The Earth, the Sun and the Moon are part of the solar system. There are 7 other planets in the solar system.

The Universe: The solar system is part of the universe. The universe is huge. It contains billions of stars and planets.

Figure 11.3   Model text on the Universe

Look more closely and you can see how carefully this information text has been written to be at the right level of difficulty for the middle of the reception year. Most of the sentences are simple and short. Internalising such sentences will help the children write in sentences as well as engaging them and their parents with interesting facts about the universe we live in.

Warren Farm Primary in Birmingham makes sure the parents are involved from reception to Year 6. Every term, a Talk for Writing practical afternoon event is held related to a unit each class has been working on. Because the events are practical, dads as well as mums get involved. The school closely evaluates parent participation and has an impressive 95% attendance record at its regular parent events. This is particularly good given the fact that, with 67% of pupils on free school meals, the school serves an area of significant deprivation and has one of the lowest baselines in the country. Displays help the parents understand the process that is helping their children learn across the curriculum. The pictures on the next pages from two different parent events illustrate how involved the parents become in working with their children. This helps the process to continue at home as the parents' comments below suggest.

At the Year 4 Evacuees event, Glen Miller's rhythmic *In the Mood* accompanied the entrance of the children with their iconic evacuee labels and little suitcases. The children performed the letter and then their parents were invited to join the children in making artefacts associated with the era, based on the children's research and instructions: a poster encouraging rural residents to take in an evacuee, a gas mask, an identity card, and a spinning top. The last three items were to be included in the children's suitcases. Popular wartime tunes by Vera Lynn and Marlene Dietrich alongside *Land of Hope and Glory* helped maintain the atmosphere, while somewhat dry chocolate cake, baked according to the limitations of wartime rationing, helped the children understand the era they were studying. The level of parental concentration on the tasks in hand had to be seen to be believed as, hopefully, video clips 43 and 44 and the pictures below convey.

Figure 11.4   Parents watching their children imitate a text

Figure 11.6   Parents and children working together at the workshop

Figure 11.5   Two of the children dressed as evacuees

A knock-on bonus of such events is that the children and their parents now have a shared interest in discussing how the unit develops and what areas are being focused on. Enthusiastic parental feedback on the event reflects how engaging and useful the parents had found it:

- *It gave me time to spend with Aliscia and learn what she is doing at school – made me understand the work she does.*

- *Rielly has been talking about this subject since starting to learn it. It was great to come in and see it all put together and how they'd learned it.*

And, of course, it gets the conversation going about families' own memories of the war: 'My father was in the RAF in the Second World War. I have his RAF jacket he wore at the time. My father and mother got married at this time. Found the workshop great.'

Figure 11.7   Fathers as well as mothers working with their children at a workshop

In May 2014, it was the turn of the Year 3 parents, but this time the theme was fairy tales. Twenty-nine parents or grandparents attended and all the evaluations of the event were very positive: they all said that they would like the opportunity to come into school to see their child learning a new story. When you read through the comments about why they enjoyed the workshop, overwhelmingly it is the opportunity to see how their child learns and to share the learning with them that is appreciated. As one parent expressed it: 'It's enabled both father and child to work together in creative activities', as the picture here illustrates. Another simply commented: 'It was very good working with my child. I learned something new.'

In the words of Jim Dugmore, headteacher at Porter Croft School, Sheffield, the storytelling root of Talk for Writing is 'the gateway: it has enabled us to establish positive relationships so that parent and teacher alike can share secrets about how we can help each child move forward'.